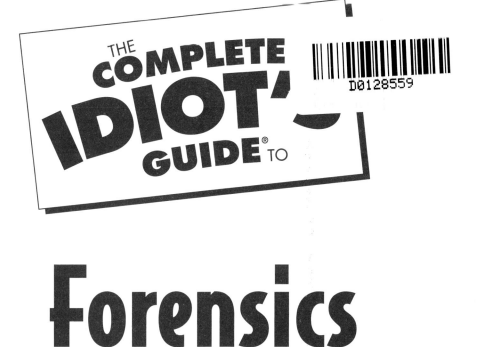

THE COMPLETE IDIOT'S GUIDE® TO

Forensics

Second Edition

by Alan Axelrod and Guy Antinozzi

A Member of Penguin Group (USA) Inc.

To Anita and Ian.—AA
To Jennifer, Rudy, Joshua, Salvatore, Vincent, Vito, Dominic, Luca, Anthony, and Mia.—GA
And to the officers and forensics professionals who serve and protect.—AA and GA

ALPHA BOOKS

Published by the Penguin Group

Penguin Group (USA) Inc., 375 Hudson Street, New York, New York 10014, USA

Penguin Group (Canada), 90 Eglinton Avenue East, Suite 700, Toronto, Ontario M4P 2Y3, Canada (a division of Pearson Penguin Canada Inc.)

Penguin Books Ltd, 80 Strand, London WC2R 0RL, England

Penguin Ireland, 25 St. Stephen's Green, Dublin 2, Ireland (a division of Penguin Books Ltd.)

Penguin Group (Australia), 250 Camberwell Road, Camberwell, Victoria 3124, Australia (a division of Pearson Australia Group Pty. Ltd.)

Penguin Books India Pvt. Ltd., 11 Community Centre, Panchsheel Park, New Delhi—110 017, India

Penguin Group (NZ), 67 Apollo Drive, Rosedale, North Shore, Auckland 1311, New Zealand (a division of Pearson New Zealand Ltd.)

Penguin Books (South Africa) (Pty.) Ltd, 24 Sturdee Avenue, Rosebank, Johannesburg 2196, South Africa

Penguin Books Ltd., Registered Offices: 80 Strand, London WC2R 0RL, England

International Standard Book Number: 978-1-59257-677-7
Library of Congress Catalog Card Number: 2007924621

09 08 07   8 7 6 5 4 3 2 1

Interpretation of the printing code: The rightmost number of the first series of numbers is the year of the book's printing; the rightmost number of the second series of numbers is the number of the book's printing. For example, a printing code of 07-1 shows that the first printing occurred in 2007.

Printed in the United States of America

Note: This publication contains the opinions and ideas of its authors. It is intended to provide helpful and informative material on the subject matter covered. It is sold with the understanding that the authors and publisher are not engaged in rendering professional services in the book. If the reader requires personal assistance or advice, a competent professional should be consulted.

The authors and publisher specifically disclaim any responsibility for any liability, loss, or risk, personal or otherwise, which is incurred as a consequence, directly or indirectly, of the use and application of any of the contents of this book.

Most Alpha books are available at special quantity discounts for bulk purchases for sales promotions, premiums, fundraising, or educational use. Special books, or book excerpts, can also be created to fit specific needs.

For details, write: Special Markets, Alpha Books, 375 Hudson Street, New York, NY 10014.

Publisher: *Marie Butler-Knight*
Editorial Director: *Mike Sanders*
Managing Editor: *Billy Fields*
Executive Editor: *Randy Ladenheim-Gil*
Development Editor: *Megan Douglass*
Production Editor: *Kayla Dugger*
Copy Editor: *Jennifer Connolly*

Cartoonist: *Shannon Wheeler*
Cover Designer: *Bill Thomas*
Book Designer: *Trina Wurst*
Indexer: *Tonya Heard*
Layout: *Chad Dressler*
Proofreader: *Aaron Black, Mary Hunt*

Contents at a Glance

Contents

Appendixes

Foreword

In 1943, the great American psychologist Abraham Maslow drew up a list of what he considered the most basic human needs. These included physiological needs such as breathing, drinking, eating, and the like; safety needs, including physical security; love and social needs; a need for respect and self-respect; a need to increase knowledge; a need for aesthetic satisfaction—for beauty; a need to strive toward what Maslow called self-actualization; and a need for spiritual fulfillment, which Maslow called self-transcendence.

There is a great deal to think about in this list, and certainly law enforcement—of which forensics and criminal investigation are such vital elements—grows directly from and contributes to the "safety needs" Maslow identified. But as comprehensive and thought provoking as his list is, the psychologist left out two major items: the need for truth, and the need for justice. They are the human needs at the very heart of forensic science.

Science is a search for truth—objective, above prejudice, and beyond passion. Forensics puts that search in the service of justice, which is the application of truth (likewise above prejudice and beyond passion) in an effort to identify the guilty, to exonerate the innocent, to redress as far as possible injury and wrong, and to protect and continually improve our society and civilization.

Modern forensics brings to bear contributions from virtually every branch of science to illuminate the darkest and most desperate of human deeds and to discover the truth in situations in which the truth has been hidden, whether by nature, by deliberate criminal action, or both. Having discovered the hidden truth, forensics then seems to make it available to the cause of justice.

This book by Alan Axelrod, a writer and teacher, and by Guy Antinozzi, a veteran criminal investigator, is an exciting and authoritative introduction to criminal investigation and the science of forensics. It focuses on the historical background behind modern criminal investigation, brings readers up to date on current practices, then goes beyond to the cutting edge of forensics in the near future. Axelrod and Antinozzi capture the fascination that drives so much of what we see on television and theater screens, but they also separate the facts from the fiction, the hype from the reality, to provide a razor-sharp 360-degree picture of the extraordinarily varied work of today's forensic professionals. For anyone who wants to investigate criminal investigation, there is no better place to start than with *The Complete Idiot's Guide to Forensics, Second Edition*.

Harold Copus

FBI Special Agent (retired); managing director, HRH Risk Mitigation, Inc.; and consultant, *The Dr. Phil Show*

Introduction

Good and evil. At any time, in any place, among any people of any culture, could anything be more basic than these eternally present, perpetually warring opposites?

The closest most of us get to evil is crime. We fear it. It consistently tops the list of concerns people express in public opinion polls—and with very good reason. About 13 million people, some 5 percent of the U.S. population, become victims of crime *each year.* Of this number, 1.5 million are victims of violent crime, *each year.*

But it's not just fear that motivates our interest in this evil called crime. Most of us have, it seems, a natural need for justice. A wrong, we feel, must not remain uncorrected or, at least, unpunished. That's why crime is such a compelling subject for novels, TV shows, films, and "true crime" narratives. A crime is committed, it throws the world off balance, and we cannot rest—we'll keep turning the pages, we'll stay glued to the TV, we won't leave the theater seat to get a tub of popcorn—until the crime is solved and the balance set right again.

Crime and punishment, like good and evil, are very basic to us all, summoning up our animal instincts for survival, arousing in us a primitive hunger for vengeance, yet also calling on our noblest aspirations for justice, for healing, and for making things right again.

Basic, yes, but hardly simple. Since time immemorial, societies have searched for the cause of crime. They have sought ways to prevent crime as well as ways to cure it. Each answer offered has shown promise, but also flaws. Absolute government and dictatorship surely stamp out some kinds of crime, but they do so by holding *everyone* prisoner. Democracy brings opportunity and freedom, but that includes the opportunity and freedom to commit crimes.

Driven by the most basic of human forces, rooted in the most basic human needs, desires, and perceptions, crime and the social response to crime are nevertheless highly complex subjects. We become outraged after seeing a TV news report of some terrible crime. We fume. We demand justice *now.* But then we learn more about the background of the suspect, a life of poverty, abuse, and victimization. Or we hear that the state's evidence against him is circumstantial—a suggestive case, perhaps, but hardly airtight. Or we learn that the prosecution's main witness is himself a felon who has "cut a deal" in return for spilling his guts in testimony to convict the chief suspect. Or we listen to the prosecution's expert forensic witness interpret the evidence 100 percent one way, then listen further as the defense forensic expert reaches the opposite conclusion. And on and on it goes, the question of guilt or innocence spiraling farther and farther from what seemed the compelling core issues of simple good versus simple evil.

Most of us have strong feelings about crime, punishment, and justice. Yet, in our free society, these basic, urgent issues become so complex that we are pulled and pushed in a variety of directions and often find it almost impossible to take a stand. This book is intended to help us all sort things out.

The Complete Idiot's Guide to Forensics, Second Edition, explores the history, present, and future of police work, with special emphasis on that aspect of police work called forensics: the processes of discovering, collecting, analyzing, and presenting evidence to prove the truth or falsity of particular criminal issues in law. **Part 1, "The Usual Suspects,"** briefly surveys the scope and goals of criminology, then focuses on criminal investigation in general and forensics in particular. Here are chapters on how crimes are classified (and why it is necessary to classify them) and how modern cops attempt to profile criminals in order to understand, identify, and apprehend them.

Part 2, "On the Scene (and in the Lab)," begins with the police arrival at a crime scene and discusses how investigators size up the scene and interrogate suspects, witnesses, and victims. Chapters in this part explain just what evidence the cops look for, and how they find it, gather it, and analyze it, as well as the tools they use and the techniques they call upon.

Part 3, "The Body in Question," looks at what is often the single most compelling object at a crime scene: the body of the victim. Chapters in this part explain what investigators do at the scene and in the medical examiner's office. Special chapters are devoted to toxicology; the forensic investigation of dental and skeletal evidence; forensic entomology, botany, and geology; and the discovery, recovery, and analysis of DNA evidence.

Part 4, "The Long Arm," begins with the origin and history of the professional police force in Europe and America, then explores police operations as they are today, including police organization, police communications and intelligence gathering, the science of lie detection, and certain "extreme" investigative methods: the use of truth serum, hypnosis, and psychics.

Part 5, "Crime in a Crystal Ball," looks forward to the future of crime—with emphasis on the burgeoning areas of information and computer crime, as well as identity theft—and the future of police work and forensic science.

The Complete Idiot's Guide to Forensics, Second Edition, concludes with appendixes covering who's who in criminal investigation, milestones in crime and crime fighting, the police "Ten Code" communication system, and suggestions for further reading.

Extras

In addition to the main narrative of *The Complete Idiot's Guide to Forensics, Second Edition*, you'll find other types of useful information, including the following special features:

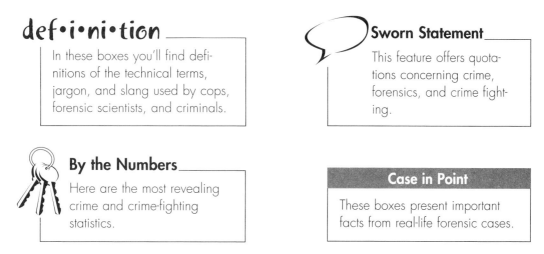

def•i•ni•tion

In these boxes you'll find definitions of the technical terms, jargon, and slang used by cops, forensic scientists, and criminals.

Sworn Statement

This feature offers quotations concerning crime, forensics, and crime fighting.

By the Numbers

Here are the most revealing crime and crime-fighting statistics.

Case in Point

These boxes present important facts from real-life forensic cases.

Acknowledgments

My thanks and respect to my co-author, Guy Antinozzi, who serves and protects.

I am also grateful for the fine work and support of the folks at Alpha, especially Randy Ladenheim-Gil, Megan Douglass, Lynn Northrup, Katherin Bidwell, and Susan Aufheimer.

—Alan Axelrod

I would like to thank the following people, beginning with my son Dominic. His enthusiasm for police work reminds me why I do what I do. My lovely wife, Jennifer, and all my sons provide the love and challenges necessary to motivate an otherwise easily complacent middle-aged man. My father, Rudy, showed me the gift of faith that guided me through some dark days. My brother Joe has become my confidant and friend. My deep respect, gratitude and admiration for Chief Rus Drew, Columbus State University Police, grows with the passing years.

Chief Henry Hope, Agnes Scott College Police, and Chief John Richey, DeKalb County District Attorney's Office, are two of the finest examples of law enforcement officers and leaders. Lieutenant Connie Rembert, Agnes Scott College Police; Captain Bobby Tribble, Walton County Sheriff's Office; and Officer Lee Swann, DeKalb

County Police, have provided support and friendship for many years. Officer Joshua Fritz, DeKalb County Police, is a fine example of the future of law enforcement.

I am honored to serve the Oglethorpe University community with the finest campus safety staff anywhere. Supervising Officers Stephen Oliver, Reginald Maddox, Aaron Melbourne, and Ernest Winston are dedicated to the university and loyal to me far beyond their compensation. My thanks go to President Larry Schall and Vice President Marilyn Fowle, who trust me to serve at Oglethorpe University and will guide us to great things.

Harold Copus and John Weeks, of HRH Risk Mitigation, Inc, are true professionals who practice the science of criminal investigation with vigor, knowledge and experience. Alan Axelrod is always pleasant and usually sarcastic. I find both qualities wonderful and refreshing. Wystan Getz is a defense attorney who serves the system by demanding accountability. My respect for him is immeasurable. Roger Guilford, Stephen Newman, and Michael Powell are loyal, fun and generous family.

Lastly, I want to mention the victims and children I have served for many years now. Your suffering has been felt, though never mentioned. It has been the job of others to weep with you and hold your hand. I have been honored by your trust to stand firm in the face of evil and injustice to help provide you the opportunity for safe passage to a better life. That some of you have made this passage makes it all worthwhile.

—Guy Antinozzi

Trademarks

All terms mentioned in this book that are known to be or are suspected of being trademarks or service marks have been appropriately capitalized. Alpha Books and Penguin Group (USA) Inc. cannot attest to the accuracy of this information. Use of a term in this book should not be regarded as affecting the validity of any trademark or service mark.

Part 1

The Usual Suspects

Just about everyone has a theory about crime: why it happens, who commits it, how to fight it, and how to prevent it. We begin by looking at some popular points of view and how these fit into the history of criminology and relate to the business of criminal investigation and the science of forensics.

In this part of the book, you'll find prehistoric and early historical views of crime and punishment, as well as the birth, evolution, and current state of criminal investigation as a field of scientific study.

Right and Wrong and Cops and Robbers

In This Chapter

- ◆ Crime: the popular view
- ◆ Criminology, criminal investigation, and forensics defined
- ◆ Some leading theories of crime
- ◆ Relation of criminology to criminal investigation and forensics
- ◆ At the crime scene
- ◆ Fantasy cops vs. real investigators

To a question recently posed by the public opinion firm Zogby International—"Have you or any member of your immediate family been a victim of nonviolent crime over the last five years?"—26 percent of Americans asked answered yes, while an additional 9 percent said they had been victims of *violent* crime. According to the public opinion analysts at Public Agenda Online, crime tops the list of what Americans say are the most important problems the United States faces in the twenty-first century. For most Americans most of the time, crime looms with greater importance than moral values, health care, poverty, the economy, education, the environment, drugs, jobs and unemployment, overpopulation, and war.

Clearly, crime is very much on our minds. And it has always been, in both a collective social sense and individually. Can you remember a time when you *didn't* know about right and wrong or cops and robbers? Yet can you answer the following questions: What, exactly, *is* crime? And what causes it?

Everyone's Got a Theory

Well, maybe you believe you *can* answer these questions. But how do you know you have the right answers? Start talking to people about crime and the causes of crime, read the popular press, turn on the TV, or think about your own experience, and you will likely discover there are at least as many opinions concerning the nature of wrongdoing and criminality as there are actual misdeeds.

Authority Figures

For most of us, our first concepts of the nature of right and wrong come from our parents and other early authority figures. At first we believe that a thing is wrong because Mom or Pop or some other important adult says it's wrong or, perhaps, punishes us for doing that thing. Many people never really move beyond this concept, and many people see no reason to move beyond it. They are content to define crime as conduct forbidden by authority. End of story.

But what authority? For some, it is nothing less than God. For others, it may be the government, it may be a king or tyrant, or it may not be a person at all, but custom and law. Act contrary to the "will" of any of these authorities, and you have committed a crime.

One of the earliest surviving documents of civilization is the Code of Hammurabi, king of Babylon, which dates from before 1750 B.C.E. The first three of the 282 laws of the Code of Hammurabi are …

By the Numbers

The FBI reported that 11,556,854 crimes were committed in the United States in 2005—3,899 crimes per each 100,000 inhabitants. Offenses included in the FBI statistics are the violent crimes of murder, non-negligent manslaughter, forcible rape, robbery, and aggravated assault, as well as the property crimes of burglary, larceny/theft, motor vehicle theft, and arson.

1. If any one ensnare another, putting a ban upon him, but he can not prove it, then he that ensnared him shall be put to death.

2. If any one bring an accusation against a man, and the accused go to the river and leap into the river, if he sink in the river his accuser shall take possession of his house. But if the river prove that the accused is not guilty, and he escape unhurt, then he who had brought the accusation shall be put to death, while he who leaped into the river shall take possession of the house that had belonged to his accuser.

3. If any one bring an accusation of any crime before the elders, and does not prove what he has charged, he shall, if it be a capital offense charged, be put to death.

Tabloids and TV

If most of us derive our earliest concepts of right and wrong—and, therefore, of criminality—from our parents, many of us go on to gather our first, and perhaps even our most enduring, concepts of the causes of crime from the media outlets of popular culture.

Novels, newspapers, tabloids, and television introduce us to a vast array of criminals or, at least, fictional portrayals of criminals. All of these media aim to present good stories. Now, a story may include plenty of exciting action, but such action alone is not sufficient to make a really *good* story. A good story always makes sense of the action it presents, neatly tying up any loose ends; therefore, most popular portrayals of criminal behavior include some explanation for that behavior.

Since the advent of the scientific study of psychology toward the end of the nineteenth century, many explanations have been psychological in nature. The criminal behaves as he or she does because of psychological forces over which the criminal has no control.

But the psychological explanation, although prevalent, is not the only common reason given for criminal behavior. TV and tabloids portray many people who turn to crime because they were raised in poverty or exposed to the "bad influences" of "peer pressure" in a "rough neighborhood." Some criminals are portrayed as the products of bad families, families that find crime acceptable.

> **Sworn Statement**
>
> There are two kinds of criminals: those who get caught and the rest of us.
>
> —Anonymous observation quoted in Leonard Roy Frank, ed., *Random House Webster's Quotationary* (New York, 1999)

Still other popular images of the criminal include those who are wicked for some unknown reason: a genetic flaw, perhaps, as in the 1956 film *The Bad Seed*, in which a little girl proves literally to be a born criminal. Another familiar criminal image is the product of the Judeo-Christian tradition, which divides the world into those who walk the godly path of righteousness, and those who, for some reason known perhaps only to God, turn away from the straight gate and follow the way of the devil.

Gloomiest of all the popular images of criminality is the explanation that wrongdoing is not aberrant at all, but rather part of human nature; that is, anyone would commit a crime if that person were certain he or she could get away with it.

Your Own Perspective

It is, of course, ultimately your own experience that filters all of the concepts, half-concepts, and vague thoughts about crime and criminality. You may come to favor this view or that, based on people you have known and things you have seen.

If you are a certain kind of person, you may try to look at everything from a fresh perspective. Maybe crime and criminality are not about bad individuals behaving badly, but about society labeling certain behavior as criminal and thereby *creating* criminals. Maybe treating someone as if he or she is deviant can, by and by, *make* that person deviant. Or perhaps at least some crime is merely a definition used by society's "haves" to control society's "have nots." In this connection, the writer Howard Scott wryly observed, "A criminal is a person with predatory instincts who has not sufficient capital to form a corporation."

Order and Law

While it is hardly difficult to find disagreement over the nature and causes of crime and criminality, just about everyone agrees that this behavior must be a central focus of any society and civilization. Crime, whatever it is, whatever its causes, must somehow be dealt with.

There was a time in which dealing with crime was simple. The king declared this and that wrong and therefore punishable. Or the high priest declared this or that a sin and therefore punishable. Doubtless, there are still places in the world where this system is applied. But in a modern democracy such as ours, simple tyranny does not hold. Crime and criminality, therefore, become proper—and urgent—subjects for rational, scientific inquiry: hence criminology.

Many people think about crime, but for most people, "criminology" never gets beyond an image like this: an urban cop from 1940.

(Image from Arttoday.com.)

What Is Criminology?

Defined at its broadest and most basic, *criminology* is the systematic inquiry into the causes of crime.

An eighteenth-century Italian, the Marchese Cesare Beccaria, is generally credited with having introduced the rational, systematic study of crime and punishment with a 1764 book titled —what else?—*On Crimes and Punishments.* Thus, criminology is a fairly youthful science, yet it has branched out to encompass many and varied approaches. However varied, criminology generally addresses three main areas:

def•i•ni•tion

Criminology is the systematic inquiry into the nature and causes of crime, typically with the object of creating social strategies to prevent crime and to respond more effectively to it.

1. Crime causation, sometimes referred to as criminogenesis, or the branch of criminology devoted to studying the causes of crime. Most criminologists consider this the heart of their discipline.

2. The sociology of law—that is, how crime and law relate to society and the particular values of a given society.

3. Social responses to crime—how the police, courts, and correctional institutions cope with crime.

What Is Criminal Investigation?

The principal objective of criminology is to create theories of crime causation. It is hoped that such theories will ultimately serve a practical purpose, suggesting ways in which crime can be prevented, predicted, and appropriately responded to by police, the courts, and lawmakers.

Criminology looks at the big picture, identifying trends and searching for meaning. However, criminology is not about solving individual crimes. That is the province of *criminal investigation*. Although the theories of the criminologist may assist and inform the work of the criminal investigator, criminal investigation is more practical than theoretical, and, in its most modern application, the practical aspects of criminal investigation are highly technical and scientific. Traditionally, criminal investigation has encompassed the tools, techniques, and processes of solving crimes—identifying the perpetrator or perpetrators and providing the legal evidence to bring him, her, or them to justice. Over the past quarter century, these tools, techniques, and processes have become increasingly sophisticated and specialized as the science of *forensics*.

def•i•ni•tion

Criminal investigation is the general process of discovering, collecting, identifying, preparing, analyzing, and presenting evidence, often directly from or related to a crime scene, to prove the truth or falsity of an issue of law.

Forensics is an approach to criminal investigation that uses the tools, techniques, and processes of science and technology to identify, recover, and analyze crime scene evidence so that this data can be presented effectively in a court of law.

When It Comes to Crime, Everything's Relative

Now that we've defined criminology (as the study of the causes of crime in general), criminal investigation (as the practical business of solving particular crimes), and forensics (as the scientific study of evidence), let's return to the issue we opened with: just what *is* crime?

The Difference Between Right and Wrong

It is a cornerstone of our legal system that only individuals determined to be "competent to stand trial" can be validly judged guilty or not guilty of a crime. Among the most basic determinants of such competence is the ability to "distinguish right from wrong."

Yet the fact is that the difference between right and wrong is not always clear-cut, even to sane and intelligent people. And the relation between what is right and legal and what is wrong and illegal is not absolute. For example, almost all societies in all recorded times have deemed premeditated murder both wrong and illegal. But earnest, well-meaning people disagree on whether abortion is premeditated murder and, therefore, both wrong and illegal. If the anti-abortion lobby secures legislation outlawing abortion, does that make abortion wrong? Or if the pro-choice lobby succeeds in upholding the legality of abortion, does that make abortion right?

Case in Point

In recent years, the state of Oregon and the United States Department of Justice have come to loggerheads over the legality of physician-assisted suicide. In 1994 and again in 1997, the citizens of Oregon voted to permit doctors to aid terminally ill patients to end their lives; but on November 6, 2001, then-U.S. Attorney General John Ashcroft issued a directive stating that prescribing, dispensing, or administering federally controlled substances to assist suicide violated the federal Controlled Substances Act (CSA). Oregon challenged this directive in the federal courts. When the Oregon statute was upheld in 2002, Ashcroft filed an appeal in the 9th U.S. Circuit Court of Appeals. The appeal court upheld the Oregon statute in 2004, whereupon Ashcroft filed another appeal, which was rejected. Ashcroft then appealed to the U.S. Supreme Court, which, on January 17, 2006, upheld the 9th U.S. District Court of Appeals' decision. Oregon's law therefore remains in effect. Yet does this complex deliberative process answer the root question: is physician-assisted suicide inherently criminal?

While most of us would agree that the definition of crime should relate in some way to concepts of right and wrong, the relation is not as absolute as most of us would like it to be. At any given moment, people may legitimately disagree on what is wrong and what is right and, therefore, on what is criminal and what is not. When the perspective of history is taken into account, the issues become even more complex. For instance, in seventeenth-century Europe, the most common of all crimes was witchcraft. Today, many people would dismiss witchcraft as mere superstition, and those folks who still take it seriously might regard witchcraft as a sin, but not as a crime.

Just as we may venture outside of our own point of view or out of our own historical period to get a radically different perspective on the definition of crime, so we might travel to a different culture. Theft, most of us would agree, is a crime. Yet if we lived in a communal society such as that of the aboriginal people of Australia, who have no concept of private property, theft not only would not be a crime, it would not even be a concept, because it would be totally without meaning.

Is That Legal?

If absolute concepts of right and wrong cannot be looked on as the foundation for an absolute definition of crime, what about taking the less ambitious approach of simply defining crime as whatever the state calls crime? That is, if an act is against the law and is subject to a specific, state-sanctioned penalty, it is therefore a crime. Criminologists call this the "formal legal" definition of crime, which holds that crime is defined by the laws of a particular state.

While such a definition may serve in a pragmatic and immediate context, it is not very satisfactory in a moral or philosophical sense. In Nazi Germany, for example, it was a "crime" to give aid and protection to Jews, Gypsies, Communists, homosexuals, and other "undesirables." Closer to home, in 1955, Rosa Parks, an African American, was arrested for and convicted of refusing to yield her seat to a white passenger on a Montgomery, Alabama, city bus, a clear violation of the city's segregation ordinance. Until very recently, in Afghanistan, under the rule of the fundamentalist Taliban government, it was a crime for a woman to seek an education. By the formal legal definition, these are all crimes. But who among the readers of this book would truly consider them so?

Where's the Harm?

An alternative to an absolute right-versus-wrong definition of crime and a narrow formal legal definition is the "social harm" concept, which defines a crime as any action (or, for that matter, inaction) that causes some type of harm. Assault causes harm and is, therefore, a crime, but so is negligence—the failure to act in a given situation—because it, too, causes harm.

Right Is Right!

In our quest for a definition of crime, we might revisit the right-versus-wrong argument and make it less absolute. While there may be no universal standard for unfailingly telling right from wrong, there are certain *cross-cultural norms* by which some acts (not all) are always (or almost always) deemed crimes. Murder, for instance, is a crime from Atlanta to Zanzibar.

def•i•ni•tion

In criminology, **cross-cultural norms** identify certain acts as universally deemed crimes, regardless of cultural or historical context.

Check the Label

A more radical perspective altogether rejects crime as a thing in itself and holds that crime exists when a social response to an act brands it as criminal. This is known as the "criminal labeling approach." In civilized society, crime is defined by society. In the absence of a label, a given act is not a crime.

Right Is Human

For some, the only significant definition of crime is an act that violates human rights. The "human rights perspective" defines crime as any act that violates human rights, regardless of whether a particular state authority or jurisdiction deems the act a crime. From this perspective, the persecution of the Jews in Nazi Germany; the Montgomery, Alabama, segregation ordinances; and the Taliban's strictures against female education are all crimes—even though they were perfectly legal in Germany, Alabama, and Afghanistan.

Case in Point

While it's unlikely criminologists will ever agree on a single definition of crime, it doesn't mean criminology is a failed science. Of greater value than defining crime once and for all is the ongoing *attempt* to define it. This ensures that thought on the nature and causes of crime will continue to evolve, perhaps yielding more effective approaches to preventing and dealing with criminal behavior.

Deviance Is Normal

Yet another approach defines crime as deviance, but also defines deviance as a normal response to oppressive or inherently unequal circumstances. That is, the dominant group in a society attempts to restrict human diversity of language, experience, or culture in order to retain its dominance. This restriction is achieved by classifying certain manifestations of diversity as deviance and by deeming deviance as criminal. Criminologists call this definition of crime the "human diversity approach."

The Professor and the Cop

Can the cop on the beat or the judge on the bench afford the luxury of theorizing about the nature and causes of crime? Is there a point at which criminology and criminal investigation meet? Does criminology have immediate, practical value?

Criminology in Theory

As an academic pursuit, criminology is a specialized branch of sociology. Formulating theories of crime and criminality is, in part, an academic end in itself, its goal neither more nor less than attaining a fuller understanding of society. But most academic criminologists attempt to reach beyond the merely academic. They try to evolve the big picture of crime and its relation to society, not for the purpose of helping the patrol officer in the squad car, but for viewing momentous social issues in new ways. For example, a criminologist might speculate on the wisdom of building more and bigger prisons when imprisonment has failed to achieve a dramatic reduction in crime. The object of such speculation, on a theoretical level, is not to improve this or that aspect of the penal system, but to invite profound rethinking of society's entire approach to crime and punishment.

Criminology in Practice

Not all criminologists are theoreticians. So-called vocational or professional criminology does not shy away from theory, but, in contrast to strictly academic criminology, it does seek to apply theory directly to practices employed by various professionals within the criminal justice system, including criminal investigators, beat cops, prosecutors, judges, and lawmakers.

Sleuths and Scientists

While criminologists ponder the causes of crime, criminal investigators focus on the results of crime for the purpose of identifying and apprehending the perpetrator, and ultimately bringing him or her to justice. In the process, side benefits of a particular investigation may include deriving some lessons on how to prevent certain crimes in the future and how to identify patterns of criminal behavior that might assist investigators in solving future crimes. However, the main purpose of criminal investigation is implied in the verb *investigate* and, in particular, in the Latin root from which it is derived: *vestigare*, "to track or to trace." The ultimate purpose of such investigation is implied by the Latin root of the word "forensic," *forensis*, which conveys the sense of a forum, a place in which facts and findings—evidence—are presented publicly.

Criminal investigators, including detectives and forensic scientists, track and trace a particular crime both to identify and apprehend the criminal, but also and always to gather and analyze evidence such that it can be effectively presented in a public forum (the courtroom) to bring justice by convicting the guilty.

Crime Scene

Most criminal investigations begin at the scene of a crime. Virtually all human activity, including crime, leaves a trace of some sort. Television and movie depictions of so-called "professional criminals" notwithstanding, most criminal activity is carried out by ordinary people in the heat of desperation. Perpetrators make mistakes. They leave fingerprints, they make noise (which a witness hears), they leave something behind. Crime is typically a messy business.

Even those criminals who go about their activities with cool competence create evidence in the very act of committing the crime. There may be bloodstains, footprints, body hairs, clothing fibers, and other examples of *trace evidence*.

Detectives and forensic scientists alike regard the crime scene as a kind of book. The print on the page may be faint and incomplete. The language may be strange and difficult to parse. But still, the scene is there to be read—if one possesses the skill, experience, and tools to read it.

def•i•ni•tion

Trace evidence is extremely small matter left at a crime scene, such as bloodstains, body hairs, and clothing fibers.

Just the Facts, Ma'am

The category of forensic scientists include specially trained crime scene technicians as well as pathologists and laboratory scientists who do the closest "reading" of the crime scene and various items of evidence recovered from the crime scene. Operating in close cooperation with the scientists, detectives at some point in the investigation shift their focus from reading the scene to seeking suspects, victims, and witnesses. They ask them questions, and they listen first and foremost to the spontaneous statements that are made as close to the time of the crime as possible.

Goals of Criminal Investigations

Criminal acts vary widely, as does the quality of crime scenes and the presence and reliability of witnesses. But all criminal investigations have similar general goals:

1. To determine, first of all, if a crime has been committed

2. To obtain, legally, evidence and information to identify the person or persons responsible for the crime

3. To find and arrest the suspect or suspects

4. To recover property, if any has been stolen

5. To present the prosecuting attorney with the best possible case

Get Real: The Truth About Criminal Investigation

We've seen all this a thousand times on television and in the movies: Sherlock Holmes in his deerstalker cap or Columbo in his wrinkled trench coat with his eagle eyes riveted on this piece of evidence or that, the one clue that, for the super sleuth, immediately reveals the identity of the criminal.

Real investigations are typically much harder work and much less instantly revealing. It is also a fact that many crimes cannot be solved, even by highly skilled investigators. Some crime scenes present insufficient evidence and offer no witnesses. That is a hard reality not very conducive to an exciting hour of television.

Fantasy Cops

The classic criminal investigator of pulp fiction and pulp film operates on sheer intuition and an uncanny ability to "think like a criminal."

While it is true that intuition and empathic imagination—an ability to put oneself in the place of another—are valuable qualities in an investigator, they are hardly enough. Real-life detectives are patient, careful, and observant of detail. They have a talent for obtaining and also retaining information. They have a detailed familiarity with the mechanics of crime, with the way particular criminal acts are usually done. Yet they remain open-minded and objective. They deal with intensely emotional situations in a logical way. While they obtain vast amounts of information, they are selective and systematic and refuse to be overwhelmed. Their work is occasionally exciting, but it is always hard.

Police professionalism grew up alongside the academic development of criminology and the professionalization of criminal investigation. Reform-minded bureaucrats and politicians (like Teddy Roosevelt, who was appointed a New York City police commissioner in 1889) did much to bring scientific knowledge and discipline to modern police work. This contemporary political cartoon shows Commissioner Roosevelt as the ever-watchful Cheshire Cat.

(Image from Arttoday.com)

Pressures, Dangers, and the Nitty-Gritty

Gathering information, scrutinizing the crime scene, finding and following up on leads, and doing research is hard and painstaking work. But as grueling as gathering, evaluating, sorting, and analyzing evidence are, and as demanding as finding witnesses and suspects can be, all of this is only part of what makes the work of a criminal investigator difficult.

There's the added grind of the nitty-gritty, of ensuring that all the paperwork is executed correctly and completely, that no suspect's civil rights have been violated, and that no evidence has been obtained or handled in a legally questionable manner. There are a hundred traps to avoid, and while the legal system is set up to ensure that the innocent are not erroneously punished, it is all too easy for some oversight, some investigative lapse, to implicate the innocent or to set a guilty person free. That is the reality of criminal investigation.

> **Case in Point**
>
> Criminal investigations are carried out under pressure—pressure from prosecutors and defenders, pressure from politicians, pressure from the press, pressure from the public—and the work can be dangerous. Suspects don't generally sit still and politely await arrest.

The Least You Need to Know

- Crime is a big part of civilized life, yet it is a phenomenon surprisingly difficult to define.

- Criminology studies the causes of crime, whereas criminal investigation discovers, collects, prepares, identifies, and presents evidence relating to a particular crime.

- Forensics is the application of scientific method and technology to criminal investigation.

- The fantasies of novelists and screenwriters notwithstanding, crime scene investigation is hard and painstaking work, rarely glamorous, and often dangerous.

2

Crimes to Order

In This Chapter

- ◆ Why classify crimes?
- ◆ The major crimes against persons
- ◆ The major crimes against property
- ◆ Drugs and crime
- ◆ The white-collar offenses
- ◆ Victimology: a new focus on the victim

A brontosaurus was lumbering in the background while a pterodactyl soared overhead. Vines clung from trees in a primordial mist. Lugg clubbed Ugg on the head and dragged her by her hair into his cave. The local law enforcement officer who responded to the scene after Ugg woke up did not complete a Domestic Violence Incident Report. While there may have been a need for record keeping and criminal statistics in the Stone Age, there were so many other needs that this mundane practice didn't become popular until much later.

Today it seems that we have become obsessed with numbers and statistical record keeping. From elections to grocery shopping, many of our daily activities are recorded, processed, disseminated, and utilized to affect our lives in countless ways. And that includes how we classify crime—the topic of this chapter.

Classifying Crime

For today's law enforcement professional, numbers are everything. How many tickets does a traffic officer write? How many cases does a detective close? Where should uniform patrol be increased? Where can it be decreased in order to increase it somewhere else? What are the crime patterns? Do property crimes increase in a particular area when school is out of session or as the holidays approach?

You get the idea. It may seem as if we are drowning in numbers and losing focus on the important issues. But compiling and analyzing statistics, especially statistics on distinctly defined types of crime, are aimed at achieving two goals. First, they help police agencies set law enforcement priorities and genuinely realizable goals. Second, the careful classification of crime aids criminal investigators and forensic scientists by associating specific types of evidence with specific types of crime. For example, when investigators are brought in to examine a fire of suspicious origin, they focus their investigation on looking for and analyzing the types of evidence commonly associated with arson. These include the remains of incendiary devices (timers, candles, wire, and so on), traces of accelerants (gasoline, lighter fluid, kerosene, and so on), and remnants of bombs or Molotov cocktails (glass fragments, for example). By analyzing such evidence, investigators may determine not only that the fire really was an act of arson—a crime as opposed to an accident—but they may also find out something about the perpetrator. For instance, if sophisticated incendiary devices (electronic timers, say) are found, the arsonist is probably highly "organized," a professional. If, however, nothing more than matches and gasoline are discovered, the arsonist may well be a "disorganized" amateur who simply used materials at hand to commit the crime. Moreover, by investigating what remains of the arsonist's materials, it may be possible to determine where they were purchased—a first step to determining who purchased them. Or by patiently recovering glass fragments from a shattered Molotov cocktail, it may even be possible to recover fingerprints.

Knowledge of crime classification allows investigators to obtain intelligent search warrants. The U.S. Constitution forbids unreasonable searches, and judges are very wary about issuing "blanket" search warrants. If, however, investigators know that they are looking into a case of arson, they can obtain very specific warrants, authorizing them to search for such evidence as the components of incendiary devices, how-to books, computer evidence (a hard disk showing that the suspect has surfed the Internet for incendiary recipes, for example), accelerants, and other types of physical evidence that will allow investigators to compare material found at the crime scene with material found in a suspect's house or place of business.

What's the Point?

There was a time when an officer's career could have been made or unmade by the number of traffic citations she wrote—or to whom they were written. Those days are mostly gone, but the numbers are still important. If an officer works diligently in an area with moderate to heavy vehicle traffic, the number of observable traffic violations is legion. The issue becomes one of common sense. A prudent officer will enforce the traffic laws and make a useful impact on the safety of the driving public, but the officer will not be so zealous as to be seen as heavy-handed. A gentle touch is often best. Besides, a traffic pullover is the most dangerous of police-initiated encounters with the public.

Case in Point
Nothing is ever routine, including the traffic pullover. The vehicle must be guided to a stopping point that will provide the officer with room to maneuver. This is not to say that the driver will in fact stop. If she flees, the officer must follow the SOP (standard operating procedures) of the department when deciding whether to give chase. If she slows but fails to pull over promptly, the officer must expect a "bush bond," in which the driver exits the rolling vehicle and flees on foot. Even if the driver does pull over, the situation may still be dangerous. A sizable fraction of people stopped for traffic violations are, in fact, guilty of something far more serious and do not want to be caught.

Setting Priorities

During the 1980s, driving under the influence of alcohol (DUI) became the focus of a passionate crusade both inside and outside of law enforcement. The crime that was once seen as a social faux pas now became a heinous offense. Earlier, police officers had given rides home to drivers who had had too much to drink. Now DUI enforcement became a high priority. Officers were establishing traffic safety checkpoints—roadblocks typically set up to check drivers for alcohol intoxication and for such violations as failure to wear safety belts or to possess a valid driver's license, registration, and insurance identification card—to apprehend and jail offenders. Some civil libertarians have challenged the checkpoint as a violation of the constitutional presumption of innocence.

Another example of making and revising priorities is the so-called war on drugs. In the nineteenth century and early twentieth, before passage of the Pure Food and Drug Act of 1906, cocaine was considered an innocuous pick-me-up and was even an ingredient in Coca-Cola—just the thing to make it the "pause that refreshes." During the last two decades, however, the war on drugs, especially cocaine and its derivatives, has consumed an incredible proportion of the time and budget of law enforcement agencies.

def•i•ni•tion

Quality of life offenses generally include such misdemeanors as littering, defacing property with graffiti, and panhandling. During the last decade of the twentieth century, New York City pioneered the vigorous prosecution of such offenses—a controversial policy which, some argued, drained law enforcement resources and others claimed greatly improved the livability of the city.

Even more recently, following the horrific terrorist attacks on New York and Washington on September 11, 2001, terrorism has become an urgent law enforcement priority, severely straining local policing budgets and manpower.

The point is not that fighting drug-related crimes and preventing acts of terrorism are invalid priorities, but they are relatively recent priorities, and, like every priority, they exact a price on law enforcement at every level, from the cop on the street to the courts to the corrections system. Focusing on one type of crime inevitably removes the focus from some other type. In many jurisdictions, the rates of various categories of violent crime, which had been on a generally downward trend, have recently begun to rise again. Many believe this is the result of the refocusing of police priorities.

Predictions as Prevention

When we decide that certain behaviors are negative, we also decide that actions should be taken to suppress them. New York City was the first of the nation's law enforcement jurisdictions to determine that *quality of life offenses* should be prosecuted vigorously. This was a huge leap for a municipality that many had written off as a wasteland of crime and an example of the degradation of modern society. As many see it, police policies under former mayor Rudolph Giuliani made the city not only more livable, but may well have served as a basis for the reconstruction necessary after the attack on the World Trade Center on September 11, 2001. It is conceded, even by many skeptics, that policies focusing on quality of life offenses at the very least compel municipal leaders to seek alternatives to the graffiti, panhandling, and public disorder that were once thought to be inevitable features of urban life.

The Stat Keepers

The crime analysis and police management process known as COMPSTAT was developed by the New York City Police Department. The essence of the process is to collect, analyze, and map crime data and other essential police performance measures on a regular basis and hold police managers accountable for their performance as measured by these data.

The four principles of COMPSTAT express the rationale for keeping accurate crime statistics:

1. **To obtain accurate and timely intelligence.** Officers at all levels of the police department must understand when (time of day, day of week, week of year) various types of crimes have been committed as well as how, where, and by whom they have been committed.

2. **To formulate effective tactics.** Having collated, analyzed, and mapped intelligence, the department's commanders must develop effective tactics for dealing with the problems that are revealed. To bring about permanent change in crime conditions, tactics must be comprehensive, flexible, and adaptable to changing trends. They must also involve other law enforcement agencies such as the FBI, DEA (Drug Enforcement Agency), and ATF (Bureau of Alcohol, Tobacco, and Firearms), prosecutors, probation services, other city agencies not directly connected to law enforcement, as well as the public (such as community groups, schools, and neighborhood associations).

> **Case in Point**
>
> The Federal Bureau of Investigation's (FBI) Uniform Crime Reporting program and the U.S. Department of Justice's Bureau of Justice Statistics are two key sources of crime statistics in the United States. You can access both of these sources at www.fedstats.gov.

3. **To enable the rapid deployment of personnel and resources.** Once a tactical plan has been developed, the deployment of personnel must be rapid and focused. To be effective, the response to a crime or quality of life problem demands that patrol and special units coordinate their resources and expertise and act with a sense of urgency.

4. **To promote relentless follow-up and assessment.** All actions must be relentlessly followed up and assessed to ensure that the desired results have been achieved. This is the only way of ensuring that recurring or similar problems are dealt with effectively in the future.

COMPSTAT is now being used in many police departments around the country and is having a profound influence on the way policing is done, even where the process has not been formally adopted. Today, even small to medium-size departments break down their crime statistics by geographic area, time of day, and type of crime. What was once a "rash of break-ins" is now a statistically analyzed recurring set of similar incidents—in other words, it is now evidence of potential investigative, forensic value.

Even before COMPSTAT, all law enforcement jurisdictions recognized certain broad classifications of crime. The rest of this chapter discusses them.

Crimes Against Persons

In our society, top priority is given to preventing and punishing crimes committed against persons. The most serious of such offenses is homicide.

By the Numbers

Most murderers and victims are well acquainted. According to the Bureau of Justice Statistics, between 1976 and 2004, 13.9 percent of murders were committed by strangers to the victim, whereas 51.2 percent were committed by spouses, relatives, friends, or other acquaintances. (In 34.9 percent of the cases, the relationship of perpetrator and victim was undetermined.)

Homicide

Homicide is the general term for the killing of a human being. *Murder* is a specific type of homicide: the killing of another human being "with malice aforethought" or during the commission of a felony. Another form of homicide is *voluntary manslaughter*, the killing of another human being as a result of a sudden and violent passion arising from a serious provocation. There are also two types of *involuntary manslaughter*: a killing caused by the commission of a nonfelonious unlawful act, and a killing caused by the commission of a lawful act in an unlawful manner likely to cause death. The single common element to all homicidal offenses is the death of a human being.

Robbery

A person commits the offense of *robbery* when, with the intent to commit a theft, she takes property by the use of force, intimidation, threat of force, coercion, or by sudden snatching. In *armed robbery*, the offender employs an offensive weapon or a replica, article, or device having the appearance of such a weapon. The offender who seeks to hedge his bet by using a toy gun, hoping to evade an armed robbery charge if caught, is in for a rude awakening.

Assault

Simple assault is the deliberate violent injury to the person of another or the commission of an act that places another in reasonable apprehension of immediately receiving a violent injury. *Aggravated assault* is assault with the intent to murder, rape, or rob with any weapon or any object, device, or instrument likely to result in serious bodily injury.

Sex Offenses

A man commits the offense of *rape* when he has carnal knowledge of a female against her will. *Carnal knowledge* means penetration of the female sex organ by the male sex organ. The meaning of *sexual assault* varies with jurisdiction. In some states, it is virtually synonymous with rape, but may also encompass an assault with the clear intent to commit rape. In some jurisdictions, sexual assault is defined far more narrowly and is deemed to have occurred when any person who has supervisory or disciplinary authority over another person engages in sexual contact with that other person. *Sexual battery* is intentional physical contact with the intimate parts of the body of another person without the consent of that person. *Aggravated sexual battery* is the intentional penetration, with a foreign object, of the sexual organ or anus of another person without the consent of that person.

> **Sworn Statement**
>
> Give me a kid who knows nothing about sex, and you've given me my next victim.
> —Child molester quoted in the Child Lures Prevention website (www.childlures.com)

Crimes Against Children

Child molestation is any immoral or indecent act against, with, or in the presence of any child under age 16 with the intent to arouse or satisfy the sexual desires of either the child or the adult. *Aggravated child molestation* is molestation that physically injures the child or involves an act of sodomy.

The Serial Offender

Perhaps the most grotesquely intriguing criminal is the serial offender. While there is no universally accepted definition of this criminal, he is more often than not white, male, intelligent, attractive, and personable. (Even after these sociopathic monsters are convicted and sentenced to a life behind bars—or even to death—they are often besieged by marriage proposals from enamored female suitors.)

Serial offenses committed range from property crimes to sexual sadism to murder, or any combination of these. But the crimes committed by any one offender are typically quite consistent. The fetishes and quirks are very personal to the offender. What turns on one serial sexual sadist may disgust another. Roy Hazelwood, a former FBI special agent and profiler, describes serial sexual crimes as existing in the fantasy world of the offenders. The more complex the crime, the more complex the fantasy, and the more intelligent the offender.

Crimes Against Property

Crimes against property are second in priority only to crimes against persons. Note that robbery is classified as a crime against a person, whereas burglary is deemed a crime against property.

Burglary

A person commits the offense of *burglary* when, without authority, with or without force, and with the intent to steal, she enters any structure, including a dwelling or a vehicle used as a dwelling.

Environmental Crime

Criminal codes relating to natural resources regulate such areas as parks, historic sites, and recreation areas; mineral, water, and forest resources; soil erosion and sedimentation; waste management; air pollution; asbestos safety; underground storage tanks; oil spills; and sewage holding tanks.

Environmental laws are complex and vary greatly from jurisdiction to jurisdiction. For example, in many states it is a misdemeanor to operate without authorization any motorized vehicle or machine on sand dunes or beaches. Similarly, it is unlawful to enter a park without complying with all the rules, regulations, and permits regarding use of the park. It is unlawful to violate laws regulating the archaeological exploration or excavation of a historic site.

Arson

The basic definition of *arson* is simple: it is the willful and malicious burning of property. The crime, however, is often quite complex, because the motives of arson are many.

Some arsonists are motivated by excitement. They may be thrill seekers, attention seekers, or even driven by sexual perversion (achieving sexual gratification by setting and watching fires). Some arsonists are motivated by revenge, perhaps personal retaliation for some wrong, perceived or actual; perhaps retaliation against a corporation or institution; or perhaps retaliation against society itself. Arson may be used to conceal other crimes, including murder, suicide, breaking and entering, embezzlement, fraud, and so on. Some arsonists destroy their own property in order to make an insurance claim.

> **Case in Point**
>
> Two special types of arson are *extremist motivated*—that is, terrorism, hate crimes, or rioting—and *serial*. Some arsonists, especially those who derive sexual gratification from the offense, indulge in spree or mass arsons.

The evidence of arson is often quite apparent—the presence of an accelerant (such as gasoline) or an explosive device—at the crime scene. But because so much of the physical evidence is destroyed by the crime itself, it is often extremely difficult to trace the particular act of arson to a particular perpetrator.

The Drug Cycle

The "war on drugs" has been an essential part of law enforcement for nearly three decades. Are we winning the war? This would be easier to determine if what constitutes "victory" were clearly defined. The fact is that the objectives of the war seem to change as frequently as they are discussed.

From a tactical point of view, today's police officer is better trained and more capable of handling the dangerous situations the war on drugs often entails. Weapons are better, and training is better, but does this translate into better law enforcement?

It all depends on who you ask. Few police officers live where they work, and the war on drugs has left many cops feeling like an invading army in a very real war zone. It is hard to tell the good guys from the bad guys, and drug use is so prevalent that it alone cannot be the determinant of good versus bad. Drug dealers themselves are frequently the victims of violent crimes.

Most jurisdictions do make distinctions among different controlled substances. They are classified according to their potential for abuse, their medical importance, and their level of safety.

The Georgia Controlled Substances Act of 1974 is an example of an attempt to classify drugs according to their potential for abuse. Crimes involving drugs higher up on the schedule are deemed more serious than those involving drugs lower down:

◆ **Schedule I.** High potential for abuse, no currently accepted medical use, and a lack of accepted safety; for example, nonmedicinal opiates and hallucinogens

◆ **Schedule II.** High potential for abuse, current accepted medical use, and if abused may lead to severe physical or psychological dependence; for example, medicinal opiates, cocaine, coca leaves, and depressants

◆ **Schedule III.** Less potential for abuse, medically accepted use, and moderate to low physical dependence, but high risk of psychological dependence; for example, certain stimulants, certain depressants, and anabolic steroids

◆ **Schedule IV.** Low potential for abuse, currently accepted medical uses, and limited physical and psychological dependence; for example, serotonin inhibitors

◆ **Schedule V.** Lower potential for abuse than Schedule IV drugs, currently accepted medical use, and if abused may lead to limited physical or psychological dependence; includes substances with very limited narcotic concentrations

Generally, it is more serious to sell than to possess controlled substances, but distinctions are also made on the basis of seemingly arcane issues. For example, sellers as well as users of powdered cocaine are generally treated with greater leniency than sellers and users of the popular rocklike street version commonly known as "crack." Moreover, for many offenders, drug dealing is a way of life, and "three strikes, you're out" sentencing in some jurisdictions has put even low-level drug dealers behind bars for decades.

White-Collar Crime

White-collar crime encompasses business-related or occupational offenses such as embezzlement and fraud. Although often very serious—and costly—they are not directly violent crimes. (But who can measure the emotional violence inflicted on a victim of fraud who has lost his family's life savings?)

Fraud

Arguably, *fraud* is the most frequently perpetrated crime. Offenses range from the complicated telemarketer scam in which thousands of persons are tricked into purchasing five years of subscriptions to magazines they may never read at a price exponentially greater than they would have paid from a reputable distributor, to multimillion-dollar fraudulent insurance claims, to billion-dollar embezzlement schemes. Some authorities believe that about one-third of all insurance claims have at least an element of fraud in them. For instance, following a collision, it is very common for a person to report existing damage as damage caused by the collision under claim.

The victims of fraud are often multiple. In the case of the insurance company that pays a fraudulently inflated claim, the company is certainly victimized, but so are policyholders, who end up making up the insurer's losses by paying higher premiums because actuarial tables become skewed.

Computer Crime

Who can calculate the benefits computers have brought to commerce and the economy? Yet as wonderful as the computer is, the technology has also provided a new vehicle for criminals of many kinds. From money scams to financial transaction card fraud to identity theft to child pornography on the Internet, the surge in computer use has aided perpetrators and frustrated law enforcement officers. Many jurisdictions now have units specifically tasked to combat the crimes made popular—or even possible—by computers.

def•i•ni•tion

Victimology is the study of the victim's role in a particular crime and particular classes of crime. The objective of victimology is to use victims' experiences to prevent future crimes and to find ways to restore crime victims to wholeness.

Victimology

For centuries the focus of law enforcement has been exclusively on the perpetrator. The victim was left to fend for himself. Recently, the focus has broadened. One of the most dynamic areas in recent criminology and criminal investigation is *victimology*. The hope of this new field is that studying the victim will produce better results in crime prevention and prosecution. In effect, the victim is now regarded as part of the whole evidence picture. Victimology can fill in the pattern created by forensic analysis of physical evidence, adding a further human dimension to it.

Crime is never the victim's fault, but it is often the case that certain actions or behaviors on the part of the victim might have made the victim vulnerable. Learning from victims' actions may aid in preventing crime.

Victimology also strives to help the victim heal after the offense. More and more jurisdictions are offering victims financial assistance, psychological counseling, and other help.

Victimology promises to be an increasingly active area in criminology as well as in all phases of the criminal justice system.

The Least You Need to Know

- To begin to understand crime, including the nature of the evidence typically associated with crime, it is first necessary to obtain reliable statistics on crime pegged to time, place, and circumstance, and to organize and analyze the data obtained.

- Police agencies and the criminal justice system as a whole give top priority to addressing crimes against persons, which put lives at jeopardy.

- Crimes against property are the most common and numerous offenses.

- The "war on drugs" is a relatively new priority for law enforcement, which many feel consumes an inordinate proportion of police, court, and penal resources.

- White-collar crimes are nonviolent but costly, ranging from scams perpetrated against individuals to embezzlement (typically a crime against a corporation) to massive frauds committed by some of the nation's wealthiest and biggest companies.

- Increasingly, crime statistics are being analyzed not just to understand criminals, but to learn more about victims in order to address their needs; this is known as victimology.

Profiling the Bad Guys

In This Chapter

- ◆ Criminal profiling and forensic psychology
- ◆ Hollywood myth vs. nitty-gritty reality
- ◆ Evolution of profiling: from Jack the Ripper to the Boston Strangler
- ◆ FBI profiling practices
- ◆ Profiling serial offenders: the Canter method
- ◆ Turvey's Behavioral Evidence Analysis method
- ◆ How effective is criminal profiling?

If you're a fan of old detective movies, crime shows of television's Golden Age, or pulp detective fiction of the '40s and '50s, you've doubtless heard and read a lot about "MO." It's short for *modus operandi* (Latin for "method of operating") and refers to a once commonly held assumption that individual criminals or types of criminals almost invariably behave in the same way. That is, a given repeat offender or class of offender always leaves a recognizable signature on each crime committed. The clever detective arrives on the scene of the crime, looks around, instantly recognizes a familiar MO, then goes out and gets his or her man. Piece of cake.

Most criminal investigators today regard the concept of modus operandi as too simplistic to be of much practical use. But far from obsolete is the idea that offenders motivated by certain emotional drives, offenders shaped by certain elements in their current life and in their background, leave a recognizable signature on the crimes they commit. In contemporary criminal investigation, the modus operandi concept appears as the much more sophisticated and refined process of criminal profiling, which we'll discuss in this chapter.

Psychology Gets a New Branch

In a German courtroom in 1896, physician Albert von Schrenk-Notzing testified in the sensational case of a man accused of murdering three women. Citing research into memory and suggestibility, Schrenk-Notzing argued that pre-trial publicity had made it impossible for witnesses to distinguish between what they actually saw and what they read in newspapers. This instance of expert psychological testimony is generally considered the birth of *forensic psychology*—the application of psychological principles and knowledge in the legal sphere.

def•i•ni•tion

> **Forensic psychology** applies psychological principles and knowledge in the sphere of law.

Today, forensic psychologists (generally persons holding a doctorate in clinical psychology who have devoted special study to forensic psychology) and forensic psychiatrists (medical doctors specializing in psychiatry who have focused on forensic matters) study and testify about matters of criminality, criminal responsibility, a defendant's competency to stand trial, sentencing, and assessment of future risk (is a convicted person likely to offend again?).

Some forensic psychologists and psychiatrists help to process crime scenes from a psychological point of view in an effort to determine what the nature of the crime indicates about the personality—and likely identity—of the perpetrator. Such forensic psychologists attempt to define and classify the range of criminal behavior and are often referred to as "criminal profilers."

Today, criminal profiling is the most widely familiar specialty in forensic psychology; however, most of today's profilers are not psychologists by profession, but specially trained criminal investigators with knowledge of certain principles of psychology and, when necessary, a willingness to consult with forensic psychologists and forensic psychiatrists.

Criminal Profiling: Fact vs. Fiction

Let's get the inevitable pun out of the way fast: these days, *criminal profiling* is a high-profile investigative technique. The public is fascinated by it and sees TV news magazine stories about it, watches movies about it (such as the 1999 Denzel Washington vehicle, *The Bone Collector*; or Morgan Freeman in *Kiss the Girls*, 1997; and *Along Came a Spider*, 2001) and TV cop shows built around it (aired from 1996 to 2000, *Profiler*, for example, was about a sexy forensic psychiatrist, haunted by the murder of her husband, but possessing an uncanny knack for nailing "the criminal mind."). Even more recently, the CBS television series *Criminal Minds* focuses on the FBI's Behavioral Analysis Unit.

def•i•ni•tion

Criminal profiling uses crime scene evidence and other (mainly psychological) data to indicate the type of person likely to have committed a crime under investigation.

Welcome to Hollywood

As portrayed in popular fiction, film, and TV, detectives are cops who operate on (invariably brilliant) hunches, while "profilers" are detectives whose hunches are raised to the *n*th degree by a combination of nerdy scientific savvy and paranormal psychic ability. They arrive at a crime scene, slip on the latex gloves, pick up a few pieces of evidence, stand back and survey the scene, frown, grimace, then raise their eyebrows and declare, "The doer is a white guy, early twenties, brown hair, brown eyes, and a fan of *Seinfeld* reruns. Let's go get him!" (See Chapter 20 for more on psychic detectives.)

And if it's never quite this simple on the more sophisticated shows, well, the loose ends are nevertheless almost always tied up before the last commercial break.

A Dose of Reality

Thus spake Hollywood. In reality, however, profiling is first and foremost painstaking detective work, which begins with a by-the-book analysis of physical evidence at individual crime scenes in the light of certain principles of psychology. By inductive reasoning—that is, reasoning that uses specific physical facts to build generalizations—the criminal profiler begins to identify the tendencies and typologies that characterize various classes of offender.

It is only after carefully analyzing many crime scenes that the criminal profiler can, with some confidence, attempt to reconstruct the behavior of a perpetrator at a particular crime scene and, from this reconstruction, draw inferences about his motivation.

No reputable criminal profiler believes in the old-time definition of MO, that a certain type of criminal behavior is always and inevitably the result of the same motivation. On the contrary, it is assumed that a given behavior may have resulted from any number of motives. Say an investigator finds a body with its eyes covered by a cloth. Does this reveal a significant psychological kink in the offender? Or does it mean that the offender knew the victim and didn't want to be recognized?

Usually, the most that can be expected from real-life criminal profiling is a narrowing of the range of suspects. Although this is no investigative silver bullet, it is a valuable tool, because it allows police agencies to focus their limited resources more efficiently. If the perpetrator is likely to possess characteristics A, B, and C, detectives don't have to hunt for suspects who partake of the rest of the alphabet.

Sworn Statement

The criminal profiler should ... have [some] understanding of ... psychology: the study of individual behavior; sociology: the study of group behavior, groups being comprised of individuals; criminalistics: a general term for the scientific study of recognition, collection and preservation of physical evidence as it is related to the law; ... forensic pathology: a branch of medicine that applies the principles and knowledge of the medical sciences to problems in the field of law .... Anyone without specific training from qualified experts, or experience in at least the above fields is not, in my opinion, capable of the complex processes involved in rendering a criminal profile.

—Brent E. Turvey, M.S., in "What Is Criminal Profiling?"

A Short History of Criminal Profiling

Ask most law enforcement professionals who "invented" criminal profiling, and the credit will probably be given to the Behavioral Sciences Unit (BSU) of the Federal Bureau of Investigation, based at the FBI Academy in Quantico, Virginia. While it is true that a number of FBI special agents, including Roy Hazelwood and Robert Ressler, among others, have pioneered contemporary profiling, the idea of creating criminal profiles was born long before the FBI even came into existence.

Sworn Statement

In each case the mutilation was inflicted by a person who had no scientific nor anatomical knowledge. In my opinion he does not even possess the technical knowledge of a butcher or horse slaughterer or any person accustomed to cut up dead animals.

—London Metropolitan Police surgeon Dr. Thomas Bond, in reference to the work of Jack the Ripper

Looking for the Ripper

The most famous early historical example of profiling is the work of London Metropolitan Police surgeon Dr. Thomas Bond, who in 1888 performed the autopsy of Mary Kelly, the last victim of Jack the Ripper. Bond's autopsy led to the conclusion that, contrary to what many believed, the Ripper had no knowledge of surgical technique. But Bond went beyond this to reconstruct certain aspects of the crime and, based on wound patterns and the use of a sheet to cover the victim's face, he advised police to seek a quiet and inoffensive-looking man, neatly dressed, and in his middle age.

Based on his examination of all of the Ripper's victims, Bond concluded that the crimes were the work of the same perpetrator, a man of "great coolness and daring."

This 1888 cartoon from the British humor magazine Punch *is titled "Blind Man's Buff" and depicts what the public perceived as the utter confusion of the police in their failed pursuit of Jack the Ripper.*

(Image from ArtToday)

While Bond's analysis was thought-provoking, it did not assist police in tracking the Ripper. He was never brought to justice.

A Profile of Der Führer

Something very like modern profiling was employed in the study of another infamous murderer, Adolf Hitler. During World War II, the precursor agency to the CIA, the Office of Strategic Services (OSS), called on psychiatrist Walter Langer to "profile" Hitler in an attempt to gain a strategic edge against German forces. "If Hitler is running the show," OSS officials asked Langer, "what kind of person is he? What are his ambitions? We want to know about his psychological make-up—the things that make him tick. In addition, we ought to know what he might do if things begin to go against him."

Langer made a number of fascinating speculations, the most intriguing of which involved predicting what would happen to Hitler in the end. Langer believed that Hitler was too healthy to die of natural causes (recently discovered evidence suggests that he actually suffered from Parkinson's disease and other ailments). While he did not rule out the possibility of assassination, he did conclude that Hitler, in defeat, would never seek refuge in another country, because the dictator was convinced that he was the savior of Germany. Langer predicted that Hitler would commit suicide if defeat seemed inevitable. This, of course, is precisely what Der Führer did.

Mad Bomber of New York

On November 16, 1940, someone walked unseen into the 64th Street offices of Consolidated Edison, New York City's electric power generating company, dropped his toolbox, and walked out again. Workers opened the toolbox and discovered an unexploded pipe bomb with a note wrapped around it: "Con Edison crooks, this is for you." The NYPD Bomb Squad was summoned but, finding no fingerprints or other evidence, let the matter lie.

One year later, an unexploded alarm clock bomb was found in a gutter just outside another Con Ed building, this one on 14th Street. Three months after this, the police received a letter: "I will make no more bomb units for the duration of the War—My patriotic feelings have made me decide this—Later I will bring the Con Edison to justice—they must pay for their dastardly deeds."

True to his word, the perpetrator the press dubbed the "Mad Bomber" planted no more bombs during World War II, but he did continue to send letters (each signed

"F.P.," for "Fair Play") to various individuals, newspapers, movie theaters, Con Edison, and the police. Then, on March 29, 1950, a bomb was discovered in Grand Central Station. During the next half-dozen years, 30 more were found, in phone booths, in the public library, in subway stations, and in movie theaters (here the Mad Bomber would slit a seat, tuck in a bomb, then disappear through a fire exit). Up to this point, none of the Mad Bomber's devices had actually exploded, but on December 2, 1956, the detonation of one in a Brooklyn movie house injured six people, three critically. At last the police were driven to take unconventional action. They called on Dr. James Brussel, a Manhattan forensic psychiatrist.

Brussel intensively reviewed the massive 16-year case file on the Mad Bomber, including his many letters. After some deliberation, Brussel delivered a remarkably detailed and specific criminal profile: the Mad Bomber was a middle-age man, heavyset but meticulous in grooming, self-educated, and of Slavic, Roman Catholic background. Brussel believed that he was single and living with a brother or sister in Connecticut. He suffered from an *Oedipus complex*. Brussel also concluded that the bomber had worked for Consolidated Edison or one of its subsidiaries.

Dr. Brussel had some pointed recommendations for the detectives. He told them not to keep the profile confidential, but to publicize it widely so that the bomber, antagonized, would be lured out of cover. In addition, he urged them to search Con Ed files pertaining to former employees. Just as the detectives were leaving with their marching orders, Brussel added: "One more thing. When you catch him, and I have no doubt you will, he'll be wearing a double-breasted suit. And it will be buttoned."

def•i•ni•tion

In psychoanalytic theory, an **Oedipus complex** is the unconscious sexual desire in a child, especially a boy, for the parent of the opposite sex. Unresolved, the Oedipus complex may result in an adult neurosis.

The police reluctantly followed Brussel's recommendation about publicizing the profile and, as the doctor had predicted, the stories so irked the Mad Bomber that he revealed himself by sending to a newspaper a detailed account of his motive: an accident he had suffered while working for Con Ed and what he alleged was the company's plot to cheat him out of workmen's compensation.

The police consulted Con Ed files and arrested George Metesky, a heavyset bachelor living in Waterbury, Connecticut. At the time of his arrest, he was wearing a double-breasted suit. It was buttoned.

Committed to an asylum, Metesky was released in 1974 and returned to Waterbury, where he lived quietly until his death, at age 90, in 1994.

Boston Strangler

In Boston, on June 14, 1962, the body of Anna Slesers, age 55, was discovered by her son. She had been strangled with her own belt. Before the end of June, three other Boston women—ages 85, 68, and 65—were discovered strangled to death.

The press began referring to the unknown assailant as the Boston Strangler, and police called in a team of forensic psychiatrists to create a profile of the killer. The psychiatrists concluded, among other things, that the murderer was acting out a hatred of his mother, and his next two murders, during August 1962, both of elderly women (75 and 67), seemed to bear this out. But on December 5, 20-year-old Sophie Clark was found strangled and, on the 31st, the body of Patricia Bissette, 23, was found.

Stymied, police again called on Dr. Brussel. Whereas the earlier profilers had concluded that the serial killer was between 18 and 40 and suffered from delusions of persecution and a hatred of his mother, Brussel believed that the murderer was about 30, of strong build and average height, clean shaven, with thick dark hair. He was, Brussel thought, of Spanish or Italian heritage and a paranoid schizophrenic.

Despite possessing this profile, the police turned up nothing as five more women, ranging in age from 19 to 69, were found strangled in Boston. The break in the case came not from the profile, but from the perpetrator himself.

On October 27, 1964, posing as a detective, Albert DeSalvo entered a young woman's home. He bound her and began to assault her sexually. Then, as suddenly as he had attacked her, he stopped, said "I'm sorry," and left. The woman subsequently described him to police, and he was soon identified by other rape victims. He was apprehended for the rapes, but he was not suspected of being the Boston Strangler until he voluntarily confessed. The police were impressed not only by the detailed nature of his confession, but by how well he fit Brussel's profile.

Because there was no evidence to corroborate his confession, DeSalvo was never tried for the stranglings, but he was tried for robbery and rape and sent to prison for life in 1967. Six years later, he was murdered in his cell by a fellow inmate.

Although he fit the forensic psychiatrist's profile to a tee, nobody personally acquainted with DeSalvo ever believed he was the Boston Strangler—not his wife, his former employers, his lawyer, his prison psychiatrist, and not even police officers who knew him as a small-time burglar. Furthermore, no physical evidence connected him to any of the murders, and there were no eyewitnesses to place him anywhere near any of the crime scenes.

Some experts now believe that the murders were perpetrated by more than one person. But why would DeSalvo have confessed to horrendous crimes he didn't commit? Some point out that he believed the rape convictions would send him to prison for life in any event. By confessing to the sensational Boston Strangler crimes, he could sell his story to support his family financially. Besides, the high-profile stranglings were a "step up" for a petty criminal.

FBI Crime Scene Analysis

In the 1960s, Howard Teten, an investigator with the San Leandro (California) Police Department, worked with the School of Criminology of the University of California to develop a systematic approach to profiling. In 1970, after Teten became an FBI special agent, he initiated what would become the bureau's famous profiling program, working in conjunction with Pat Mullany, a specialist in abnormal psychology. The FBI's profiling methods were further refined in the late 1970s by John Douglas and Robert Ressler, who introduced the "organized/disorganized method," still a cornerstone of the FBI profiling procedure.

FBI Crime Scene Analysis begins by distinguishing between an "organized" and "disorganized" crime scene. Organized offender characteristics include:

- Average to above average intelligence
- Adequate level of social competence
- Prefers skilled work
- Sexually competent
- High birth-order status
- Father had/has stable work
- Childhood discipline inconsistent
- Mood was controlled during the crime
- Used alcohol in connection with the crime
- Situational stress precipitated crime

- Lives with partner

- Is mobile; owns a car in good condition

- Follows crime in the news media

- May change jobs or leave town after the crime

Disorganized offender characteristics include:

- Below average intelligence

- Socially inadequate

- Works at unskilled labor

- Sexually incompetent

- Low birth-order status

- Father has/had unstable work

- Received harsh discipline as a child

- Mood was anxious during the crime

- Minimal use of alcohol in connection with the crime

- Situational stress played little role in precipitating the crime

- Lives alone

- Lives or works near the crime scene

- Not interested in following the crime in the news media

- Significant behavior change follows the crime; may resort to drug or alcohol use

Between 1979 and 1983, agents from the FBI's Behavioral Sciences Unit interviewed incarcerated offenders about their backgrounds, crimes, crime scenes, and their victims. They supplemented the interviews with reviews of court transcripts, police reports, and psychiatric and criminal records. Using this data, they developed a six-step "Crime Scene Analysis" procedure for building a suspect profile:

1. **Inputs.** The first step is collecting and assessing materials relating to the case under investigation, including crime scene and victim photographs, a thorough background check of the victim, autopsy reports, and other forensic data.

2. **Models.** The modeling phase requires arranging the data gathered in the input stage into a logical, coherent pattern for analysis.

3. **Assessment.** Using the sorted and arranged data, the profiler attempts to reconstruct the sequence of events and the behaviors of the perpetrator as well as the victim. The object is to determine the role each played in the crime.

4. **Profile.** Based on the reconstruction of the crime, a list of background, physical, and behavioral characteristics is prepared. This is the profile of the perpetrator. The profiler tries to advise police officials on how to identify, apprehend, and then interview the suspect.

5. **Investigation.** In this stage, the profile is fully integrated into the investigation of the crime. If the profile fails to turn up suspects—or if new evidence comes to light—it is reevaluated and, possibly, modified.

6. **Apprehension.** Any suspects who are apprehended are cross-checked against the profile to assess how closely the suspect's characteristics correspond with it.

Investigative Psychology: The Canter Approach

David Canter is a British psychologist long associated with the University of Surrey, where, under the auspices of Scotland Yard, he developed a leading method of psychological profiling designed especially to identify serial rapists and murderers.

Canter is best known for his work in nailing John Duffy, England's "railway rapist," during the 1980s. By identifying certain features of Duffy's crimes—location, timing, method—Canter established that the offender had a troubled, childless marriage, that he was interested in martial arts, and that he was employed as a semiskilled laborer. Using this and other information, police were able to pick Duffy out of a field of 1,999 suspects.

def•i•ni•tion

The **five-factor model** is the basis of the criminal profiling method developed by David Canter. It evaluates evidence of interpersonal coherence, the significance of the time and place of the crime, criminal characteristics, criminal career, and the offender's forensic awareness.

Canter's method is based on what he calls the *five-factor model*, analysis of five key aspects of the interaction between the victim and the offender: interpersonal coherence, significance of time and place, criminal characteristics, criminal career, and forensic awareness. Let's take a closer look at each.

Interpersonal Coherence

Canter believes that features of an offender's criminal activity relate to features of his activity in noncriminal situations. For example, the most infamous serial killer of the 1970s, Ted Bundy, apparently selected victims who somehow resembled a former girlfriend. Canter makes the assumption that offenders deal with their victims in ways that are similar to how they deal with people in their everyday lives.

Significance of Time and Place

Because the offender chooses the time and place of the crime, this information may reveal information about the perpetrator's mobility and where he lives or works. The choice of time and place may also suggest how the offender views his surroundings and may say something about the offender's usual schedule: when he is (legitimately) at work, for example.

Criminal Characteristics

This is a catchall category in which the investigator may list characteristics that seem significant and compare these to the evidence found at the crime scene. The FBI's organized/disorganized categories are examples of criminal characteristics that might be considered.

Criminal Career

Based on the crime scene evidence, does it seem likely or unlikely that the offender has committed other crimes? Is he a career criminal? A serial offender?

Forensic Awareness

This is strongly related to the "criminal career" category. The investigator looks for signs of the perpetrator's awareness of police techniques relating to the collection of evidence. Such awareness strongly suggests a serial offender as opposed to someone who committed an isolated or random crime on impulse or because of opportunity.

Behavioral Evidence Analysis: The Turvey Approach

Brent E. Turvey is a California-based private criminal profiler who has extensively interviewed convicted sex offenders and serial killers in an effort to understand characteristics common among them. He developed Behavioral Evidence Analysis (BEA), a four-step profiling method. It begins with a new concept called equivocal forensic analysis, the assumption that any given piece of evidence may suggest more than one interpretation, then narrows this down and proceeds through analysis of victimology, crime scene characteristics, and offender characteristics.

Equivocal Forensic Analysis

Turvey assumes that physical evidence found at a crime scene is typically equivocal in nature; that is, any given piece of evidence may suggest more than one interpretation. Therefore, the first step in analysis is to list the possible interpretations and assess the most likely one.

Victimology

After thoroughly evaluating evidence related to the crime scene, Turvey turns next to the victim, profiling him or her in much the same way and with the same thoroughness as the perpetrator is profiled. Assessing how, where, when, and why a victim was chosen suggests a wealth of information about the offender. For instance, the physical build of the victim implies much about the physique and strength of the offender and whether or not he worked alone or with others. The presence or absence of signs of struggle may suggest whether or not the victim and offender were acquainted with one another.

Crime Scene Characteristics

Crime scene characteristics are, according to Turvey, the "distinguishing features of a crime scene as evidenced by an offender's behavioral decisions regarding the victim and the offense location, and their subsequent meaning to the offender." Is there evidence to suggest that the scene of the crime has special significance for the offender? How does this crime scene compare with the scenes of prior, apparently related, crimes? Does the crime scene reveal little forensic information? This is significant, in that it may suggest that this scene is only one of several scenes involved in the crime under investigation.

Offender Characteristics

Using data and conclusions derived from the first three steps, the investigator now attempts to create a picture of the characteristics of the offender. The features that make up this picture typically include the following:

- Physical build and other characteristics

- Gender

- Presence and type of vehicle used

- Offender's residence or workplace in relation to the crime scene

- Level of skill

- Criminal history, repeat or serial offender

- Aggressiveness

- Medical history

- Marital status

- Race or ethnic origin

Profiling Scorecard

Because criminal profiling is almost always just one element in any criminal investigation, it is difficult to assess how effective or ineffective it is in bringing about an arrest. Moreover, the quality of the profiling depends on the quality of the crime scene and crime scene investigation. The skill, knowledge, experience—and, yes, luck—of investigators also vary widely.

Case in Point

The FBI musters a few agents who specialize in criminal profiling. A number of private investigators market themselves as criminal profilers and are hired on a case-by-case basis by local police departments. In large urban departments, some detectives receive training as criminal profilers.

Nevertheless, research conducted in the early 1990s strongly suggests that trained profilers provide more useful and more valid criminal profiles than general clinical psychologists or even detectives do. While it is clear that criminal profiling does not magically deliver the offender into police custody, profiling often significantly improves the odds of making an arrest and doing so with less time and less wasted effort than would be the case without the profiling information, especially when the perpetrator is a repeat or serial offender.

The Least You Need to Know

♦ Criminal profiling employs meticulous analysis of crime scenes in order to reconstruct offender and victim behavior and draw conclusions about the characteristics and identity of the perpetrator.

♦ Although the FBI Behavioral Sciences Unit brought profiling to a high level of sophistication in the 1970s, the technique was used at least as early as 1888 in the case of Jack the Ripper.

♦ Alternatives to "FBI Crime Scene Analysis" include the Canter method of investigative psychology and Brent Turvey's Behavioral Evidence Analysis approach.

♦ Criminal investigation involves too many variables to permit an unambiguous assessment of the effectiveness of profiling, but most experts believe that, especially in serial cases, criminal profiling is a significant aid to investigation.

Part 2

On the Scene
(and in the Lab)

Edmond Locard, the French police official who established the world's first crime lab in 1910, proclaimed the chief assumption of forensic science. "Every contact," he said, "leaves a trace." Crime, especially violent crime, is a profound and terrifying contact between assailant and victim. Criminal investigators, including forensic scientists, look for the traces of this contact, collect them, examine them, and use them to solve the crime and secure justice.

This part tells what patrol officers and detectives do when they arrive at a crime scene; how investigators "read" that scene and question witnesses, victims, and suspects; and how evidence is gathered, processed, and analyzed. A special chapter is devoted to the history and present practice of fingerprint identification and analysis.

Chapter 4

The Arrival

In This Chapter

- Crime scene roles
- Processing the scene
- Investigative pitfalls
- Learning from the O. J. Simpson and JonBenét Ramsey cases

As with any big event, the entrance is often the most important moment in the crime scene investigation. How first responders enter the scene sets the tone for the entire investigation. The initial responding officer, the lowest-paid officer holding the lowest rank, makes decisions that will affect the rest of the case or, more critically, whether or not a criminal case can even be made.

Safety comes first. A hot crime scene may include injured victims and may yet harbor dangerous perpetrators. And once the scene is secured, it becomes a matter of keeping your eyes open and taking care not to compromise any pieces of evidence. This chapter covers the initial investigative assessment and continues through the "processing" of a crime scene—the gathering of evidence for subsequent analysis and ultimate use at trial.

Who's on Call

Responding to a crime involves a number of professionals, typically beginning with the dispatcher, who takes the emergency 911 call and relays vital information to a responding officer or officers. In the case of any major crime, other investigators are called in, including detectives, investigators from the prosecutor's office, and, depending on the nature of the crime, the medical examiner and his or her staff.

Uniformed Officers

Uniformed police officers hold the most important job in law enforcement. Under-paid, overworked, stressed, tired, and often young, they are also brave, dedicated, trained, and mature beyond their years.

When an officer leaves the academy, he or she is faced with a tangled web of complex laws and even more complex human emotions, which make for a degree of confusion greater than what a rookie in any other field faces. In law enforcement, your mistakes shoot at you. You must make quick and positive decisions at the most inopportune of times. It is an awakening akin to a cold slap in the face when a new officer arrives at a violent domestic disturbance, a grisly murder scene, or a horrific traffic accident. The thought runs through that officer's mind that *someone—please!*—should call 911. Then it hits the rookie: *Well, someone already did.*

Case in Point
How does a lowly uniformed officer keep a superior from mucking up the crime scene? By issuing a judicious reminder that, since all officers on scene may be called on to testify, the superior's presence will probably mean a subpoena to a court appearance. No overworked cop likes to appear in court, and a word to the wise is usually sufficient to discourage unwanted interference from on high.

The training calls for the officer to be calm, to look for and aid injured victims, to apprehend the perpetrator, and to preserve the crime scene. Sometimes the mere presence of the officer is a sufficient calming force to comfort the victims. As for the perpetrator, he may be sitting in a chair, dazed, surveying the damage he has just done, or he may be attempting to flee or has fled. The emotions of all parties simmer, boil, and swirl. Amid the chaos, the uniformed officer must conduct a security sweep, care for the injured, and begin the process of calling for backup and investigative help, if needed. While doing all of this, he or she must take steps to secure the scene so that it is not contaminated in ways that might hinder forensic investigation or compromise the value of evidence that must ultimately hold up in court.

In addition to securing the scene for investigation by the forensics team, the uniformed officer should also act as the first investigator. Only the victim and the offender are closer to the crime than the first responding officer. His or her trained eye and skill at recording events can mean the difference between a successful prosecution and the failure of justice.

One of the most difficult but most critical duties of the uniformed officer is to secure the crime scene and control access to it. This means keeping nonessential persons out—including the overly inquisitive fellow patrol officer, the caring neighbor, the distraught relative, the pushy media personality, and even the micro-managing police chief about to breathe down the investigator's neck.

Assuming the absence of an obvious threat—for example, gunfire—the uniformed officer begins by determining the location and condition of the victim or victims. If he or she is confronted by an "active shooter," the officer must attend to that danger first. If not, the officer next takes these steps:

- Determines if the suspect is still at the scene.

- Determines if any weapon is involved.

- Determines what, if any, crime has occurred.

- Summons an ambulance if the injuries require one.

- Separates the victim, suspects, and witnesses.

- Prevents communication between the parties. This includes removing the victim and witnesses from the suspect's line of sight and range of hearing.

- Takes care to disturb no evidence and summons other investigators, as required, if the dispatcher has not already done so.

Case in Point

One of the toughest judgments an officer must make is to employ a level of force appropriate to the situation. Take the job of separating the parties at the scene. Simple? Not always. The officer must go about this without provoking violence or further violence and in a way that keeps fellow officers in his or her line of sight and range of hearing. This is particularly critical in responding to domestic violence incidents. These calls are often the most volatile, unpredictable, and dangerous. It is common for the responding officers to be attacked not only by the offender, but by the victim they were sent to protect—once it dawns on her that her husband, boyfriend, or partner is about to go to jail.

While the uniformed officer does all of this, he or she must also keep in mind the report that will soon have to be written. Older cops tell this to the rookies: "If it is not in the report, it did not happen." That is, in court, little or no weight will be given to any police testimony that is not documented in the on-the-scene report.

Detectives

Many uniformed officers want to be detectives—or so they think, until they actually get that promotion. The hours are long, the frequent calls to crime scenes are burdensome, and the responsibility is tremendous. Detectives usually have at least three years of law enforcement experience before they are even considered for the position. In large jurisdictions they may be assigned to a specialized unit: Homicide, Burglary, Auto Theft, White Collar, or Narcotics. In many smaller departments they need to be an expert in whatever crime they are called to investigate.

Upon arrival at the scene the detective gets the first explanation of the event from the responding uniformed officer. The better the job the officer has done, the better understanding the detective will have of the crime scene and the events that took place.

All detectives have their own personal style. Some are gruff, some are smooth, but all the good ones have the practical knowledge of a seasoned street officer; a grasp of the forensic sciences; the legal knowledge of a prosecutor; and an ability to place people, events, and tangible and intangible evidence in space and time in order to put together an investigative scenario of the criminal event.

The detective begins by making certain that all of the duties of the patrol officer have been effectively completed or are on their way to being completed. A good detective not only knows that the case depends on what the responding patrol officer has done, but also remembers what it was like to be in uniform. Rapport and cooperation between patrol officers and detectives are essential.

After getting a rundown from the patrol officer, the detective does the following, generally in this order:

◆ Determines if immediate judicial action is required, such as securing a search warrant.

◆ Reinterviews the victim(s).

◆ Determines the status of the alleged perpetrator. Is the perpetrator in custody? Is the perpetrator a juvenile? Has the perpetrator been read his or her Miranda rights? (We'll discuss Miranda rights in Chapter 5.)

- ◆ Determines if the witnesses are only that or are more deeply involved in the commission of the crime.

- ◆ Contacts appropriate forensic technicians.

- ◆ Reports the early status of the investigation to supervisors, uniformed officers, detectives, and staff.

- ◆ Determines if other law enforcement agencies should be notified, such as federal, state, county, or municipal departments.

- ◆ Controls the flow of information and media access.

- ◆ Develops theories about the incident based on the evidence.

The more serious and complicated the crime scene, the more time is taken to gather and document evidence, and the more forensic specialists may be required, either on the scene or in the lab. In some cases, the detective is competent to assess and gather all relevant physical evidence. Usually, however, one or more forensic technicians will be called to the scene. Indeed, on a homicide scene, the detective may choose not to gather or disturb the evidence, but to leave this to forensic technicians and criminalists, who are forensic technicians specially trained not only in the collection and preservation of physical evidence, but in some of the more advanced aspects of forensic science, including the performance of some types of physical and chemical analysis. Criminalists are often called on to give expert testimony in court. Also typically present at homicide scenes is someone from the medical examiner's office. Although the medical examiner may perform a detailed autopsy in the morgue, a trained forensic pathologist can tell much about the circumstances of death by first examining the body at the scene.

Police Lab Personnel

In large departments, forensic technicians and criminalists are full-time investigators exclusively assigned to crime scene evidence gathering and analysis. They are usually assigned to every busy shift and remain on call at off hours. Smaller departments rely on regular detectives to do crime scene technical work.

Many forensic technicians (and all criminalists) hold academic degrees in the forensic sciences, but their qualifications run deeper. These are the people who can leave a bloody homicide scene and wolf down a piece of cold pepperoni pizza in the car. They are as caring and committed as most folks—probably more so—but they are conditioned to be clinical and deliberate. If they ever complain, it is only about other law enforcement officers messing up *their* crime scene.

Medical Examiner's People

The role of the medical examiner (ME) has changed dramatically in the last several decades. The professional ME is now usually a physician specializing in pathology and specially trained in forensic science (see Chapter 10). The investigators working for the medical examiner are usually former detectives with a background in homicide investigation.

Once on the scene, the ME's personnel can generally determine whether the murder occurred at that location or somewhere else. They are able to differentiate between a homicide and a suicide by the evidence available, both tangible and intangible. These investigators live with death. It is a part of their daily lives. Personally, they range from profoundly focused to overwhelmingly morbid. Professionally, they perform invaluable work in determining the cause of the event and the responsible party.

Prosecutor's People

Once the work of the police and medical examiner is finished, the prosecutor's investigators evaluate the case to ensure that it is ready for trial. These investigators are usually former detectives. They are still certified law enforcement officers, with full powers of arrest, but they've found a job with regular hours.

The trend today is for the prosecutor's office to get involved early in the case. Investigators from the prosecutor's office may be present at a traffic safety checkpoint (roadblock) or assigned to a homicide or narcotics task force. This proactive approach allows the early input of the office that has the ultimate responsibility and accountability for law enforcement.

Criminalists

As mentioned earlier, *criminalists* go beyond the work of forensic technicians to examine and identify physical evidence in order to reconstruct a crime scene. This evidence may be a weapon, a piece of clothing, a bloodstain, hairs, fibers, drugs, or even a vapor in the air. The objective is to use the evidence to establish a link between the suspect and the victim. Typically, criminalists work at a crime laboratory and receive the collected evidence from crime scene investigators; however, some criminalists collect physical evidence at crime scenes, but they do so only as the investigation progresses.

def•i•ni•tion

A **criminalist** examines and identifies physical evidence in order to reconstruct a crime scene. Criminalists often specialize in serology (body fluid evidence), DNA typing, trace evidence, firearms and tool marks, impression evidence, or drug identification. They are qualified to give expert testimony in court.

Pitfalls

Investigating crime is a high-stakes occupation. Do the job right and lives may be saved and justice served. Make a mistake—or a misjudgment—and people can get hurt or a criminal can walk free. The job has to be done quickly and efficiently, but also painstakingly—not an easy combination.

Inside the Pressure Cooker

Try to imagine the pressure on a law enforcement officer assigned to solve a crime or end a crime spree. Maybe the case in question is a high-profile serial murder investigation. Maybe it's a "routine" rash of convenience store robberies. To the officer in charge, the responsibility is great in either instance.

Throughout the investigation, the officer is considering not only the present victims, but future ones as well. If the suspect is not located, properly treated, and fully investigated, the officer knows only too well that many more horrible things may take place.

def•i•ni•tion

Sunshine laws is a general term for legislation mandating free and open public (including media) access to many aspects of the police investigative process. The idea is to eliminate any dark corners of the criminal justice system by "letting the sunshine in."

Media Spotlight

These days, the media is rarely friendly to law enforcement. At one time, a local reporter was assigned to the police beat, and usually felt like "one of the boys." Today, the relationship between police and media is more adversarial. With the advent of *sunshine laws*, the reporter is no longer solely reliant on the willingness of the police to provide information. Since the reporter is no longer dependent on the police for access to information, the climate of collegial cooperation has all but disappeared.

Why buy lunch for a detective when you can force the release of information by other means?

Police officials want to be responsible and responsive to the public, but the wrong information published at the wrong time can seriously compromise a case, making the work of the forensics team more difficult, either in the investigative stage or when the matter goes to trial. While the prospect of police acting omnipotently or in secrecy is appalling, unbridled criticism in the press undermines police effectiveness, not to mention department morale, and the public's trust and willingness to cooperate with law enforcement professionals.

Chain of Custody

Chain of custody is a concept that is drilled into police officers from their first days in the academy to the last day of their career. The idea is this: evidence is subject to loss, damage, contamination, tampering, or the suspicion of any of these things. Therefore, it is critically important to control the evidence and to be accountable for that control. Chain of custody is a complete and seamless record of all investigative and judicial personnel who have had custody of a piece of evidence.

The chain of evidence concept is simple in theory, but it is often complicated in practice. Once evidence is obtained, the goal is to seize it properly and use it against the accused. If the evidence is tangible—for instance, a gun, fingerprints, or a bloody shirt—it is seized, logged, secured, and processed. At the appropriate time, it is brought to trial to be used in the prosecution of the case. At each step, every time the evidence changes hands, it must be accounted for. The person who releases the evidence to the next person must sign a release, and the receiver must sign a receipt.

In the case of intangible evidence, such as a statement, the material must be reduced to writing or video and/or audio recording. Each time a transcript is shared or a tape passed on, the same releases and receipts must be signed.

Of O. J. and JonBenét

Throughout this book there are examples of cases investigated, solved, brought to trial, and successfully prosecuted. Sometimes, however, the public hears most about the cases that show everything that can go wrong and demonstrate just how high the investigative stakes are.

The nearly year-long trial of O. J. Simpson for the brutal murder of his ex-wife, Nicole Brown Simpson, and her friend, Ronald Goldman, in 1995 was nationally televised and followed by the public like a soap opera.

The Los Angeles Police Department (LAPD) presented prosecutors with what lead prosecuting attorney Marcia Clark called a "mountain of evidence" against Simpson. Bloodstains found at the crime scene were tested to determine blood type and to provide DNA samples. Bloodstains were found in Simpson's white Bronco SUV, on a pair of socks in his bedroom, on a pair of gloves, at the crime scene, in his driveway, and in his house.

DNA samples taken from blood at the crime scene were compared to samples from O. J. Simpson, Nicole Brown Simpson, and Ron Goldman. While expert witnesses for the prosecution testified that the DNA definitively linked O. J. Simpson to the murders, defense witnesses supported the claim that crime scene samples were mishandled, contaminated, or even planted as part of a racist police conspiracy.

Shoe-print evidence found at the scene (see Chapter 8) indicated that the murderer wore size 12 Bruno Magli "Lorenzo" shoes, and snapshots by a photojournalist showed Simpson wearing such shoes—but the actual shoes were never recovered, and the jury seemed unimpressed.

One of the most critical pieces of evidence presented was a pair of bloody gloves. The left-handed glove was found outside Nicole Brown Simpson's residence, and the right-handed glove was recovered from O. J. Simpson's estate. During a June 15, 1995, court session, Simpson put on the gloves, which appeared to be too small. The prosecution pointed out that the gloves, having

Sworn Statement

If it doesn't fit, you must acquit.

—O. J. Simpson attorney Johnnie Cochran, regarding the infamous glove evidence in his summation to the jury

been drenched in blood, had shrunk. The defense turned the evidence against the prosecution, however, claiming that if the glove didn't fit, Simpson could not be the killer.

To the stunned dismay of many, O. J. Simpson was acquitted of murder charges, the "mountain of evidence" notwithstanding. Physical evidence could not overcome the jury's suspicion that the LAPD was a racist organization quite capable of framing a high-profile black celebrity.

By the Numbers

Forensic evidence is not always compelling. In a CNN poll taken shortly after the O. J. Simpson verdict, 62 percent of whites believed that Simpson was guilty, whereas only 14 percent of African Americans believed him guilty. Twenty-one percent of whites and 66 percent of African Americans stated their belief that he was innocent. To the question "Was Simpson framed by the LAPD?" 62 percent of whites answered no, and 65 percent of African Americans answered yes.

Similarly dismaying was the tragic case of JonBenét Ramsey, a six-year-old girl found, on December 26, 1996, strangled and sexually assaulted in the basement of her family's Boulder, Colorado, home. Physical evidence abounded, including a purported ransom note, a ligature around the girl's neck, and the body itself. Yet the crime scene was poorly processed, access to it poorly controlled, and cooperation among local law enforcement agencies and between the police and JonBenét's parents—who were treated by some officials as suspects, but were never arrested—seemed to range from grudging to nonexistent. On August 16, 2006, John Mark Karr confessed to the murder but, based on forensic evidence, officials concluded that this was a false confession. Karr's DNA did not match DNA trace evidence found at the murder scene.

In a situation characterized by many investigative errors, the physical evidence proved sufficient to eliminate one suspect—Karr—but consistently insufficient to identify any other suspects. Despite the forensic resources devoted to the case as well as intense public pressure, the murder of JonBenét remains unsolved as of 2007.

The Least You Need to Know

- A 911 call mobilizes an array of law enforcement professionals, beginning with uniformed officers, then continuing to detectives and other investigative specialists.

- Although the uniformed patrol officer soon relinquishes responsibility for the crime scene to other investigators, his or her actions as the first to respond often determine whether or not the case will be solved, suspects apprehended, and offenders successfully prosecuted.

- Complex or serious crimes are investigated by forensic specialists, criminalists, and the medical examiner in addition to detectives.

- Investigating a crime requires individual expertise and collective cooperation among a variety of law enforcement officials. When the expertise is seriously in doubt or cooperation breaks down, crimes remain unsolved and suspects walk free.

Chapter 5

Bringing Method to the Madness

In This Chapter

- The crime scene: a systematic approach
- The importance of recording the crime scene
- The linkage principle
- The police report
- Interrogation: techniques and objectives
- Searches and the law

So much goes on during a criminal investigation that it is essential to filter the information coming in. This is the only way to separate useful information from the garbage. Information gathered is—or can lead to—inculpatory evidence, legally incriminating facts that may be used to prove an allegation of guilt. An investigation may also turn up exculpatory evidence, which suggests that the accused is innocent of the charges or at least not guilty beyond a reasonable doubt—and guilt beyond a reasonable doubt is the only legally acceptable standard for conviction.

Whether inculpatory or exculpatory, evidence must be probative; that is, it must have more value in providing information than in creating a sensational or emotional effect. While the investigator will use and filter all the information provided, he or she must always weigh the value of the evidence and its usefulness in prosecuting the case at hand. This chapter explains how investigators develop compelling probative evidence.

Crime Scene

The crime scene is a site of great contradiction. To the perpetrator, it is the place where his future has changed. For the victim, it may well be the place where life ended and the future became an impossibility. But for the forensic team—detective, crime scene technician, medical examiner, criminalist, and perhaps other specialized forensic investigators—it is a place of possibility, of science, and the practice of a craft requiring much training and expertise. The crime scene tech wants to know what the responding officer found, and what—she hopes—he did not touch or contaminate. She knows what the detective will be looking for, and she knows what the courts will allow. She expects to be grilled by the defense attorney and cajoled by the prosecutor. She expects to be questioned repeatedly by those who know much less than she. She knows that the crime lab personnel will second-guess her actions and wonder why she used one technique rather than another.

Primary and Secondary Crime Scenes

The site of the first or original criminal activity is called the *primary crime scene*. This may not be the location to which the technician is first called, but it is the site where the criminal activity took place. Any locations associated with the primary crime scene are called *secondary crime scenes*.

Macroscopic and Microscopic

The macroscopic crime scene is the crime scene at its largest, most comprehensive level. It may be composed of many smaller crime scenes. For example, the scene of a shooting in which shots were fired by several persons is the macroscopic crime scene, whereas investigators treat each of the shootings as smaller crime scenes within that larger, all-encompassing scene.

The microscopic crime scene is the smallest area under examination above the molecular level. The area around a gunshot wound, for example, or the fiber evidence left behind in the trunk of a car or

def•i•ni•tion _____

The site of the first or original criminal activity is the **primary crime scene**. All other sites associated with the primary crime scene are classified as **secondary crime scenes**.

the footprint made by a fleeing suspect are all examples of a microscopic crime scene—even though they may not literally require the use of a microscope to investigate.

Crime Scene Search

Before a crime scene technician or other forensic investigator can begin to collect and analyze evidence, the evidence has to be found. There is only one right way to search a crime scene: systematically. There are several methods. The method chosen is determined by the layout of the scene, the preference of the investigator in charge, and the personnel available.

Crime scene investigators may make a *spiral search*, starting from the outside of the crime scene and walking in a spiral path toward the center.

Sometimes the *grid method* is used, in which the scene is divided into a grid, so that the search can be conducted grid square by grid square. This is very useful in large crime scenes, especially outdoors, where small items of evidence may otherwise be easily overlooked.

A *strip* or *line search* is made by walking a straight line from one corner (let's say the lower right) of the crime scene to the upper right corner, making a U-turn at the end of the walk, then walking back across the crime scene a few feet to the left of the original path. At the end of this line, the investigator turns back again, a few feet to the left of the downward path and walks up the scene. The process is repeated until the entire scene has been covered, right to left.

Finally, a crime scene may be divided into *quadrants* or *zones*, each of which is thoroughly searched.

Common sense is important in crime scene searches. First, it is essential to have enough personnel to conduct a thorough and complete search. You get one chance at the search. Once the scene is released, returning to it is usually not an option. In some cases, it may be possible to seal off a scene for hours, even days. Outdoor scenes and places of public activity (a train station or airport concourse, for example) cannot be isolated for long periods. But even when a scene can be effectively sealed for an extended period, it is always best to gather evidence when it is at its freshest.

Second, the layout and nature of the scene often dictates the type of search employed. A search for a spent shell casing in a parking lot cannot be conducted in the same manner as a search for a small body part in a wooded area. For example, investigators searching in a stream always walk upstream; otherwise, the silt they kick by walking in the water will cloud the water.

Sorting Out the Mess

Thinking of the crime scene in macroscopic and microscopic order and making a systematic search are ways of sorting out and interpreting the reality of a crime.

Crime is rarely neat. Most often, crime involves some passion. Whether a husband butchers his wife and her lover after finding them together, or a lone computer hacker finds a way to compromise the identity and assets of hundreds of people, the motivating passion exists. Passion leads to excitement, excitement leads to mistakes, mistakes lead to trace evidence, and trace evidence provides the crime scene investigator with the target of his pursuit.

Much of what we see on fictional television shows based on forensics is just plain silly, but the episodes in which the crime scene technician attempts to recreate the steps of a criminal event are truest to life.

A good criminal investigator asks, "When did passion take over from reason in the commission of the act?" "When did rage supersede restraint?" "What would happen if someone crossed the line by committing a certain criminal act?"

> **Sworn Statement**
>
> The study of crime begins with the knowledge of oneself.
>
> —Henry Miller, *The Air-Conditioned Nightmare*, 1945

It is not easy to put oneself in the mind of a criminal committing a heinous act, but that is precisely what investigators do every day on the job. On the old *Dragnet* TV show, Detective Sergeant Joe Friday admonished witnesses to tell him "Just the facts, ma'am." While it is true that investigators look for facts, hard and cold, they analyze them with imagination, always making an effort to get into the minds of both suspects and victims.

Physical Evidence—and How to Use It

The analysis of physical evidence determines what happened at a crime scene. The crime scene is a canvas painted upon by the perpetrator and influenced to some degree by the victim. By examining the physical evidence, investigators attempt to answer questions such as these:

- Did the victim flail around, fight back, or simply comply?

- How strong or weak was the killer?

- Does the evidence suggest wild passion or cold, calculating precision?

- Was there a sexual element in the crime?

- Did the burglar leave anything behind?

- Did the offender use the toilet before he left the scene? (A surprising number do.)

- Did he raid the victim's refrigerator? (And many do this, too.)

Modus Operandi

Physical evidence may reveal much about the perpetrator's method—what crime writers like to call the criminal's modus operandi, his way of operating.

Determining a modus operandi is especially useful in following the trail of a serial criminal. That person may not follow the usual rules of social behavior, but he still follows certain rules, rules laid down by the drive and perversion of the serial criminal.

All About Linkage

At bottom, crime scene investigation is about linkage, connecting together persons, objects, and the scene. Unless the evidence obtained at a crime scene can be associated with a particular suspect, all the investigative activity is no more than an empty exercise. The goal is ever and always to link the physical evidence obtained at the crime scene to a particular suspect and to do so with sufficient probative value that a jury will be convinced that the suspect committed the crime.

While other factors may be involved in a jury's determination of guilt beyond a reasonable doubt, none is more compelling than good, solid physical evidence. A bloody knife with the suspect's fingerprints on the handle, a computer hard drive holding thousands of child pornography images, the paint scraping of a second vehicle found on the car of a hit-and-run/vehicular homicide suspect—all such items are extremely compelling.

This has always been the case, but it is especially true in the current legal climate, in which eyewitness testimony, law enforcement accounts, and even confessions are subject to close and skeptical scrutiny.

Recording the Scene

The crime scene itself is the first piece of evidence that the investigator comes upon after the original call for assistance, which typically provides only the location and a few limited details. The scene is, therefore, a critical piece of the puzzle and may provide perspective for understanding the events that occurred. Who did what, where, and why may be explained to a large extent by the physical geography of the location. However, the only way that most juries, who are the final arbiters of fact in a criminal proceeding, will get to observe the crime scene is through photographic evidence; therefore, it is essential for the investigator to be able to reproduce the crime scene for the jury in as much detail as possible and in a fair and probative manner.

Case in Point

One of the most important aspects of crime scene photography is perspective. The photographer uses objects of known size—rulers, pencils, quarters, and so on—to provide a sense of scale that puts the evidence into perspective. A photograph of a laceration next to a 6-inch ruler provides a vivid and yet objective image of the extent of the injury.

Investigative Photography

Photographs are excellent evidence—if they are properly taken, produced, and explained. There is an accepted method of crime scene photography used in most jurisdictions in the United States. The purpose of photographing the crime scene is to make a record of the scene to create a vivid demonstration and description for a jury. The crime scene photographer sets out to photograph the scene much as an average person would approach that scene. Thus, the first photos are overviews, which present the big picture, the crime scene as it fits into the surrounding landscape or cityscape.

After documenting an overview, the photographer captures the midrange. These photos are of a particular room or area, and they constitute a sequence of photographs taken to show the immediate area of the incident. Midrange photographs may be taken of each room in a house to show how the rooms relate to one another. Generally, the photographer moves logically, from outside to inside.

After the midrange photos have been made, the photographer turns to close-ups, images of particular pieces of evidence. In a domestic violence investigation, for example, these photographs may be of bruises and other injuries. In the case of homicide, blood-splatter patterns are especially important, as are close-ups of such evidence as fingerprints (see Chapter 7).

These are six of some 80 photographs taken at the scene of a death ruled a suicide. Notice the orderly approach to the scene, beginning with an overall view of the room, then focusing on the victim, then on relevant artifacts associated with the victim—body-building supplements and books (including several addressing dark and violent subjects).

(Photos courtesy of Bobby Tribble, Clarke County [Georgia] Coroner)

Crime Scene Sketches

Sketching the crime scene is one of the first things a crime scene tech does as she organizes her thoughts, especially when working a complicated scene.

On-the-scene sketches are also helpful supplements to photographic evidence. Most useful is a carefully measured overhead plan of the scene, showing how one relevant element relates to another—for example, the position of a body relative to a gun on the floor and relative to windows and doorways.

def•i•ni•tion

Computer-aided imaging employs CAD (computer-aided design) software to create accurate, clear, and rapid renderings of crime scenes.

Investigators do not attempt great feats of artistry in making crime scene sketches, but they do try to create a sketch that accurately portrays and conveys the physical facts, that clearly relates to the sequence of events at the scene, and that precisely establishes the location and relation of pieces of evidence.

Sketches have value in investigation, as aids to thinking through a problem. They also help the jury fit separate pieces of evidence into the big picture.

Computer-Aided Imaging

Today's investigators often make use of *computer-aided imaging* to render more accurate and realistic sketches. Special drawing software specifically adapted to the requirements of police officers and lawyers speeds up the sketching process and makes it more accurate. The presentation is often neater and clearer. Best of all, the software makes it easy to create three-dimensional full-perspective renderings from two-dimensional floor-plan sketches. Such sketches are typically easier for a jury to understand.

This computer-aided 3D rendering of a crime scene employed Crime Zone software from the CAD Zone company.

(Image courtesy of CAD Zone, Inc.)

Taking Note

One of the first things police officers in the academy are cautioned about is this: *if it's not in the report, it didn't happen.* Seasoned investigators take ample notes, because they realize that if they don't write it down—*now*—it is probably not going to get into the final report. Gone are the days when police officers were trusted implicitly and their testimony taken as gospel. The juries of today give police testimony little, if any, more credibility than that of any other witness. The credibility comes not from the badge, but from the documentation, recording, and reporting. It must be routine, systematic, and reliable.

Those Pads—and What Investigators Write on Them

The paper pad is one of the most essential tools of police investigation. Of course, it does little good without a pen, but even in an era of tight city budgets pens are still being provided to police officers.

The investigator—typically the first officer on the scene, or the detective that follows her—records the name, street address, date of birth, Social Security number, telephone number, and whatever other information relevant to the investigation the subject provides. Some pads have preprinted blocks for this information. It may seem like a very easy thing to do, writing down the personal information someone provides to you; however, it is remarkable how many people forget their birth date or even their own name when talking to a police officer, especially after involvement in a violent crime. Also, in many jurisdictions today, people of various cultures and nationalities coexist, and many languages are used. If the officer and the victim or witness do not speak the same language the same way, the possibility of confusion and misinformation is dramatically increased.

The practice of taking notes has become such an integral part of criminal investigation that defense attorneys often demand the policeman's pad as an actual part of the report. In the past, the notepads were discarded. Now they are kept in a secure location and indexed for use at a later time.

Reducing It to Words

Many officers would rather conduct an operation into a very dangerous location than write a report afterward. Usually, by the time detectives have achieved that rank they have found a style that helps them struggle through the mundane task of report writing. The preferred style is neither flashy nor complicated. It is not filled with police jargon or unfamiliar code signals. Like any good writing, it is clear, concise, and truthful.

It is very difficult, if not impossible, to present to a jury evidence that did not find its way into the police incident report. Another real-world fact is that the time between the event and the trial is often so long that unaided memory fails the testifying officer. Commonly, investigators are asked to relay their recollections of events based upon a review of their police report prior to testimony. If a report is not sufficiently clear and detailed in the first place, the testimony will be that much less convincing. Juries do not look favorably upon testifying officers who seem unsure of the facts or, worse, appear to be making up the evidence as they go along.

Asking Questions

The trained investigator—whether cop or criminalist—is a difficult person to be around. The children of such a person can always be sure of some type of interrogation upon returning home after being out: "Where were you? Who were you with?" The assumption is that everyone is lying, at least a little bit. Whether or not this assumption is warranted is arguable. What is not arguable is that a generous helping of skepticism can go a long way in testing the veracity of another person.

It's amazing the things people lie about. The secrets we wish kept are often of such a trivial nature that one would think they mean nothing. To the police interrogator—and that is what a good investigator needs to be, an interrogator (as asker of questions and interpreter of answers)—these lies are the doors that open to the truth.

If you can get to what people are lying about, then you can get to the truth: Who is being protected and why? What motive is there for not coming clean? These are the questions the experienced investigator seeks to answer.

"You Have the Right to Remain Silent"

Miranda v. *Arizona* was the 1966 United States Supreme Court case that affirmed an accused person's right to be explicitly informed of the Fifth Amendment right to avoid self-incrimination by remaining silent.

When an accused person is in custody and is subjected to police interrogation, a *Miranda warning* is given to remind the accused of his or her Miranda rights. If the Miranda warning is not given and the right to remain silent is not freely and voluntarily waived, then any statement made by the defendant or any subsequent evidence garnered by his statement cannot be used against him in court.

def•i•ni•tion

A **Miranda warning** is issued to any suspect taken into police custody and subjected to police interrogation; it advises the suspect of his constitutional rights to remain silent (to avoid self-incrimination) and to legal representation. The warning is named after the landmark 1966 Supreme Court decision in the case of *Miranda v. Arizona*.

Most police officers carry the Miranda warning on a printed card:

> You have the right to remain silent.

> Anything you say can and will be used against you in a court of law.

> You have the right to an attorney.

> If you cannot afford an attorney, one will be appointed to represent you if you wish.

> You can decide at any time to stop answering questions if you wish.

Miranda can be tricky. Key terms to remember are *custody* and *interrogation*. Miranda applies only when the suspect is actually in custody or, more commonly, under arrest, and responding to police questions. It is not necessary, nor is it good police practice, to "Mirandize" everyone at a crime scene automatically and perfunctorily.

The most remarkable thing about Miranda is that so many accused individuals still talk, even after they are warned. Is it because they are sure that they are much smarter than the police officer? Or do they have a sudden, urgent need to bare their souls? Whatever the motive, suspects talk, and talk a lot. Often, the overworked and weary investigator secretly longs to say, "You have the right to remain silent. Why don't you exercise it?" Of course, he or she says no such thing and goes right on listening, sometimes late into the night.

Productive Questioning

One of the most valuable lessons an investigator learns is to avoid asking questions to which he or she does not already know the answer. It is critical to direct the flow of information. Rare is the subject who freely divulges truthful, useful, and concise information. It is far more common for the suspect to talk around the questions. This can lead to the truth, but not without some nudging.

Often, the first task is simply to get the person talking. The detective must figure out what sort of
persona he or she needs to project in order to get
through to the suspect—a parental figure, a confes-
sor, an intimidator, or even something of a friend and
ally. The detective tries to be whatever it takes to get
the tongue wagging. In this role playing, the suspect
often unknowingly assists the interrogator. Appealing
to the bravado, pride, machismo, the need for understanding, or insecurity the suspect exhibits is often
effective in overcoming a reluctance to talk.

If interrogators should be good questioners, they must be even better listeners.
Interrogators avoid questions that produce nothing more than a yes or no. Instead,
they ask open-ended questions that keep the conversation going.

Look Me in the Eye

Interrogators use many methods to assess the truthfulness of a suspect. Kinesics is one
effective method all experienced investigators use, whether they call it by that name
or not. Kinesics is the formal study of nonverbal communication, what is familiarly
called "body language." There is a lot to be learned from the suspect's movements,
expressions, and gestures in response to questions or what psychologists call other
"stressors." The suspect may touch his nose, touch his mouth, grab his neck. He may
cross his arms over his chest, or may laugh inappropriately. He may avoid eye contact
or chew on his lip when being spoken to. Various protective and evasive movements
are innate human responses to stressors. They are hardly proof of guilt, but they are
indicators of a lack of truthfulness. Deception detection, really a subfield of forensic
psychology, has received increasing attention in recent years; see Chapter 19.

In jurisdictions that encompass culturally diverse populations, the interrogator must
also be aware of how culture and tradition may influence gestures. For example, in
some cultural traditions, it is considered impolite to look someone in the eye. The
interrogator needs to be certain that a suspect who appears evasive is not merely acting as a result of upbringing and background.

Search Me

In criminal investigation, a search is a quest for information. As defined in the landmark Supreme Court case of *Elliot* v. *State*, a search is "an examination of a person's

house or other buildings or premises or of the person for the purpose of discovering contraband, illicit or stolen property, or some evidence of guilt to be used in prosecuting a criminal action with which the person is charged."

There is usually little glamour in searching a person's body, dresser drawers, closet, garbage can, vehicle, or file cabinet. The hoped-for result is to find probative evidence, seize it, then use it in a trial. If the evidence located is formidable enough, the accused may plead guilty, and a trial may be avoided.

The Fourth Amendment

All search and seizure law in the United States stems from the Fourth Amendment, which guarantees that people shall "be secure in their person, houses, papers and effects, against unreasonable searches and seizures." The framers of the Constitution wanted to ensure that people would be free from governmental interference in their personal liberties except for those instances in which *probable cause* has been established and a judicial officer has issued a warrant ordering that interference.

As a result of the Fourth Amendment, it is assumed that people have a right to a reasonable expectation of privacy. While not unlimited, this right to privacy cannot be violated lightly and must be intruded upon only on the basis of probable cause.

A search of a person may be conducted after an arrest has been made. A search of a premises may be conducted after a judge issues a search warrant. Both of these

def•i•ni•tion

Probable cause is a collection of facts that would lead a reasonable person to believe that a crime has been committed or is about to be committed. This is a standard less than a certainty, but more than a probability.

instances require preexisting probable cause that a crime has been committed. The Bill of Rights permits no general or blanket warrants. The law enforcement officer must swear that the facts are such that they reasonably justify the search in *this* particular case. The judge reviews the affidavit of the applying officer and grants the search warrant if it is deemed that probable cause of the alleged criminal activity exists. It is not legally sufficient to justify a search after the fact. That is, an officer cannot present the judge with a piece of probative evidence found in an illegal search and ask the judge to issue, in effect, a retroactive search warrant. The probable cause must exist prior to the search.

What Investigators Look For

The search warrant lists items or classes of items to be seized. These may include, for example, narcotics, weapons, "fruits of a crime," money, or clothing. The warrant may also specifically list various ordinary items from which forensic scientists may recover such trace evidence as blood, semen, hair, and so on. In such cases, a criminalist is usually part of the search team. In addition, the searching officer may seize contraband, stolen property, or evidence of another crime. Once the object or objects named in the warrant are found, the search is ended. However, items that are in plain view may also be seized, even though they are not specifically named, provided that they fit into the general categories of objects that may be taken.

Investigators must conduct the search in a systematic manner. No rummaging or ransacking is allowed, and the search must be carried out with reasonable care to avoid damage to property. (This is not always possible. If the police have demonstrated probable cause to search for a body buried in the basement, they are authorized to take sledgehammer and jackhammer to the basement floor.) A copy of the search warrant must be served upon the person whose premises are being searched, and an inventory of the items taken must be left with that person. If no one is present during the search, a copy of the search warrant must be left in a conspicuous place, along with an inventory.

How They Look

A systematic search may be done in a circular pattern or a grid pattern. There is no one right way to do it, and the search is typically tailored to the specific layout of the area to be searched.

To keep to a minimum the number of officers that need to be subpoenaed when the case comes to trial, there is usually one "finding officer" assigned when a search is being conducted. All searchers report to that officer, and he or she takes primary responsibility for anything recovered. The idea is to be thorough, but also to keep the search manageable.

Special Searches

Most searches are routine hunts for particular evidence in a residence or place of business. A few are more specialized.

In the Garbage

A *garbage pull* is one of the least pleasant types of search. It is often part of a narcotics investigation, in which suspects discard drug-related paraphernalia and, if cornered, even the drugs themselves.

The most important factor in a garbage pull is to be certain that the garbage searched actually belongs to the subject of the investigation and that the garbage has been legally abandoned by having been placed in a location for pickup by sanitation workers. Searching through abandoned garbage does not require a warrant.

A garbage pull may yield such evidence as drug residue, packaging materials, and many other indicators of illegal drug transactions or manufacture. Trash is also a treasure trove of materials of interest to a forensic accountant, an investigator who specializes in the interpretation of financial transactions from such fragmentary evidence as discarded receipts, credit card and bank statements, and the like.

def•i•ni•tion

A **garbage pull** is police jargon for a search through trash or garbage in an effort to find evidence.

Working a garbage pull is hard, time-consuming, unpleasant, and often subject to stringent challenge from defense attorneys. Therefore, it is usually conducted as a last resort and bolstered by a good deal of other investigation.

Vehicle Searches

Often the most useful vehicle search is not a search as defined in legal terms and is therefore not subject to the Fourth Amendment strictures against unreasonable searches and seizure. Vehicles impounded, for whatever reason, are subject to an inventory, an administrative procedure conducted to catalog the contents of vehicles for safekeeping purposes. No search warrant is required, and anything found during this administrative procedure may be used as evidence. Performing a close search for trace evidence, such as fibers and fluids, may require a search warrant, however.

Suspect Searches

It is legally permissible for a police officer to intrude upon the personal body space of a suspect if the officer has what is called in law "reasonable articulable suspicion" of criminal activity and that suspicion is particularized to an individual. In such a case, the officer may stop the person for a brief period to investigate further. If the officer can justify his or her belief that the person may be armed and therefore poses a threat, the officer may "frisk" the person for weapons.

This situation is known as the *Terry Stop*, named after the 1968 Supreme Court case of *Terry* v. *Ohio*. Although frisking a suspect is not a search, it does come under the Fourth Amendment. If, during the "pat-down of the outer clothing for weapons," the officer immediately recognizes an object to be contraband without squeezing, sliding, or otherwise manipulating it, the officer may seize that item and use it as evidence against the person. This is called the "plain feel doctrine," which was allowed after the 1993 U.S. Supreme Court decision in *Minnesota* v. *Dickerson*.

Once a person is taken into custody or arrested, it is assumed that probable cause existed prior to this action and, at this time, a suspect is subject to a "search incident to a lawful arrest." This is a constitutionally unlimited search and may be conducted at the scene or, later, in a more secure location.

Case in Point
In *Terry v. Ohio* (1968), the U.S. Supreme Court ruled: "Where a police officer observes unusual conduct which leads him reasonably to conclude in light of his experience that criminal activity may be afoot and that the persons with whom he is dealing may be armed and presently dangerous, where in the course of investigating this behavior he identifies himself as a policeman and makes reasonable inquiries, and where nothing in the initial stages of the encounter serves to dispel his reasonable fear for his own or others' safety, he is entitled for the protection of himself and others in the area to conduct a carefully limited search of the outer clothing of such persons in an attempt to discover weapons which might be used to assault him."

Dead Body Searches

If a garbage pull is unpleasant and arduous, searching a dead body can be downright gruesome, especially if the body is in an advanced state of decomposition.

Like any other search, the dead body search is conducted systematically, usually beginning with the clothing. Obvious targets of a search include the wallet, identification papers, and personal effects. The investigator is also careful to search around and under the body after it is removed. Beyond these searches, most further investigation is carried out by the medical examiner (see Chapter 10).

Release the Hounds!

The bond between human beings and dogs is older than history, and the working relationship between canine (K-9) officers and their "partners" (that's how they invariably think of their dogs) is especially strong. Police use dogs not only to assist in tracking, apprehending, and controlling suspects, but also in conducting specialized searches.

With their keen sense of smell, dogs can be trained to search for very specific items, from human suspects, to narcotics, to explosives. Dogs can search large areas more efficiently than human beings can, and, in the instance of an explosives search, they can do so in a way that minimizes the risks to police officers.

Savvy criminals have sometimes attempted to foil dog searches by masking narcotics and even explosives with other odors. However, because dogs can distinguish more than one odor simultaneously and to a degree far beyond that of human beings, such masking efforts fail.

By the Numbers _____

According to a 1990 study conducted for the Lansing (Michigan) Police Department, a single K-9 team typically completed building searches seven times faster than four officers working together. The dog team found hidden suspects 93 percent of the time, while human officers found them 59 percent of the time.

Just because a dog isn't human doesn't mean that dog searches are immune from the Fourth Amendment. The courts consider dogs to be agents of the police and, therefore, dog searches require probable cause. Unlike human officers, however, no dog has ever been subpoenaed to testify in a criminal trial.

The Least You Need to Know

- Carefully, accurately, and concisely recording the crime scene, in pictures and words, is not only an aid to solving the crime, but essential to prosecuting suspects.

- The goal of any crime scene investigation is to identify evidence linking a suspect to the scene.

- Investigators must take careful notes, which become part of the record of the criminal investigation; from the beginning of their training, police officers are admonished: _If it's not in the record, it didn't happen._

◆ Searches and interrogations must be thorough and efficient, and they must be conducted within the strictures of the Bill of Rights, particularly the Fourth and Fifth Amendments.

◆ The typical search is of a dwelling or other building; special searches range from sifting through garbage, searching on and around dead bodies, and using dogs to track suspects or to sniff out explosives or narcotics.

Chapter 6

Gathering the Evidence

In This Chapter

♦ Tools of the investigator's trade

♦ A catalog of physical evidence

♦ Discovering and collecting physical evidence

♦ Importance of the "chain of custody"

Edgar Allan Poe is best remembered for his gothic short stories (such as "The Pit and the Pendulum") and his gothic poetry ("The Raven" comes instantly to mind), but, as the Mystery Writers of America recognized when they named their annual mystery fiction award "The Edgar," Poe is also celebrated as the inventor of the detective story.

In 1841, Poe published in *Graham's Lady's and Gentleman's Magazine* (of which he happened to be editor) "The Murders in the Rue Morgue." In it, he introduced the key elements that would become so very familiar in detective fiction: the exquisitely sensitive, brilliant, eccentric investigator (C. Auguste Dupin) who calmly surveys the scene of a bizarre and utterly baffling crime, hones in on precisely the handful of cryptic clues that have escaped the attention of the ordinary policemen, and rapidly works backward from these clues (with nary a misstep) to discover the process, motive, and perpetrator of the crime.

Real-life criminal investigators do, in fact, embody some of the characteristics of Dupin, Sherlock Holmes, Hercule Poirot, or any of a number of other fictional detectives. A good investigator needs a sharp mind and a sharp eye, a large helping of intuition, and a flexible imagination. But, most of all, he or she needs a willingness to do the often hard, tedious, and always meticulous work of gathering evidence for analysis—because, in the court room, eccentricity, acute imagination, and keen intuition count for precisely zip.

An Investigator's Toolkit

A crime is committed in a big city. Investigators pull up to the scene, one of them—sometimes a cop or detective but often a civilian crime scene technician—carrying an aluminum case, bigger than an attaché but smaller than a suitcase. Ah, what high-tech investigative wonders must it contain?

Few, if any.

For the most part, investigators bring to the scene cameras, a set of simple tools, and an array of containers.

Chalk, Tweezers, Wrecking Bar ...

The standard investigative toolkit holds tools for gathering evidence, not for analyzing it. Accordingly, the typical kit contains little more than the following:

> **Case in Point**
>
> At present, most police departments use conventional film cameras rather than digital cameras, because many courts do not admit digital images as evidence and, even when they do, a defense attorney may point to the ease with which digital images can be altered.

- **Angle mirror, with collapsible handle.** This device is handy for looking into difficult-to-get-at places and for getting a quick look at the underside of vehicles.

- **Bloodborne pathogen protection kit.** This is used to protect the evidence gatherer from disease. The kit generally includes such items as fluid solidifying reagent; biohazard scoop; disposable biohazard gown, shoe covers, and bonnet; an assortment of biohazard bags; disposable clean-up towels; exam-quality gloves; a clear plastic eye shield; antiseptic cleansing wipes; and germicidal wipes.

- ◆ **Body fluid collection kit.** This kit is used to collect wet or dry stains on crime scene surfaces—such as walls, doors, floors, window frames, and so on—that cannot be readily transported to the crime laboratory for analysis. This kit typically includes rubber gloves, a vial of distilled water, sterile envelopes, and sterile cotton swabs. The kit may also contain instructions for collecting dried stains and wet stains.

- ◆ **Camera (still) and film.** Investigators take a lot of still pictures. (Well-funded departments send along a trained crime scene photographer to take the pictures.) Often a video camera is also included, because it can provide a good overall picture of the crime scene, one that clearly shows the layout of an area or a room, the relation of one object to another, the location of doors and windows, and so on. The investigator can also supply a running spoken commentary as he or she pans the camera over the scene.

- ◆ **Chalk.** Yes, investigators really do draw a chalk or, sometimes, tape outline to mark the position of bodies or other objects before they are removed from the scene. In crime scenes, the position of a body or other objects in relation to the rest of the crime scene tells a story. It is crucially important to note and record this.

- ◆ **Compass.** This piece of equipment is essential for determining directions and accurately reporting the orientation of bodies or objects at outdoor crime scenes. At some scenes, especially in rural or semiwilderness settings, it is helpful to have GPS (geographical positioning satellite) directions provided by a portable GPS receiver, which can pinpoint the exact longitude and latitude of the scene or scenes involved in a crime.

- ◆ **Containers and envelopes.** Much of the investigator's toolkit consists of nothing more than bags, boxes, bottles, envelopes, and other scrupulously clean, sealable containers to carry small pieces of evidence, especially trace evidence, away from the scene.

- ◆ **Crayon, markers, pencils, pens.** All evidence containers must be clearly and completely labeled. Most police departments provide printed labels with spaces for the required information.

- ◆ **Fingerprint kit.** This includes the various developing powders, chemicals, and lifting tapes discussed in Chapter 7. Some investigators are equipped with a special fingerprint camera, usually a Polaroid-type camera fitted with a macro lens designed to work at close range, to record prints developed at the scene.

- ◆ **Flashlights.** These light sources will do for a start. Investigating and recording some crime scenes requires setting up portable lighting equipment or the use of special forensic light sources, which will be discussed in a moment.

- **Knife.** An ordinary jack knife or Swiss Army knife can be used for many investigative tasks.

- **Magnifier.** Sherlock Holmes wasn't the last detective to make use of a magnifying glass. Some investigators use handheld magnifiers, some employ hands-free magnifiers that fit like goggles or glasses for locating minute or trace evidence, such as hairs and fibers.

- **Measuring tape, rulers, protractors.** Recording precise distances and dimensions is crucial in crime scene investigation. Evidence that is recorded at the scene is often photographed with the inclusion of a ruler in the picture. A protractor is necessary for measuring angles.

- **Picks.** The investigator may need lock picks to gain access to locked rooms or cabinets. He or she may use dental picks to collect (scrape and pry) certain kinds of evidence.

- **Plaster.** Plaster of Paris and other molding substances are commonly used to obtain casts of footprints, tire tracks, and the like.

- **Pliers.** Gathering some evidence requires prying and twisting.

- **Rope or tape.** Fluorescent rope or bright yellow crime scene tape are required to mark off and protect the crime scene.

- **Scissors.** A basic investigative tool.

- **Screwdrivers.** These are often necessary to access evidence.

- **Sexual assault kit**. Hospital emergency rooms and rape crisis centers have such evidence-gathering kits, as do crime scene evidence gatherers. The kit is often referred to as a SAFE (Sexual Assault Forensic Evidence) kit, and its purpose is to preserve physical evidence to be used in criminal proceedings. The kit typically contains cotton swabs, urine collection containers, and sterile sample containers and sealable envelopes for holding physical evidence such as hair, semen, blood, and body tissues.

- **Sketching supplies.** Paper, graph paper, pencils, and so on are used to make a quick sketch of the scene, mainly for purposes of orientation and layout.

- **Spatula.** This tool may be used to dig, scoop, or otherwise gather evidence.

- **Tweezers (forceps).** Indispensable for picking up small evidence items without contaminating them.

- **Wrecking bar.** This may be used to pry open doors, windows, and so on.

Forensic Light Sources

If the notable absence of high-tech equipment disappoints you, take heart. Most investigative kits also include a very cool *forensic light source* or two.

A forensic light source is a powerful portable lamp that contains ultraviolet (UV), visible, and infrared components of light. Using optical filters, the investigator can select (tune) individual color bands (wavelengths) to enhance the visualization of evidence by means of fluorescence (making the evidence glow), absorption (making the evidence appear darker), and oblique lighting (making small-particle evidence more apparent).

def•i•ni•tion

A **forensic light source** is a powerful portable lamp whose spectrum contains ultraviolet (UV), visible, and infrared light components, which can be selectively filtered (tuned) to provide narrow portions of the spectral band for investigative purposes.

Forensic lighting is especially useful in detecting latent fingerprints (see Chapter 7), especially on surfaces that are difficult to dust and lift, such as thin plastic bags, rigid duct tape, thin aluminum foil, heavily grained wood, concrete walls, and brick walls. Investigators lightly dust such surfaces with a special fluorescent powder, which glows under ultraviolet light to reveal the fingerprint.

Such body fluids as semen, saliva, and vaginal fluid are naturally fluorescent under ultraviolet light. Precisely filtered forensic light sources can reveal the presence of these dried fluids on carpeting, mattresses, clothing, and so on.

In its natural state, blood does not fluoresce under UV light but, using the appropriate filter on the forensic light source, blood traces appear to darken, making it much easier to detect and photograph them. (See Chapter 9 for a discussion of how investigators detect blood traces and analyze blood splatter evidence.)

Strong oblique lighting of a surface tends to reveal small particles such as hair and fibers, which may then be collected as evidence. Some hair and fibers also glow under ultraviolet light.

By adjusting the filters on a forensic light source, bruises and wound patterns, invisible under normal white light, may be revealed. Bite marks, shoe marks, and other distinctive wound evidence may also become visible or more clearly defined. Exposing a suspect's palm may reveal a bruise pattern that links him to the use of a bludgeon-type weapon.

What *Is* Evidence, Anyway?

Evidence is anything that helps to establish the facts of the crime under investigation. As discussed in Chapter 5, some evidence is more valuable in a legal sense (more "probative") than others. In addition to witness, victim, and suspect testimony (all promising sources of probative evidence), investigators gather physical evidence, especially of the following types.

Case in Point
Many a poorly trained sleuth has been unable to resist the urge to measure a shoe print by attempting to fit his or her own shoe into the suspect's print. The result? A ruined piece of evidence.

Shoe and Tire Impressions

Shoe soles and heels leave characteristic prints and impressions, as do tire treads. If a pattern found at the scene can be linked to shoes worn by the suspect or a vehicle driven by him, a strong connection to the scene is made. If the prints are on smooth surfaces, they are photographed. They may also be lifted, using special transparent adhesive tape.

On soft surfaces, such as earth, shoes and tires make an impression rather than a print. These are photographed at the scene. An investigator will also usually make a plaster cast of such prints. Some investigators use dental casting material, some use Plaster of Paris.

In the increasingly specialized world of forensics, investigators can call on specialists in shoe prints and tire prints—forensic footwear examiners and forensic tire examiners. Footwear specialists are not only experts in methods of photography, casting, and lifting, but also in the chemical enhancement of impressions; footwear manufacturing methods as they relate to the examination; the evaluation of classes of footwear and the identifying characteristics of footwear; and footwear sizing issues. Tire examiners often have extensive experience in the tire industry, which has given them a background in tire manufacturing, tire re-treading, and tire wear patterns, as well as the recovery and enhancement of tire tread evidence.

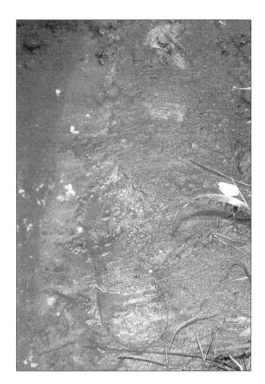

Shoe impressions are typically subtle. An investigator would do her best to make a usable casting of this print in wet, sandy soil.

(Photo by Guy Antinozzi)

Tools and Tool Marks

Tools are commonly used to force entry into buildings or rooms. Any tools found at a crime scene—pry bars, screwdrivers, and the like—need to be collected as evidence and, certainly, dusted for fingerprints. Pieces of broken tools are also important and are collected by investigators. Sometimes it is possible to match a broken tool piece to the rest of a tool found in the suspect's possession.

Tools leave characteristic marks on anything they are applied to. A screwdriver used to pry open a window, for instance, will leave an impression in both the window and sill. These marks need to be noted, photographed, and, perhaps, even cast. They may be matched to a tool found in the suspect's possession.

Sometimes it is possible to match marks on a tool with marks left on the object to which the tool was applied. For example, the sledgehammer used to open a strongbox or safe will leave an impression on the metal of the safe, which may be matched to the surface of the hammer head. If that safe was painted, it may be possible to find traces of the paint on a hammer known to be owned by the suspect.

As in the case of forensic footwear examiners and forensic tire examiners, there are investigative experts who specialize in analyzing tool-mark evidence. The individuals are usually members of the Association of Firearms and Tool Mark Examiners (AFTE), a professional organization dedicated to the exchange of information and developments; the standardization of theory, practice, and techniques; the dissemination of information at annual training seminars; and the publication of a professional journal that covers the latest developments in the field.

Broken Glass

Broken glass is nasty stuff. It adheres to shoes and clothing. Finding shattered glass at a crime scene and tiny glass fragments embedded in the sneaker soles of a suspect can provide a strong evidentiary link between crime and suspect. Large fragments of glass are routinely dusted for fingerprints.

The pattern created by broken glass says much about how the glass was broken and from what direction it was hit. Was it broken from the inside of the building or the outside? Was it hit from above or below?

The size and shape of bullet holes in glass indicate the direction of the bullet's travel and the angle of fire. If the bullet does not shatter the glass, it leaves a conical hole, the smaller hole at the point of entry, the larger at the point of exit. It is even possible to estimate the velocity of the bullet from the appearance of the hole. The faster the bullet, the smaller the cracks will be and the tighter the hole at the point of entry. This information, in turn, enables an investigator to estimate the distance from which the shot was fired.

Soils and Minerals

Fans of Sir Arthur Conan Doyle will remember that Sherlock Holmes was always interested in mud and soil tracked into a crime scene. Holmes was an expert on soils and could tell at a glance where, geographically, a particular sample came from. No one expects a criminal investigator to possess Holmes's encyclopedic knowledge of soils and minerals, but investigators are careful to collect any soil or mineral deposits they find at a crime scene. These can be submitted to a forensic geologist for identification, who may be able to provide analytical results linking a suspect to the scene (see Chapter 13).

Not all soil or mineral samples are of natural origin. They may be traces of cement, plaster, or even building insulation. All of this is typically collected and analyzed. If necessary, investigators may consult the FBI Laboratory, which maintains extensive databases on construction materials, or may call upon the expertise of materials manufacturers or people in the building trades.

Cigarette Butts

Sherlock Holmes was also an expert on rare tobaccos, and he carefully analyzed the butts of certain exotic cigarettes left at a crime scene. Today, cigarette butts provide evidence Holmes never dreamed of. Saliva deposits on a cigarette are a rich source of DNA evidence. Many people involved in a crime are nervous, and many people smoke when they're nervous. Investigators eagerly collect and carefully bag any cigarette butts found at the crime scene.

Sworn Statement

I get to the scene. I look at an ashtray—how they put out a cigarette butt. Which one is still warm? The way each of us puts out a cigarette butt shows certain habits. Then we look for whether there's lipstick or grease on it. You sort it out before you send it to the laboratory. If you do the work, you already know how many people sat in there and smoked, and whether or not there were females or auto mechanics. Then if I go to a suspect's home, I look at the way he or she puts out a cigarette to see if there are similarities with what we found. You make an interpretation of existing patterns.

—Dr. Henry C. Lee, forensic scientist

Rope and Tape

Rope and tape are often used to bind the hands and feet of a victim. Burglars may use tape to hold back a door latch. Tape must be dusted for fingerprints, of course, but tape as well as rope evidence are always carefully collected because it may be possible to match the type of tape or rope found at the scene with materials in a suspect's possession or known to have been purchased by him. Tear patterns in tape or fraying patterns on rope found at the scene may be matched with material associated with the suspect. As with other manufactured materials, the FBI Laboratory maintains comprehensive data on tape and rope. Manufacturers may also be consulted.

Alcohol

Driving Under the Influence (DUI) is one of the most commonly charged offenses. Usually a type of machine called a breathalyzer is used to measure the percentage level of alcohol in a suspect's system by analyzing a sample of breath. The record provided by this machine is evidence usable in court. Another way of measuring someone's blood alcohol level (BAC) is with a blood test. Unlike the breath test, which can be performed in the field, at the moment of arrest, the blood for the test is almost always drawn in a hospital emergency room. It is then sent to the crime lab for analysis. Urine samples may also be used to charge this offense.

Drugs

Drugs associated with a crime scene are always important, whether the drug in question is an illicit substance or a prescription product. This material is carefully collected and sent to the lab for analysis.

Whenever marijuana, narcotics, or other controlled substances are seized by officers, they are field tested before charges are brought by the police. Later, the seized marijuana or controlled substances are sent to a crime lab for thorough analysis. Some large local police agencies have their own marijuana testing labs, but usually the state crime lab is involved. This places a huge burden on the scientists at the crime lab, and it often takes many months for evidence to be processed and the results of analysis delivered. Prosecution cannot be completed until the testing is done.

Weapons and Ammo

Most violent crimes involve firearms. Ballistics, the forensic analysis of firearm-related evidence, can often match a bullet to a gun (see Chapter 8), but first the evidence must be collected.

Investigators look for any weapons left at the crime scene. These may be dusted for fingerprints at the scene, but they must be handled carefully, so that they can be examined further by ballistics experts. The investigator also typically notes at the scene the make, caliber, model, type, and serial number of any weapons found.

Investigators carefully comb the crime scene for bullet holes, bullets lodged in holes, and spent cartridge casings. The position of all bullets and cartridge casings found must be carefully marked and photographed before this evidence is collected and sent to the lab for analysis.

Clothing and Laundry Marks

Clothing may provide a wealth of evidence. Clothing fibers may connect a suspect and victim. A piece of torn clothing—even a thread or two—left at the scene may point to a suspect.

Many professional laundries and dry cleaners use readily identifiable marking systems. The standard systems are on file with the Laundry and Dry Cleaning National Association, and the FBI and other police laboratories also maintain files of marking systems. Such markings can help identify clothed unknown human remains. It should be noted that many laundry marks are visible only under ultraviolet light.

Hair and Fibers

Hair and fibers can provide much valuable evidence because they are often shed ("transferred") by a perpetrator during a struggle or even in casual contact with the victim or with objects at the crime scene (see Chapter 8). However, this kind of trace evidence requires both a keen eye to locate and great care in collecting. Often, the best thing to do is to collect any objects that may be expected to harbor hair and fiber evidence and carefully bag the entire object for later laboratory analysis.

Hairs and fibers that are definitely located at the scene are collected with tweezers and put in appropriate envelopes or other containers.

Blood and Body Fluids

The analysis of blood and other body fluid evidence is discussed in Part 3. On the scene, the principal task is to identify the presence of body fluids, which can be collected for analysis.

Blood makes obvious stains—so obvious that perpetrators often try to wash away any blood evidence. Investigators use forensic light sources and chemical agents (Luminol is the best known) to reveal the presence of blood traces. Even with a cleaning so thorough that the visible stains have been entirely eradicated, hemoglobin in the blood leaves traces that fluoresce when treated with Luminol or that turn color when treated with other substances, such as Orthotolidine.

These days, blood and body fluid evidence is more important than ever, because DNA analysis can often provide positive identification of the human source of the evidence.

Case in Point

Famed forensic investigator Dr. Henry C. Lee was called in on a murder case that lacked a body. (Without a corpse, it is difficult to obtain a homicide conviction.) A 16-year-old girl who worked at a massage parlor was called out on a job. When she failed to return, the police were summoned. Officers found nothing at her client's house. Frustrated, detectives called Lee. "When I got to the basement, I said it was just too clean. It had a wall-to-wall carpet that had recently been shampooed. It was kind of wet." Lee tested the carpet with Orthotolidine, which turned blue, indicating blood traces. Investigators cut the carpet and discovered a pool of blood beneath it. The amount of blood, 2,000 cc, was ample trial evidence of murder. A person who lost that volume of blood *had* to be dead.

Fingerprints

Finding fingerprints is almost always a prime focus of evidence gathering. The process of lifting and analyzing fingerprints is discussed in the next chapter. But before fingerprints can be lifted and analyzed, they must be found. This often requires a long and exhausting search. Think of all the fingerprints that accumulate in an average room. Investigators rarely attempt to cover an entire room, but instead focus on areas and objects most likely to be associated with the crime. Even so, identifying the pertinent prints and eliminating the prints of others—say, the homeowner and family—can be a massive chore.

And this assumes investigators are lucky enough to find *any* usable prints. Most fingerprints on most surfaces are fragmentary smudges, not neat, full-finger patterns.

An Unbroken Chain

Finding and analyzing evidence is only half of the investigative process. Correctly handling and presenting evidence is vital to the probative value of the material. If a defense attorney can create in the mind of the jury a reasonable doubt that evidence was handled properly, the value of that evidence shrinks—perhaps to zero. A significant portion of the successful defense in the infamous O. J. Simpson murder trial was based on the questionable handling of physical evidence.

Evidence, from discovery to courtroom presentation, is supposed to be subject to a flawless chain of custody—a complete record of precisely who had custody of the evidence at each stage of handling. Any weak, let alone broken, link in this chain admits the possibility of accidental contamination or deliberate tampering and provides the basis for a defense argument of reasonable doubt.

Examining Evidence

As soon as an item of evidence is discovered, the investigator, after initially examining it, labels it, preferably with a department-standard card or label. Typically, the label includes the investigator's signature, certifying the authenticity of the evidence and making him or her the first link in the chain of custody. A label or card accompanies the evidence wherever it goes. Each person who subsequently examines the evidence item—including other investigators, forensics experts, and lab technicians—signs the evidence card, noting the date and time the item came into his or her possession.

City of Decatur Police
Decatur, Georgia

EVIDENCE   Case No. _____
Evidence Description _____
_____

Place Evidence found _____
_____

Date & time of recovery _____
Suspect _____ Offense _____
Victim _____
Evidence recovered by _____
                    Signature, rank
          CHAIN OF POSSESSION ON REVERSE SIDE

CHAIN OF POSSESSION OF EVIDENCE
Signatures required

From	to	date	time

RELEASED TO: _____

Standard two-sided evidence tag.

(Image courtesy City of Decatur [Georgia] Police Department)

Preserving and Storing Evidence

Contrary to what some defense attorneys might claim, evidence is rarely subject to deliberate tampering. However, too often, delicate evidence suffers from poor or careless handling.

Guy Antinozzi logging evidence. Notice the telephone, radio, camera, narcotics test kit, and two-hole punch, all essential investigative tools.

(Photo by Sgt. Connie Rembert, Agnes Scott College Police Department)

Medical and some narcotics evidence is perishable and must be carefully preserved in storage. Investigations may consume days, weeks, months, or years. It may take many months for a case to come to trial, then the trial itself may be subject to multiple delays. Even after conviction, the appeals process can span years. Through all of this, evidence must be preserved under proper conditions.

Labels fall off. Ink on labels smudges, fades, becomes illegible. Improperly sealed containers allow liquids (body fluids, for example) to evaporate. Envelopes containing trace evidence become unsealed. In everyday life, these things happen all the time. In police work, they can destroy evidence—and thereby wreck a case.

Many police departments have adopted the kind of modern methods of inventory control retailers use, logging in each piece of evidence into a computer database and printing out a unique, machine-readable barcode label for the item. Centralizing the evidence inventory in this manner helps ensure an unbroken chain of custody.

Presenting Evidence

At trial, physical evidence is *discussed* by the attorneys for the prosecution and the defense, but it is usually first *presented* by the police officer who discovered the evidence.

When an officer presents physical evidence in court, he or she is asked to identify the item. The officer examines the object, making certain that it is authentic and unaltered. The officer is then usually asked to describe exactly where the evidence was found. He or she may be asked to establish the chain of custody from discovery to the present.

It is not the officer's job to analyze the evidence or to draw conclusions from it in testimony. The officer establishes the context of the item within the crime scene and the item's authenticity. After this, it is up to various forensic expert witnesses to persuade the jury of the meaning or significance of the evidence. Then, in the end, it is the jury—not the evidence, not the investigator, not the forensic expert—that convicts or acquits the defendant.

The Least You Need to Know

- Before physical evidence can be analyzed, it must be found and collected. This requires a few simple tools in the hands of diligent, sharp-eyed, experienced, and patient investigators.

- The potential range of physical evidence is huge, encompassing anything the victim and perpetrator used or came into contact with.

- Equal in importance to collecting and analyzing physical evidence properly is handling and storing it in ways that preserve an unbroken chain of custody.

- The police investigator usually presents the physical evidence in court, saying how, when, and where it was recovered and establishing its authenticity; a forensic expert is then usually responsible for conveying to the jury the analytical significance of the evidence item.

Chapter 7

The Fingerprint Story

In This Chapter

- ◆ Early criminal identification and the Bertillon System
- ◆ A brief history of fingerprinting
- ◆ Detecting fingerprint evidence
- ◆ Classifying prints
- ◆ Role of the computer in fingerprint identification

Hear the words "criminal investigation" and, chances are, fingerprints leap to mind. As the layperson (or "civilian," as cops call someone who isn't a cop) sees it, investigating a crime and identifying fingerprints, like salt and pepper at the dinner table, go together.

The association seems so natural that it's hard to imagine a time when fingerprinting was a novel idea, let alone a revolutionary one. After all, archaeologists have discovered evidence suggesting that interest in fingerprints dates to prehistory. On a Nova Scotia cliff face, for example, there is a petroglyph (stone drawing) showing a hand with exaggerated fingerprints—whorls and loops—presumably the work of prehistoric Native Americans. In ancient China and Babylon, fingerprints were routinely impressed on clay-tablet documents, perhaps for purposes of authenticating them (or perhaps merely out of superstition). Inked fingerprints are present on Chinese documents of the Tang Dynasty (618–907).

In this chapter, we'll look at the history of fingerprint identification and the role it plays in criminal investigation.

Early Criminal Identification

There is ample archaeological and historical evidence of an age-old belief that each human fingerprint is unique. In the fourteenth century, a Persian physician and government official put the belief in writing, observing that no two persons have identical fingerprints.

As we shall see later in this chapter, the seventeenth-century Italian anatomy professor Marcello Malpighi made careful observations concerning fingerprints and even described their features with terms very much like those fingerprint experts use today, calling them "loops and spirals."

More recently, in 1858, the chief administrative officer of the Hooghly district of British India, frustrated by the natives' habit of voiding contracts and other legal instruments simply by denying the authenticity of their signatures, required businessmen to place their fingerprints on contracts in addition to their signatures. This, the official declared, would surely "frighten [the signer] out of all thought of repudiating his signature."

Yet well into the nineteenth century, there seems to have been little interest in using fingerprints to help identify the perpetrators of crimes. This does not mean there was a lack of concern about identifying criminals. More than 2,000 years ago, the Roman legions tattooed mercenary soldiers as a means of discouraging desertion—the tattoo would unmistakably identify the runaway as a deserter.

This was, in effect, preemptive criminal identification—a way of discouraging an act *before* it was committed. But many early societies used mutilation (amputating the hand of a thief, for example) or branding as a way to stigmatize offenders. The purpose was not only to punish wrongdoing, but also to discourage repeat offenses and to put the public on guard in the presence of the offender. In the event of a repeat offense, the mutilation or brand made it easier to identify the perp. As civilization progressed beyond the brutality of mutilation and branding as punishments for crime, career criminals found it easy to disguise their identity and blend in with the law-abiding crowd. Even when a *recidivist* was apprehended, there was no guarantee that officials would connect him with his past criminal record. Thus, many repeat offenders were treated with the leniency accorded first timers.

def•i•ni•tion

A **recidivist** is a repeat criminal offender.

The "Father of Scientific Detection"

Alphonse Bertillon (1853–1914), a Frenchman, the son of a physician whose rather erudite hobbies were statistics and anthropology, decided to find a way of identifying known criminals. In 1878, shortly after he became a clerk in the Paris Prefecture of Police, Bertillon undertook the monumental task of rationalizing the police department's chaotic records and slipshod methods of identifying prisoners. After seven years on this job, he formulated the identification method that earned him the title of "Father of Scientific Detection."

The *Bertillon System*, or *bertillonage*, had nothing to do with fingerprinting. Instead, it relied on anthropometry, a carefully formulated combination of physical measurements made by procedures Bertillon standardized. These included (for example) measuring the width of the skull, the length of the foot, the length of the forearm from the elbow to the tip of the middle finger (the biblical "cubit"), the length and girth of the trunk, and the length of the left middle finger. Along with hair color, eye color, and front- and side-view full-length and head-and-shoulder photographs, these

def•i•ni•tion

The **Bertillon System,** also called **bertillonage,** was a systematic method of measuring certain key features of the human body and classifying them rationally as a means of positive identification.

key measurements were recorded on standardized cards. Bertillon divided each of the measurements into small, medium, and large groupings, thereby placing the dimensions of any person into one of 243 distinct categories.

The Bertillon System accomplished several important things. It ensured that a good description of each prisoner would be obtained, it focused on features that could not be readily disguised or altered, and it introduced a significant degree of objectivity into criminal identification. While any number of people might be of similar height and build, it was believed highly unlikely (maybe even impossible) that any two people would exhibit the same *relationship* among all of the features Bertillon measured.

Perhaps most important of all, the Bertillon System made it relatively easy to identify repeat offenders. Once arrested, a suspect was measured, described, and photographed. The completed Bertillon card was indexed and placed in the appropriate category. Statistically, in a file of, say, 5,000 criminal records, each primary Bertillon category would hold only about 20 cards. Police officials had to compare the description and photos of the present prisoner not to 5,000 others, but to about 20.

One of the facial features Bertillon focused on was the nose. He recognized 15 distinct types, as illustrated here.

(Image from the authors' collection)

Not only did the Paris prefecture adopt the Bertillon System (in 1882), but much of the world quickly followed suit. It was introduced into the United States in 1887 by Major R. W. McClaughry, warden of the Illinois State Penitentiary, and it rapidly caught on nationwide.

At first, the universal acceptance of the Bertillon System discouraged the development of alternative systems of identification, including fingerprinting. But, after some years, the Bertillon System began to prove increasingly unwieldy. In large jurisdictions, criminal identification still consumed inordinate amounts of time as clerks searched for matching cards. There was also the ever-present problem of the accuracy of the measurements. The Bertillon System required exact training, which was often imperfect or simply unavailable. The result was flawed measurements and inaccurate data.

Then came the real bombshell: although the likelihood of any two individuals possessing identical relationships among the various features Bertillon measured was remote, it was not impossible. Bertillon measurements were not absolutely unique. Instances of mistaken identity were rare, but they did happen.

In the United States, the beginning of the end of reliance on the Bertillon System came in 1903. A man named Will West was sent to the Federal Penitentiary at Leavenworth, Kansas. He denied that he had ever been incarcerated there before, but his Bertillon measurements matched those on file for a William West. Moreover, the photographs of the new prisoner looked very much like those on file for William West. About to call Will West a liar, the clerk flipped over the card for William West. It noted that he was currently in custody at Leavenworth Federal Penitentiary. The case of the two Wests simultaneously demolished the certainty of Bertillon measurements and encouraged adoption of fingerprint identification.

Fingerprinting: A Short History

Fingerprinting for criminal identification began to catch on in England and the United States at the beginning of the twentieth century, and in 1924, the United States Congress enacted legislation creating the Identification Division of the Bureau of Investigation (the federal law enforcement agency that was renamed the *Federal Bureau of Investigation*—the FBI—in 1935) as a central repository of fingerprint files. How did law enforcement finally catch up with the long history of general interest in fingerprints?

Malpighi's Treatise

Marcello Malpighi was an Italian anatomy professor at the University of Bologna who made a number of important medical discoveries, including observations relating to the structure of the skin (the "Malpighi layer," a deep layer of the epidermis, is named after him) and the existence of capillaries, a key to understanding the human circulatory system.

In a treatise of 1686, he published another discovery, which, at the time, must have seemed rather minor: the human fingertips, he wrote, were characterized by distinctive patterns of spirals and loops and whorls.

Purkinji and Herschel: Fingerprinting Becomes an Identification Tool

Malpighi suggested no practical application for his observations on fingerprints, and it wasn't until 137 years later, in 1823, that John Evangelist Purkinji, a professor of anatomy at the University of Breslau, published a thesis in which he identified nine distinct fingerprint patterns. Even prior to Malpighi, the uniqueness of each human fingerprint was theorized. What Purkinji showed was that, while fingerprints were indeed unique from person to person, they were not simply random, but formed recognizable categories of patterns. Most modern fingerprint classification systems are based on Malpighi's patterns (see "The Nine Basic Patterns" later in this chapter).

Yet even this insight seems to have gone nowhere. Certainly, it did not lead Purkinji or any of his contemporaries to suggest that fingerprints, unique but capable of categorization, could be used for personal identification.

Thirty-three years later, it was Sir William Herschel, the British administrator in colonial India, who first deliberately used fingerprints for the purpose of positive identification. He was unfamiliar with Purkinji, and his idea of asking an Indian businessman, Rajyadhar Konai, to put his inked palm (not just his fingers) on the back of a contract so that he couldn't later repudiate it, was something of a whim. But when Herschel saw that Konai was so impressed that he swore he would never repudiate the contract, Herschel made it a rule that all contracts he witnessed had to be signed *and* printed—although he decided that the print of the right index and middle fingers, not the whole palm, would be sufficient (and a lot less messy).

Over his years of public service in India, Herschel accumulated a sizable fingerprint collection, which he offered as empirical proof of what had often been asserted in theory: that each fingerprint was unique as well as permanent to the individual.

Faulds and Galton: The Classification of Fingerprints

Purkinji had demonstrated recognizable pattern types in fingerprints, and Herschel had empirically proved that each fingerprint was unique and, therefore, uniquely useful for purposes of identification. In the 1870s, Dr. Henry Faulds, British surgeon-superintendent of Tsukiji Hospital in Tokyo, Japan, put these two concepts together.

After studying finger marks left on certain examples of prehistoric pottery, Faulds not only recognized the importance of fingerprints as a means of identification, but set out to devise a method of classifying them.

In 1880, he proposed in a scientific journal that printer's ink could be employed to make fingerprints usable for identification. He may also have been the first person actually to determine identity on the basis of a fingerprint clue when he matched to its owner a greasy fingerprint left on an alcohol bottle.

In the same year that he published his early work on fingerprinting, he sent an explanation of his system of fingerprint classification to no less a figure than Sir Charles

Darwin, creator of the theory of evolution. Old and ailing, Darwin apologized to Faulds that he was unable to devote time and attention to his ideas on fingerprinting, but he promised to pass the information to his cousin, Sir Francis Galton.

Galton was a prominent anthropologist, and he was quite excited by Faulds's work. Building on it and on his own observations, he published in 1892 a book simply titled *Fingerprints*, in which he clearly identified the characteristics by which fingerprints could be identified. He called these characteristics *minutiae*, but today they are referred to as *Galton's Details*, some of which remain the basis on which fingerprints are classified.

def•i•ni•tion

Galton's Details, named for the nineteenth-century fingerprinting pioneer, Sir Francis Galton, are distinctive features of fingerprint patterns that can be used to compare and match sets of fingerprints for identification purposes. Galton's Details are also called **minutiae.**

FBI on the Case, 1924

Britain's famed Scotland Yard began systematically using fingerprint identification early in the twentieth century, and various police and correctional agencies in the United States began to follow suit. In 1924, Congress funded the creation of the Bureau of Investigation's Identification Division, which immediately took custody of 810,188 fingerprint files, mostly from the Leavenworth Penitentiary.

As the automobile became a fixture of American life, more criminals crossed state lines in the commission of crimes, and the centralized, federalized fingerprint collection became increasingly important in law enforcement. Investigators not only concentrated on obtaining and classifying prints, but began developing techniques for finding fingerprints on weapons and on other features of crime scenes.

By the Numbers

Currently, FBI files bulge with more than 250 million sets of fingerprint records, including criminal and civil prints (prints of government employees and applicants for federal jobs). The FBI receives more than 34,000 fingerprint cards from various federal, state, and local agencies *every* workday. Pile up all of the fingerprint cards on file with the FBI, and you'd have 133 stacks, each as tall as the Empire State Building. The increasingly widespread adoption of electronic scanning of fingerprints promises to put an end to inked cards.

Finding the Prints

Few criminals are either sufficiently stupid or obliging to go about their business with ink on their fingers (although bloodstained or dirty finger and palm prints are sometimes clearly visible at crime scenes). The unfortunate fact is that, at many crime scenes, no fingerprints are found at all and, even when they are, they may not be clear enough to use. Even assuming that good prints can be found, they are of limited use if matching prints are not on file. (While such prints can't be used immediately to identify a known perpetrator, they can be filed and compared to fingerprints taken from suspects who are subsequently apprehended.)

Visible, Invisible, and Plastic

Latent fingerprints are what criminal investigators seek as evidence. These are fingerprint impressions transferred to a surface, either by the natural oils and sweat on the ridges of the fingertips or by dirt, blood, or other substances on the fingers. Latent prints may be visible, invisible, or plastic:

♦ **Visible fingerprints** are made by stained or dirty fingers. They are usually found on smooth, glossy, or light-colored surfaces.

♦ **Invisible fingerprints,** made by natural oils or sweat, are typically found on nonporous surfaces and must be rendered visible either by dusting or chemical processing.

♦ **Plastic fingerprints** are print impressions left in soft materials, such as tar, wax, soap, or even dust.

Dusting for Prints

Special powders are used to "develop" invisible prints left on hard, nonabsorbent surfaces such as glass, tile, mirrors, and painted wood. The powder is carefully dusted onto the surface using a fine brush. It reacts with deposited skin oils, adhering to oils or sweat and thereby revealing an impression of the print.

Fingerprints revealed by dusting are carefully photographed. In addition, they may be lifted, using a special transparent adhesive tape. The tape is applied to the dusted print, lifted off, and the resulting image is immediately transferred to a fingerprint card. The photograph or card is analyzed to determine the classification of the print, and it is then compared to prints that are on file.

Example of a lifted fingerprint.

(Image from the authors' collection)

Chemical Processing

To develop invisible prints that may have been left on soft, porous surfaces such as cardboard, paper, or cloth—substances that don't work well with powders—special chemical agents are used.

Iodine vapors react with skin oils to stain the invisible print brown. For iodine fuming, iodine crystals are loaded into a special fuming cabinet (if the object to be examined is small enough to take to the crime lab and fit into the cabinet) or into a fuming gun (which can be used at the crime scene). The image that results from fuming quickly fades and must therefore be photographed immediately.

Case in Point

New high-tech methods for developing latent prints are emerging, including the use of laser technology. However, many police agencies use cyanoacrylate fuming, a fancy term for exposure to the fumes of Super Glue or Crazy Glue. Typically, Super Glue is put in a dish or on a hot plate, heated in a closed container along with the evidence, and the vapor settles on the print, forming a white outline.

Ninhydrin (Triketohydrindane hydrate) can be sprayed or brushed onto evidence or, if practical, the evidence can be dipped into the ninhydrin. This chemical reacts with amines, which are the residue of peptides and proteins that are transferred from the fingertips to an object as it is touched or manipulated. Reacting with the amines, ninhydrin turns purple, creating a fingerprint image. At room temperature, the chemical reaction ("development") takes as long as two hours, so, typically, heat is applied to hasten the reaction. While the resulting image does not quickly fade, it does lose contrast over time and, as with images produced by iodine fuming, it must therefore be preserved through photography.

Silver nitrate develops the sodium chloride (the salt that is in sweat) deposited by the fingers and produces a red-brown print. The evidence may be sprayed with a silver nitrate and alcohol solution or it may be dipped. Exposure to light speeds development. Again, however, the image is ephemeral and must be photographed.

Loops to Whorls: The Classification of Fingerprints

As we've mentioned, fingerprints are a compelling means of identification because they are unique to the individual, yet they are readily classifiable into distinct categories that greatly facilitate comparison between any latent prints recovered at a crime scene and prints on file in police agencies.

Fingerprint patterns are divided into three broad groups: loops, arches, and whorls.

Loops

Sixty to 65 percent of fingerprints are loops, a pattern in which one or more ridges enter from one side of the print, curve around, and exit from the same side. Varieties of the loop are the plain loop that enters and exits on the right, the plain loop that enters and exits on the left, the central pocket loop, the lateral pocket loop, and the twinned loop.

Arches

Arches come in two basic varieties, the plain arch and the tented arch. In either case, the pattern begins on one side, rises to a peak or arch, and exits on the other side. Arches account for about 5 percent of fingerprints.

Whorls

A whorl is a circular pattern with no entrance or exit. The two basic whorls are simple and accidental. The simple whorl exhibits only the circular pattern, whereas the accidental whorl contains more than two deltas, which are places where two lines run side by side, then diverge with a significant line that curves around and passes in front of the delta.

Sworn Statement

Fingerprints are of extreme evidentiary value in criminal investigations, because they are the strongest possible evidence of a person's identity.

—Wayne W. Bennett and Kären M. Hess, *Criminal Investigation*

The Nine Basic Patterns

Many fingerprint experts recognize even more varieties of loops, arches, and whorls than the basic patterns just mentioned; however, these patterns account for what the FBI calls the nine basic fingerprint patterns: plain arch, tented arch, plain loop (right), plain loop (left), simple whorl, central pocket loop, lateral pocket loop, twinned loop, and accidental whorl.

The basic patterns allow investigators to narrow the search for file prints that may match prints obtained from crime evidence. Once a group of possible matches is obtained, a fingerprint expert compares specific identification points, minute features within the patterns that allow for specific matching of an evidence print with a file print. Common features include islands (small enclosed ridge patterns), dots (isolated dots rather than ridge lines), bifurcations (ridges that diverge or fork in various ways), and ending ridges (ridges that don't connect, but simply dead end). Some experts recognize as many as 100 or more identification points in any given print. In order to declare a match between a file print and an evidence print, a minimum of 12 identical identification points is typically required.

The nine basic fingerprint patterns, used by the FBI and adapted from Purkinji's original classification system.

(Image from the Federal Bureau of Investigation)

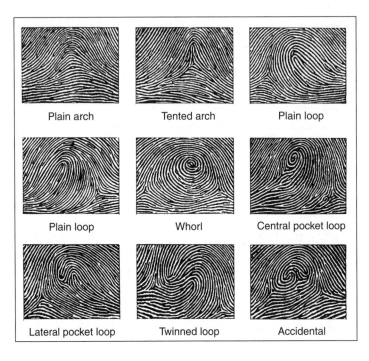

Plain arch	Tented arch	Plain loop
Plain loop	Whorl	Central pocket loop
Lateral pocket loop	Twinned loop	Accidental

AFIS: Automated Fingerprint Identification System

Fingerprint classification and matching takes skill and patience—traditionally, *a lot* of patience. Comparing evidence prints to file prints is essentially an exercise in pattern recognition, an activity in which modern, graphically oriented computer systems excel. Automated Fingerprint Identification Systems are computerized systems that electronically scan evidence prints and compare the scan to a digitized database of file prints, outputting potential matches for a human operator to examine and review.

The investigator runs the evidence print through an optical scanner that is linked to a computer. The computer program analyzes the scan for matching identification points. The computer then outputs a list of file prints that have the closest correlation to whatever criteria the investigator has specified. The computer's "word" is not accepted as law; a trained human expert always examines the prints to verify the match. AFIS technology has greatly accelerated the process of fingerprint identification.

A Word about DNA "Fingerprinting"?

In recent years, DNA evidence has become increasingly important in criminal investigation, and we often hear about "DNA fingerprinting." This process is covered in Chapter 14, and although it should not be confused with conventional fingerprint examination and analysis, there are important analogies between the use of DNA and conventional fingerprint evidence in criminal investigation. Both conventional fingerprinting and "DNA fingerprinting" analyze evidence resulting from various forms of physical contact and interaction in order to ascertain the identity of the person or persons involved in that contact and interaction. Despite the attention—especially in the media—lavished on DNA evidence during recent years, it is likely that conventional fingerprint examination will remain an important part of criminal investigation for a long time to come because most crimes, especially violent crimes, involve physical manipulation—actions that may transfer minute traces of sweat, oils, or amines to an object, but not the transfer of DNA-bearing substances.

The Least You Need to Know

- Alphonse Bertillon, a nineteenth-century French police clerk, developed the Bertillon System, the first effective attempt to identify criminals objectively and unambiguously.

- Interest in fingerprints dates from prehistory, but it wasn't until the end of the nineteenth century that it became viable as a means of identification.

- Flaws in the Bertillon System spurred almost universal adoption of fingerprint identification by the early twentieth century.

- Criminal investigators attempt to recover latent fingerprints in order to compare these with fingerprints on file, either locally or at the FBI.

- The systematic classification of a relatively small number of basic fingerprint patterns makes fingerprint identification and matching practical.

Chapter 8

Crime Lab

In This Chapter

- ◆ The field of forensics
- ◆ The modern crime lab
- ◆ Forensic chemistry
- ◆ Ballistics and firearms examination
- ◆ Analyzing prints: tools, shoes, and tires
- ◆ Arson investigation

Fans of Sir Arthur Conan Doyle's archetypal sleuth Sherlock Holmes certainly have a vivid picture of a crime lab: Holmes's London parlor at 221B Baker Street, in which flasks, bubbling retorts, and a microscope stand cheek by jowl with the detective's Meerschaum pipe and Stradivarius fiddle. Holmes routinely subjected tiny bits of evidence (today these would be called "trace evidence") to microscopic and chemical analysis, and he wrote learned treatises on such arcane subjects as how to determine what type of tobacco an offender smoked by analyzing the ashes left behind.

At one time, of course, all science was a kind of hobby, the leisure pursuit of gentlemen with time on their hands. And as a Victorian gentleman par excellence, Sherlock Holmes had plenty of time to devote to science in the service of his all-consuming avocation, crime detection.

Twenty-first-century criminal investigation has no patience with amateurs, even those on a par with Sherlock Holmes. As we'll see in this chapter, a high level of professionalism is required when so much rides on the work of the crime lab: the efficient allocation of police resources to apprehend an offender, the thorough and accurate analysis of evidence that will be used to prosecute the accused—or to exonerate the innocent—and the protection of the public safety.

Forensics: What It Is

Let us review: forensic science (sometimes simply called forensics) is the application of science—including physical, medical, and behavioral science—as it relates to the law. Scientific methods, procedures, and equipment are used in investigating crimes as well as in proving, in a court of law, the guilt of the accused.

Potentially, any field of scientific inquiry might be applied to forensic work, but it is certain disciplines from the physical and medical sciences that are called on most frequently.

def•i•ni•tion

> **Trace evidence** is extremely small physical matter (such as a carpet fiber, a hair, a chip of paint) that has evidentiary value. **Questioned documents** are any documents that may have relevance to the commission of a crime. The term is often used specifically to refer to suspected forgeries or documents that have been illicitly altered.

Physical Sciences

Chemistry and physics are the two broad fields of physical science that have the most direct application to forensics. Chemical analysis is important in analyzing the nature of *trace evidence*, including questionable substances (such as illicit drugs), hairs and fibers, firearms identification, tool marks, shoe prints, and voice analysis. It is also used to analyze *questioned documents* (documents that may be forged or may have other relevance to the commission of a crime), an area discussed later in the chapter. Specialists often study documents in which ink or paper type might hold clues as to origin, which might in turn help uncover the identity of an offender.

Medical Sciences

Homicide leaves in its wake one or more bodies, and other crimes, such as rape, typically leave fluid and tissue traces. The medical sciences have assumed such importance in forensics that they are treated in the three chapters of the next part of this book, Part 3. In this chapter, we focus exclusively on the physical sciences in the crime lab. For a discussion of the forensic application of behavioral science, see Chapter 3.

Work of the Modern Crime Lab

At its best, the modern crime lab is a state-of-the-art research laboratory. Any research laboratory needs up-to-date equipment, highly trained researchers, and a set of orderly procedures scrupulously followed. Good science depends on these things. A laboratory that puts science in the service of criminal investigation must, if anything, adhere to even higher standards. After all, the enforcement of law, the determination of guilt or innocence, and, ultimately, the safety and well-being of the public depend on the work it does.

Chemical Analysis: Trace Evidence

The chemistry section of the crime lab is equipped to subject a variety of trace evidence to analysis, including …

- **The presence and type of dyes and chemicals.** Many banks use specific dyes and chemicals in such security devices as packs of money that are rigged to explode after a certain delay period, spraying a dye marker on whomever is close to the stolen cash. Even after repeated cleaning, traces of the dye remain on skin, hair, clothing, automobile interior, and other items. Also, some cash may be treated with special dye markers, visible or invisible, so that stolen cash can be identified. The chemistry lab can analyze samples of clothing or currency.

- **Stained clothing or other items found at a crime scene.** The forensic chemist can analyze the stain to determine what it is. The presence of certain lubricant stains, for example, may provide clues to an offender's occupation as a factory worker, for instance, or an auto mechanic. Often it is possible to analyze stains with great precision, so that the substance found may be associated with a very specific activity or vocation: motor oil is chemically distinct from lubricants used in various factory processes; silicone lubricants are used exclusively in some industries, petroleum lubricants in others. The lab can also compare stains or markings to suspected sources: the stain found on a suspect's clothing may be analyzed and compared to a substance found at the scene of the crime.

- **Unknown substances** found in conjunction with a crime scene; the chemistry lab can run tests to identify them.

- **The composition of inks and papers.** For example, it may be possible to discover the author of a ransom note or a bomb threat when comparing the ink or paper with known samples.

- **Manufacturing or building materials,** many of which have distinctive chemical compositions. A forensic chemist can analyze and compare items found at a crime scene to suspected sources. Experts from specific manufacturing or building industries may also be consulted.

- **Plastics** in wire insulation and miscellaneous plastics such as buttons can be compared with known sources.

- **Duct tape,** which is sometimes used to restrain the victim of a violent crime. The lab can analyze tape samples to determine composition, construction, and color, and from this determine the manufacturer. The FBI crime lab maintains a National Forensic Tape File, with samples of virtually every known tape. If the manufacturer of the tape is known, it may be possible to identify stores in a given area that sell the tape. Investigators can call on these stores and ask questions concerning suspects.

- **Caulks, sealants, and adhesives,** which may be identified as to color, composition, and maker.

> **Case in Point**
>
> Another important source of auto-related evidence is found in fragments of trim, which can be compared with plastic remaining on the property (or person) struck in a hit-and-run case.

- **Traces of paint.** For example, the color, year, make, and model of an automobile can be determined by comparing a very small sample of paint—rubbed or chipped off, say, when the getaway car sideswiped the side of a building—to a comprehensive file of known sources. Paint on safes, vaults, window sills, and door frames can be transferred to and from burglar tools. Chemical examination of suspicious tools can demonstrate their use in a particular crime.

Chemical Analysis: Drugs, Poisons, and Other Substances

The chemistry section of the crime lab is often called on to analyze substances suspected of being—or known to be—illegal drugs. Even minute traces can be analyzed, and the chemist can usually report on the type of drug, its strength, and sometimes its probable origin.

The crime lab is called upon to perform many functions related to chemical analysis, from confirming the presence of alcohol in the blood or urine sample of an accused DUI suspect to the presence of toxicological evidence of a poisoning in a murder case.

Most of the requests are mundane. The officer obtains the body substance sample and preserves it in the manner prescribed by the crime lab (see Chapter 6). The samples are taken to the crime lab and the questioned material is analyzed. The sheer volume of material delivered to most crime labs is enough to delay prosecution of cases significantly.

A variety of bodily fluids and body parts are delivered for analysis.

◆ Blood and urine: The standard tests for the presence of illegal substances in blood and urine are *gas chromatography* and *mass spectrophotometry*. These tests produce graph-type results that show peaks and valleys, which alert the lab technician to the presence or absence of certain substances.

◆ Stomach contents: Chromotgorahy, which separates the various constituents of a fluid mixture, is used to analyze stomach—or gastric—contents, which may show a higher concentration of a suspicious substance than is present in the blood or urine.

def•i•ni•tion

Gas chromatography and mass spectrophotometry are the standard crime lab tests for detecting and measuring illegal substances in the blood. The tests produce graph-type results, the peaks and valleys of which indicate the presence and level of specific substances.

◆ Vitreous humor: The gelatinous substance present in the ocular area around the eyeball, the vitreous humor, often persists in a cadaver during and after decomposition and may be the only body fluid remaining in a corpse. Analysis of it is therefore useful in determining facts surrounding the death of the person.

◆ Bile and liver: Most metabolic processes take place in the liver. The substance it secretes, bile, often contains significant quantities of drugs or controlled substances.

◆ Hair: In recent years, kits have become available with which parents can test the hair of children they suspect of drug use; however, hair is not the most reliable specimen for forensic investigation. It is difficult to establish whether drug traces found in the hair came from ingested drugs or external exposure to drugs. Workplace testing involving hair samples is still common, but the standard for criminal forensic investigation is higher. Although hair is not considered a specimen of choice for drug testing, it often yields other important information in the crime lab.

Suspicious substances are tested in the lab or in the field using specially packaged chemical kits.

(Image courtesy of DeKalb County [Georgia] Solicitor-General's Office)

Hairs and Fibers

Like many other items of trace evidence, hairs and fibers can be difficult to locate at a crime scene. Strong lighting and careful searching are required to turn up these items. Often the extra vigilance is worth the effort, because such evidence can place a subject at a crime scene, especially in crimes of violence, in which some interchange of hairs or fibers is likely to occur. It is also possible that the suspect will inadvertently carry hair or fiber away from the scene—for example, if he kneels on a carpet.

Hair has a distinct structure, consisting of an outer cuticle (with overlapping scales that point toward the tip), a cortex (consisting of elongated cells), and the medulla (the center of the hair, consisting of variably shaped cells). Because the appearance of these structures vary, it is often possible, using a microscope, to identify an evidence strand of hair with a known source (such as the victim of a violent crime).

If blood is present on the hair, identification becomes more certain. Hair is also an excellent source of DNA evidence (see Chapter 14).

Under the microscope, it is possible to distinguish between human and animal hair, and between hair from the head, pubic hair, facial hair, and so on. Many drugs and poisons, such as arsenic, accumulate in the hair; analysis of strands is very useful to the toxicologist (see Chapter 11).

Forensic experts refer to hair specimens as "class characteristic" evidence; that is, a hair recovered from a crime scene or suspect may have enough similar properties compared with a known sample to be deemed "consistent with" the sample, but it cannot be said definitively to be a perfect match. Hair samples are very effectively used to *exclude* a suspect; for instance, Caucasian hair differs from Negroid hair, so the presence of Caucasian hair on the clothing of a homicide victim may tend to exclude a black suspect.

Nonhair fibers are of many varieties, but they fall into four major groups: mineral, vegetable, animal, and synthetic. Examples of mineral fibers are fiberglass and asbestos; vegetable fibers can include cotton, manila, hemp, and so on; animal fibers can include wool and silk; and the most common synthetics are rayon, nylon, and polyester.

After narrowing down fiber evidence to one of these four groups, the laboratory investigator can begin to compare the questioned fiber with known specimens. In some cases, it is actually possible to identify manufacturers on the basis of synthetic fiber evidence. Suspect A denies ever visiting Victim B's house. Forensic examination has recovered fibers from under Suspect A's fingernails. Analysis reveals that they are from a carpet made by Manufacturer C. Victim B's apartment has this carpeting wall to wall.

Case in Point

In 1958, 16-year-old Gaetane Bouchard, a Canadian girl, was murdered. Her ex-boyfriend, John Vollman, who lived across the border in Maine, had been seen with her just before the discovery of the murder. Flakes of paint from the place where they had been seen together were matched to Vollman's car. Also, lipstick stains matching the color Bouchard used were found on candy in the car's glove compartment. But it was strands of hair found clutched in the victim's hand that finally persuaded the jury. Using neutron activation analysis, these were matched to Vollman's hair by demonstrating an identical ratio of sulphur radiation to phosphorus. This ratio differed from the hair of the victim herself.

Neutron activation analysis, developed in the 1950s, is still a high-tech tool and is still sometimes used in the forensic analysis of hair, fiber, and some other trace evidence. The evidence is bombarded with neutrons inside the core of a nuclear reactor. The neutrons collide with the components of the trace elements, exciting them so that they emit gamma radiation of a characteristic energy level. By examining these energy levels, the investigator can measure every part of the sample, no matter how small. A single hair reveals 14 distinct components.

Polarized Light Microscopy

Light from most sources, such as the sun, radiates in waves that vibrate in all directions. This light may be polarized by filtering it so the vibrations of the light waves occur on a single plane. Polarized light can be used to analyze so-called anisotropic materials, which include 90 percent of all solid substances. In contrast to isotropic materials, which include gases, liquids, unstressed glasses, and cubic crystals, anisotropic materials have optical properties that vary with the orientation of a polarized light source. This means that the combination of a polarized light source and a special microscope can be used to study a wide variety of natural and industrial minerals and composites (such as cements, ceramics, mineral fibers, and polymers) as well as crystalline or highly ordered biological molecules, including DNA, starch, wood, and urea. Such analysis can reveal the effects of various chemical and physical processes, making it possible in some cases to link a substance found at a crime scene (or associated with a victim) to a suspect or object associated with him.

Voice and Image Analysis

The lives we live today are extensively mediated—that is, much of our reality comes to us not directly through our own ears and eyes, but via such media as television, radio, the telephone, and audio- and videotape recording. The one thing criminal investigation must account for above all is reality, and if today's reality includes electronic media, the forensic scientist must figure out ways to examine and analyze it.

Audio and video recordings are very easy to edit and alter. Advanced crime laboratories have the equipment and experts to determine whether recordings are original, continuous, unaltered, and consistent with the stated operation of the tape or video recorder purportedly used.

Evidence recordings are often made under less than ideal circumstances, using hidden microphones in noisy surroundings or hidden cameras in poor lighting conditions. Audio or video recordings may be damaged—as in arson evidence, for instance—or tapes may be deliberately erased. Crime lab experts can sometimes enhance poor-quality or damaged tapes to reduce interfering noise, to increase the readability of an image, and generally to restore and repair damaged media.

Signal analysis is another aspect of examining both audio and video recordings. It is often possible to identify, compare, and interpret such background signals as gunshots or telephone touch tones. From the sound of a gunshot, experts may be able to determine direction and even the type of firearm used. From telephone touch tones picked up on recordings, dialed phone numbers can be recovered.

Most intriguing to the public is so-called voiceprinting, which is the electronic analysis of the human voice as a graphic sound spectrograph. This spectrograph—or voiceprint—is unique to the speaker, as a fingerprint is unique to a particular finger. Any sound, including the human voice, can be represented graphically as a sound spectrograph, a distinctive pattern. As with fingerprints, no two voiceprints are exactly alike—even when a skilled mimic deliberately disguises his or her voice to sound like that of another. By comparing evidence voiceprints with known voice samples—or samples obtained from a suspect in custody—it is often possible to find a match. In this way, offenders such as bomb hoaxers, obscene callers, or others can be identified. Courts generally do not consider voiceprint evidence in and of itself conclusive, but voiceprint evidence does provide investigative guidance and can be presented in court as one evidentiary element among others.

Evidence in the form of conventional photography is also often submitted to the crime lab. As with electronic media, photographs can be examined for authenticity and to enhance poor images. The lab can determine if the photograph has been altered or retouched. It can often tell what type of camera was used to produce the picture. Physical examination of film and emulsion types can help determine the date of the photograph.

Voiceprints: the print on top closely matches the lower print, strongly suggesting that the two audio samples were spoken by the same person.

(Image from the authors' collection)

Firearms Identification

Most violent crimes in the United States are committed with firearms. The interiors of gun barrels are rifled (grooved) in order to make the bullet spin and thereby increase its accuracy. The rifling leaves distinctive marks on the bullet that is fired. By examining the markings on bullets recovered from a crime scene or a victim's body, investigators can often determine the make and model of the firearm used. If a suspect firearm is recovered, a ballistics expert—someone skilled in the analysis of all evidence relating to the discharge of firearms—will fire it, recover the discharged round, and compare it microscopically to the bullet from the crime scene. A positive match indicates that the crime scene bullet was fired from the suspect firearm.

Even if a suspect firearm has not been recovered, bullets and cartridges found at a crime scene can be analyzed using the Integrated Ballistics Identification System (IBIS). Maintained by the U.S. Bureau of Alcohol, Tobacco and Firearms (ATF), IBIS is a comprehensive database of ammunition that is analogous to the FBI's comprehensive fingerprint files.

Firearms, as well as ammunition, are examined in the ballistics lab. The examination begins with an assessment of the general condition of the firearm: is it functional? A trigger-pull analysis exactly determines the amount of pressure necessary to release the hammer or firing pin of a firearm. If a slightly built female defendant claims that she isn't strong enough to pull the trigger of that gun, the results of the trigger-pull analysis may demolish that defense.

Examinations can also determine whether a firearm has been illegally modified to fire in the full-automatic mode. In cases where firearm serial numbers have been filed off by an offender, analysts can sometimes restore them to legibility.

Case in Point
The analysis of rifling marks may be thought of as a branch of tool-mark identification because the subject is the imprint left by a specialized tool (the gun, with its distinctively rifled barrel) on an object (the shell casing). Today, some experts call rifling analysis by another name: ballistic fingerprinting.

Another important aspect of firearms examination is analysis of how gunshot residue is deposited on such evidence as clothing. The pattern of gunpowder and other blast residue varies with the distance between the muzzle of the firearm and the target. By comparing evidence patterns to patterns obtained in laboratory test firings, such information as muzzle-to-victim distance can be determined, along with the direction (angle) from which the shot was fired.

Firing a weapon also often leaves traces of nitrate (an ingredient in gunpowder) on the skin of the shooter.

Applying warm paraffin to a suspect's hand picks up impurities, including nitrate, from the skin and pores. The paraffin is treated with chemicals (diphenylamine or diphenyl-benzidine), which turn blue in the presence of nitrate. This tends to indicate that the suspect has recently fired a gun—although the test is by no means foolproof, since the procedure can give both false positives and false negatives. Shooting a gun is not the only way to get nitrate on the skin, and the absence of nitrate does not necessarily mean that the person hasn't fired a weapon recently.

def•i•ni•tion

Tool marks are characteristic impressions transferred from any tool to the material it has worked. The impressions left on the material may be matched to marks on the tool.

Tool Marks, Shoe Prints, and Tire Prints

Burglars and other intruders often use tools to pry open windows or doors. Just as the barrel of a gun leaves characteristic marks on the round that is fired, tools leave tell-tale marks on the material they work. Some *tool marks* are easy to identify. A suspected burglar is apprehended carrying a screwdriver with a blade one-half-inch wide and one-eighth-inch thick to pry open a window. Detectives find a one-half-inch-wide, eighth-inch-deep groove on the wooden windowsill of the victim's house.

Other tool-mark evidence is more complex and requires microscopic analysis in the laboratory. A sledgehammer was used to open a safe. The hammer left striated marks on the safe. A sledgehammer is recovered from the suspect. Microscopic examination of the striations on the safe match the striations on the hammer. Conclusion: *that* hammer imprinted *those* marks on the safe.

Shoe and tire prints found at crime scenes can be very important (see Chapter 6). From the number and direction of shoe prints, the number of offenders may be determined, along with the direction of their approach and exit. By photographing the prints and by carefully making plaster casts of them, it is possible (on the simplest level) to compare the pattern with the pattern of the suspect's shoes. It is also some-times possible to determine the manufacturer of the shoe and even the approximate weight of the offender (based on the depth of the print in a given material). It is often possible to distinguish between men's and women's shoes and, based on the size of the print, to make a guess about the offender's height and weight.

Large crime laboratories, including the FBI's facility, maintain files of shoe patterns, which can expedite the process of identifying manufacturers.

Tires, like shoes, leave characteristic prints. From the pattern of a tire print, the type of vehicle and the manufacturer (as well as year of manufacture) of the tire can be determined. It is also possible to estimate speed and direction of travel.

Case in Point

The most famous case of shoe-print evidence was introduced in the trial of O. J. Simpson for the murder of his ex-wife, Nicole Brown Simpson, and her friend, Ronald Goldman, on June 12, 1994. Prosecutors showed pictures of bloody footprints leading away from the crime scene. William Bodziack, an FBI expert on shoe prints, testified that the prints were made by expensive and relatively rare Bruno Magli shoes. Just 300 pairs were ever sold in Simpson's size 12. Simpson vehemently denied ever owning a pair of Bruno Maglis, denouncing them as "ugly-ass shoes." But in 1993, he had been photographed wearing them. The jury was apparently unimpressed by the shoe impressions, but Bruno Magli enjoyed a 30 percent increase in sales of its high-end "ugly-ass shoes" during the months following their introduction as evidence.

Questioned Documents

Many crimes and criminals leave a paper trail. Questioned documents, as we've mentioned, are documents suspected of holding evidence to a crime. Some documents are questioned because they are suspected of being forgeries. (Is the signature on that bank draft fake?) And some are questioned because they relate to a crime. (Who is the author of that ransom note?)

The questioned documents section of the crime lab analyzes paper types and watermarks, either of which may identify a manufacturer or even a particular retail supplier, and the composition of inks and pencil or crayon marks. Analysis may reveal erasures and alternations. It may also reveal the age of the document. Treatment with various chemicals and inspection under ultraviolet or black light often resurrect obliterated writing, whether it has been erased, crossed out, or written over. Used carbon paper, discarded in the trash can, may reveal an important message. The top sheet on the scratch pad left on the desk looks blank, but laboratory examination reveals the imprint of something written on a sheet that had been torn off. The impressions can be rendered visible and legible.

Case in Point

Crudely forged signatures are fairly easy to detect, especially if they have been traced or copied.

Despite some expert claims to the contrary, not all handwriting is identifiable to a specific writer, but the examination of handwriting characteristics can sometimes determine the origin or authenticity of questioned writing. Although a host of dinner club novelty entertainers would disagree, such traits as age, sex, personality, or intent *cannot* be determined from handwriting examinations. However, it may be possible to make inferences concerning the writer's level of education and place of origin—based not only on handwriting, but on such clues as spelling, grammar, and vocabulary—and it can certainly be fruitful to compare a questioned document with known samples, such as writing samples from a suspect.

In this age of the personal computer, the typewriter has rapidly become an endangered species; however, typewritten documents still sometimes figure into crimes, and skilled examiners can sometimes identify the make and model of a typewriter based on individual characteristics of certain letters.

Modern typewriters use carbon film rather than fabric ribbons, and it is sometimes possible to read the film ribbon. In some cases, it is also possible to study paper fibers picked up by the ribbon and thereby link a particular ribbon (and typewriter, and typist) to a particular document.

Many businesses print checks using checkwriter machines. A checkwriter impression can sometimes be identified with the checkwriter that produced it. The same is true of embossed or seal impressions—these can sometimes be identified with the specific instrument that produced them. Even rubber stamp impressions may, in some cases, be identified with the rubber stamp that produced it.

An offender might well attempt to destroy incriminating documentary evidence by burning it. Even in these cases, all is not necessarily lost. Sometimes it is possible to decipher information on burned or charred documents, and even if this is not possible, the charred remains of the paper may yield useful information upon chemical analysis.

Arson Investigation

Most arson and explosives-related crimes are notoriously difficult to investigate for the simple reason that the crime, if successful, destroys most of the evidence it creates.

The differences between an accidental explosion and one caused by a bomb are usually fairly self-evident. The differences between an accidental fire and one deliberately set are typically far more difficult to spot. However, trained observers learn to look for certain signs of arson:

- **Alligatoring** is the checkered appearance of charred wood that makes it look like alligator skin. Large, high-relief blisters indicate intense heat. Small, flat alligatoring indicates lower levels of heat. Intense fires are often produced by arsonists, who use accelerants (most commonly gasoline) to set the fire.

- **Crazing** is the formation of irregular cracks in glass. Extensive crazing indicates rapid and intense heat, signs of the use of an accelerant.

- The **depth of charring** tells much about the length of the burn and its origin. The longer the burn, the more likely it is that an accelerant was used.

- The presence of a **line of demarcation** between charred and uncharred material may indicate the presence of an accelerant. A puddle-shaped line of demarcation is suspicious.

- **Spalling** is the term for the breaking off of surface pieces of brick or concrete. Intense heat is required to create spalling, and brown stains around the spall area are a strong indication that an accelerant has been used.

- Multiple **points of origin**—a group of fires set in various parts of a room or building—suggest arson.

- The **color of the smoke** the fire produces may indicate the presence of accelerants. Blue smoke is typically associated with alcohol; white smoke with burning vegetable compounds, hay, or phosphorous; yellow or brown-yellow smoke with various chemicals, including sulfur compounds and gunpowder; black smoke is produced by petroleum products. The investigator must consult witnesses, including firefighters, to gather this information.

Charred materials and any suspicious stains or liquid deposits are often sent to the crime lab for analysis. Chemical tests can detect the presence of accelerants and identify what they are.

The lab is also called in to analyze debris and other materials from explosions. Specialists can often determine the materials and methods used in the construction of explosive devices. Serial bombers often build the same type of device from one crime to the next. Analyzing the type of bomb used may yield the signature of the offender.

The FBI maintains an Explosives Reference Search System as well as an extensive Explosives Reference File, which expedite identification of arson and explosive materials.

The Least You Need to Know

◆ Forensics is the application of science—especially in the physical and medical fields—to the investigation and prosecution of crime.

◆ Most forensic evidence is not in and of itself conclusive, but it can narrow the field of suspects, guide an investigation, and, as an element in a collection of evidence presented at trial, serve to convict a defendant.

◆ Modern crime labs use the principles of chemistry and physics to analyze physical evidence. They also use electronics to analyze electronic evidence, such as audio and video recordings.

◆ Because the vast majority of violent crimes are committed using firearms, ballistics (essentially the identification of firearms from bullet and ammunition evidence) is a key forensic field.

◆ Tools, shoes, and vehicle tires all leave characteristic marks or imprints, which may be studied to identify origin and association with a suspect.

◆ The investigation of arson is especially difficult, since the crime itself destroys much of the evidence of the crime.

Part

The Body in Question

No item of evidence is more revealing than the body of the victim of a violent crime. In this part, we follow the work of the medical examiner from the discovery of the body at the scene, through the forensic autopsy at the morgue, to the chemistry of homicide, and the work of forensic dentists, anthropologists, entomologists, botanists, and geologists. A special chapter is devoted to the cutting edge of forensic medicine, DNA analysis.

This is the story of how criminal investigators, medical professionals, and other forensic scientists have joined forces to disprove the old pirate saying "Dead men tell no tales." To the forensic specialist, the dead not only speak, they explain, they accuse, and they cry out for justice.

Chapter 9

House Call

In This Chapter

- ◆ Is this death a homicide?
- ◆ The victim: preliminary investigation
- ◆ Relationship of murderer and victim
- ◆ Reading the scene
- ◆ Blood evidence
- ◆ Wound evidence

A body has been discovered in a house. A call goes out to 911, and police officers arrive. They find a 60-year-old white female crumpled at the bottom of a steep, narrow stairway leading down to the cellar. Did the woman lose her footing and fall? Did she have a heart attack or stroke and then fall? Did she purposely throw herself down the stairs? Or was she pushed?

The first possibility is an instance of accidental death; the second, natural death; the third, suicide. All are sad events, but only one possibility—the last mentioned—is homicide, a criminal matter. The discovery of a corpse is not sufficient reason to launch a murder investigation. The first step is to determine whether a homicide has been committed and if so, to gather evidence found at the scene. Let's look at how this is done.

The Crime Scene

Much of the investigative work in a case of homicide is performed by the *medical examiner*, some of it on the scene, and even more in the morgue where an autopsy is performed. But the work always begins with the first police officers on the scene.

def•i•ni•tion

The **medical examiner** is typically an appointed or elected official, almost always a physician specializing in pathology, charged with determining the cause of death in criminal cases or in cases of mysterious death. In larger jurisdictions, the chief medical examiner is in charge of a staff of medical examiners.

Dying Declaration

Arriving on the scene, the officers do not take death for granted. A dead body may have been reported, but the first responding officer makes certain, by feeling for an arterial pulse, that the victim is indeed dead. If there are any signs of life, emergency aid is rendered and an ambulance summoned. If the victim is conscious, officers attempt to secure a dying declaration, which can be crucial in identifying the victim's assailant and in subsequently prosecuting him. In legal terms, a dying declaration consists of the victim's words identifying the causes or circumstances of his or her impending death. A dying declaration is compelling investigative and courtroom evidence. If equipment is available, it is often audio- or videotaped. To be admissible as evidence, courts do not require that a dying declaration was necessarily followed by death, but that it was made by someone who believed death was imminent. Furthermore, the statement must specifically concern the cause or circumstances of what the victim believed to be his or her impending death.

Protecting the Scene

The first responders act quickly to protect the crime scene so that evidence is neither disturbed nor destroyed. Because the scene will soon be teeming with investigators, people from the medical examiner's office, and others, the first to arrive determines a path to and from the victim that will least disturb evidence.

Capturing the Scene

If the victim is dead, there is no rush to remove the body from the scene. In many jurisdictions, a medical examiner, typically a pathologist, will perform a preliminary examination at the scene, and only after the examiner has completed work there is the body taken to the morgue for an autopsy.

Before the body is removed, the crime scene is photographed and perhaps videotaped. Investigators usually make simple sketches to indicate the position of the victim relative to other objects in the room or area. In many cases, if the body is lying on the floor or ground, investigators will outline with chalk or tape the victim's exact position, as an aid to investigative work after the body is removed. The result is the chalk outline that has figured in pop culture as a ghastly icon since *film noir* movie thrillers of the 1940s and is still seen on today's TV cop shows.

Checklist: Gathering Information

The FBI has drawn up a checklist of suggested investigative items to help ensure that police investigators obtain all important preliminary information at the scene of a suspected homicide. The first priority is to identify the victim. This may be possible with the help of witnesses on the scene and/or identification found on the victim—a driver's license, for example, or other wallet items. The victim's address should be determined, as well as marital status and the name, address, and phone number of next of kin.

From the very beginning, investigators carefully note the circumstances under which they were notified of the death, including the date and time of the notification and the identity of the person who made the call. It is especially important to note the relationship, if any, of that person to the deceased.

Signs of Struggle

Investigators also carefully note the date and time the body was found and the exact location of the body. If the body was found inside a place of business or a house or apartment, investigators make particular note of how entry was gained: Was the door forced or a window broken? Or are there no signs of forced entry? The first circumstance suggests that the victim and the perpetrator were strangers or that, in any case, the victim was not expecting the perpetrator to call. The second circumstance suggests that the victim and perpetrator were either acquainted or the perpetrator had presented the victim with a plausible reason for opening the door. Perhaps the perpetrator posed as a delivery person or even a police officer. It is also important to note the type of lock on the door and the condition of other doors and windows.

Exactly where the body was found is important. The basement? The bedroom? The living room? And where was the body found within the room? Sitting at a desk? Lying on a sofa? Or in the middle of the floor? Was the victim discovered face up, face down, or in some other position?

By carefully noting these details, it may be possible to begin putting together a picture of what happened. It is important to look for signs of struggle as well as the absence of such signs, because this information suggests much about the method of the perpetrator and even his attitude toward what he was doing—cool, calm, and professional; or wild, violent, and out of control.

Much can also be inferred about the relationship between the perpetrator and the victim. Signs of forced entry combined with signs of violence suggest the work of an intruder. The absence of forced entry and little evidence of a struggle suggest that the perpetrator was a trusted acquaintance, friend, associate, or even relation.

Condition of the Body

The initial investigators take careful note of the condition of the body. Was it fully clothed? Partially clothed? Naked? Was it carefully undressed, or were the clothes torn and ripped off? If so, what kind of clothes was the victim wearing, and where were they torn? Was a ligature (any kind of rope, tape, wire, or article of clothing) used to bind or strangle a victim?

Although the medical examiner is solely responsible for determining the cause of death, the first investigators on the scene typically take note of five more key items relating to the condition of the body:

1. **Is the body well preserved or decomposed?** This is important for determining the time of death. The presence of maggots, for example, may help fix the approximate time of death (see Chapter 13).

2. **How far has rigor mortis progressed?** This information can be important to the medical examiner in assessing the time of death, especially if the examiner arrives on the scene some time after the first officers do. A body is limp after death until the breakdown of certain enzymes within body tissue stiffens the corpse. This is known as rigor mortis—literally, the "stiffness of death."

Rigor begins in the jaw and head five to six hours after death, and the effect moves downward from there. By 12 hours, the upper body is generally stiff. Within about 18 hours, the entire body becomes rigid. Rigor mortis is not permanent, and it begins to disappear about 36 hours after death, typically in the same sequence in which it appeared.

Related to rigor mortis, but distinct from it, is cadaveric spasm. This is the contraction of specific muscle groups at the time of death—literally, a "death grip"—and it is most frequently found when the hand of the deceased is closed tightly around an object. Unlike rigor mortis, it does not disappear. Nor can cadaveric spasm be counterfeited. Thus, if a victim is found with a gunshot wound to the head, his hand tightly grasping the handle of a revolver, the chances are very good that the victim has committed suicide. If, however, the victim is found with his or her fingers loosely wrapped around the gun's handle, there is a distinct possibility that some other person has attempted to "stage the crime scene" by creating the appearance of suicide, presumably in an effort to hide a murder.

3. **What is the appearance and position of postmortem lividity?** When the heart stops beating, blood ceases to circulate, and, with the force of gravity, it drains to the body's lowest levels, pooling in these places. Where blood has pooled after death, the result is a dark blue or purple discoloration of the skin known as postmortem lividity. Postmortem lividity begins anywhere from one-half to three hours after death. Its spread slows after four or five hours, because blood coagulates within the capillaries by that time, and it reaches its maximum intensity after 10 or 12 hours. Because the rate of these changes in the condition of the blood is well known, lividity provides a remarkably accurate indication of the time of death.

   The location of lividity suggests whether a body was moved after death. For example, if a body is discovered on its back, lividity is expected to appear in the lower part of the back and legs, because this is where gravity would naturally cause the noncirculating blood to pool. If, however, it appears instead on the face, chest, and stomach, it is likely that the body was originally face down and was moved after death.

   The medical examiner will also note the color of the lividity. Cherry red or vivid pink lividity indicates carbon monoxide poisoning, and other poisons also impart a telltale color to the lividity.

4. **Is blood present?** If so, where? Blood evidence points to the cause of death—gunshot, stabbing, beating, etc.

def•i•ni•tion

Blunt force trauma (BFT) is injury caused by the blow(s) of any blunt instrument, such as a bat, pipe, hammer, or fist.

5. **Are wounds present?** What are their location and number? First responders typically take note of gunshot wounds, knife punctures, tears, lacerations, and *blunt force trauma* (*BFT*). The full extent and number of wounds are not always apparent until close medical examination or autopsy. We'll look further at wound evidence in a moment.

A Step Back

On the scene of a homicide, it is natural for all investigative eyes to focus on the body. But it is also important for investigators to take a step back and look carefully at the surroundings.

If the room is in disarray, furniture upset, items broken or scattered, it is evident that a struggle has taken place. If, however, the room is orderly, the implication is that the victim did not feel herself to be in danger. This may be because the victim was taken entirely by surprise and killed before she had time to react or because the victim knew the perpetrator and believed she had no reason to fear him.

Rooms, apartments, and houses hold other important clues. For example, evidence of the recent preparation of food may provide a clue as to the time of death. The presence of dated material, such as accumulated and unread newspapers or a mailbox stuffed with unretrieved items, may help fix the date of death in cases where a body is found in some state of decomposition.

Investigators ask themselves if the room or house shows evidence of robbery, or drug or alcohol use. They look, too, for evidence of sexually deviant practices, including sadomasochistic rituals that may have lethal consequences.

Stains and Splatters

Approximately six quarts of blood circulate through the body of an adult. When the body is violently pierced—by bullets, by a knife, by a blunt instrument—some of that blood is spilled. In the case of gunshots or a violent struggle, it is usually splattered rather than simply spilled.

The spectacle of a bloodstained, blood-splattered crime scene is gruesome, but it is not simply chaotic or meaningless. The location of the stains and the pattern of the splatter have a story to tell. Well-interpreted blood-splatter evidence is often compelling at trial and is deemed so important that some criminal investigators specialize in the study, analysis, and interpretation of blood splatter evidence. These detectives and forensic scientists do not depend solely on their experience at actual crime scenes, but also perform laboratory experiments to simulate attacks and study the resulting splatter patterns.

From the number and position of stains, it may be possible to determine the movements of the victim relative to his assailant. From blood splatter, it is possible to ascertain the direction from which an assault came. The distance between the victim and where the bloodstain came to rest can indicate the type of impact the victim received, the type of object that produced the wounds, the number of blows that were inflicted, and the position of the victim and assailant during and after the bloodshed.

This evidence can be compared to statements taken from witnesses and suspects. There have been many cases in which a suspect claims that the victim's death was accidental, but the location and angle of the blood-splatter pattern refutes the claim. When blood drips, it creates round stains. When blood is propelled, as from a blow, the stains are elongated—the more elongated, the harder the blow.

Case in Point

In February 2002, David Camm was tried for the murder of his wife, Kimberly, and his two children, Bradley and Jill, in their Indiana home. Blood-splatter expert Rod Englert testified that blood splatter on Camm's T-shirt was high-velocity, which could only come from the impact of a gunshot. In court, Englert used simulated blood to demonstrate to the jury how blood splatter is produced. He testified that Camm's shoes also showed high-velocity splatter, which Camm had tried to wipe off. Lead prosecutor Stan Faith remarked to a reporter: "If you have this kind of blood impact on your T-shirt, there's only one way you can get it. That's in the presence of a gunshot." Camm was convicted and sentenced to 195 years in prison.

Investigators photograph bloodstain and blood-splatter evidence and carefully study the patterns. Traditionally, investigators have attempted to evaluate blood-splatter evidence by directional analysis, using strings affixed to certain points in the splatter pattern and extending these back to a probable source of the blood. Recently, a computer software program called BackTrack has been developed to analyze splatter evidence digitally and graphically, using "virtual strings." The investigator enters into the computer the width, length, direction, and position of each blood droplet, and the software calculates an angle of attack for each droplet, then projects a flight path backward from each. Where two or more of the projections intersect, the position of the original wound can be determined.

Given sufficient time, a perpetrator may attempt to remove bloodstains and blood splatter by laundering bed sheets, blankets, and clothing, or by scrubbing walls, floors, and other surfaces. Luminol is a chemical that reacts with even trace amounts of hemoglobin, a constituent of blood, causing it to fluoresce with a bright green color. Faint bloodstains—or even invisible stains—can be clearly visualized with Luminol.

Luminol is intended to reveal the trace presence of blood that is otherwise invisible to the unaided eye. At some crime scenes or on some articles of evidence (clothing, for example), stains are clearly visible, but because of the passage of time or the effects of environmental exposure (long contact with water, dirt, exposure to the sun, and so on), it is not possible to visually identify the stains as blood. In other cases, investigators may have reason to believe that a crime scene or article of evidence was associated with a violent crime, but the traces of blood are so minute that they cannot be positively identified by sight alone. When there is doubt as to the nature of a suspicious stain, or in examining minute stain evidence, various chemicals (including leucomalachite green, phenolphthalein, ortho-tolidine, and tetramethylbenzidine) are used to make what is called a presumptive test for blood. As with luminal, these chemicals react with hemoglobin to reveal the presence of genuine blood.

Fingernails

The victim's fingernails are often repositories of key evidence. Blood may be visible under the fingernails, indicating that the victim attempted to defend herself by scratching or tearing at the attacker. This blood can be invaluable in identifying a suspect, especially with the availability of DNA testing.

Even when blood evidence is not immediately visible under the fingernails, it or other tissue may be present and can be discovered later by microscopic examination or by making a presumptive test for blood, using one of the hemoglobin tracers just discussed. Typically, the medical examiner or a technician will "bag" the victim's hands—cover them with plastic bags—before transporting the body to the morgue. This avoids contamination and the loss of important trace evidence.

Reading the Wounds

The medical examiner will thoroughly investigate all wounds at autopsy, but, based on the appearance of wounds even while the body is at the crime scene, an experienced detective can begin to make some important assessments.

Gunshot

When a gun is fired, the bullet does not simply and neatly exit the barrel. In addition to the emergence of the bullet, gases produced by the explosion of the powder expand, and metal fragments from the cartridge case are propelled out of the barrel, as are burned and unburned gunpowder, along with carbon and soot from the firing of the primer. All of this additional material leaves little trace when shots are fired at a distance from the victim. But if the skin around the wound shows a *powder tattoo* or is stained by soot and carbon, it is likely that the shot was fired from no more than 2 feet away. By test-firing in the ballistics lab and comparing the resulting powder pattern and the proportion of burned and unburned powder with the evidence on the body or clothing, it is possible to calculate with reasonable accuracy actual firing distance. If the muzzle of the weapon was in direct contact with the body, a contact wound appears, often along with an impression of the muzzle.

At the scene, investigators can use the gunshot wound evidence to make a preliminary assessment of whether the injury was self-inflicted or a homicide. A wound indicating that the gun was fired from more than a few inches away or a shot that penetrated clothing tends to rule out suicide. The location of the wound (for example, the back) or the angle of trajectory (as indicated by the shape of the wound or by the relation of the entry wound to the exit wound) may definitively rule out suicide—as would the absence of a weapon at the scene. If, however, the wound shows that the gun was held directly against the skin, and if the

def•i•ni•tion _____

A **powder tattoo** is a characteristic pattern created around a gunshot wound by soot or carbon when the shot was fired from no more than 2 feet away. Presence of tattooing indicates a shot at very close range.

wound is in the mouth or right temple (assuming the victim was right-handed; left temple, if left-handed), suicide is likely. Suicides do not generally fire through clothing, except in the comparatively rare case of purposely self-inflicted wounds to the chest. The weapon will almost certainly be present at the scene, typically grasped tightly in the hand (a result of cadaveric spasm).

Stab and Cutting Wounds

Wounds inflicted by a knife or other sharp object may be stab wounds, which are made by thrusting, or they may be cutting wounds. From the angle, location, and number of stab wounds, it is often possible to draw inferences about the height and strength of the attacker, and perhaps even something of his state of mind (cool, professional, efficient, panicky, or filled with rage). The presence or absence of defensive wounds—cuts on the victim's hands, arms, and legs resulting from his attempts to ward off the attack—suggest something about the relation of victim to assailant. Absence of defensive wounds may suggest that either the victim was taken completely by surprise and was killed before he could offer resistance or that the victim did not expect an attack because the assailant was someone the victim knew and trusted.

Except in the case of certain suicide rituals (the Samurai practice of *sepuku* or *hara-kiri*, for instance), stab wounds are seldom purposely self-inflicted. Cutting wounds, however, are often associated with suicide, especially when the main wounds are accompanied by "hesitation wounds"—less severe cuts caused by attempts to build up the resolve to inflict the deep, fatal cut.

Sworn Statement

I didn't want to hurt the man. I thought he was a very nice gentleman. Soft-spoken. I thought so right up to the moment I cut his throat.

—Perry Smith's confession in Truman Capote's *In Cold Blood: A True Account of a Multiple Murder and Its Consequences* (Random House, 1966)

As with gunshot wounds, the appearance of stabbing and cutting wounds can suggest much, even to those who arrive first on the scene. Knife wounds under (not *through*) clothing; cutting wounds at the throat, wrists, or ankles; and the presence of hesitation wounds all suggest suicide—especially if the weapon is present. Stab wounds through clothing, wounds in vital organs, disfiguring wounds, and the presence of defensive wounds all point to murder. Typically, the weapon is not present, and there are signs that the body has been moved.

As much as the crime scene and the body tell the first investigators who arrive, this information is usually no more than a prologue. It is the task of the medical examiner, as we will see in Chapters 10 and 11, to read the rest of the story.

The Least You Need to Know

- When a body is discovered, the responsibility for determining the cause of death ultimately rests with the medical examiner, but the first police investigators to arrive on the scene open up the investigation and make the initial determination that the death is or is not a homicide.

◆ Investigators examine the body as well as its surroundings for clues indicating the time and cause of death and, in the case of homicide, the relationship of the victim and the assailant.

◆ Rigor mortis and post-mortem lividity provide important indications of the time of death and whether the body was moved after death.

◆ The number and location of bloodstains and the size, location, and shape of blood-splatter patterns provide clues to the position of the assailant relative to the victim.

◆ The appearance of both gunshot and knife wounds suggests much about how the victim was killed, providing (among other things) clues that either suggest or rule out suicide and that imply the assailant was either known or unknown to the victim.

Chapter 10

Body of Evidence

In This Chapter

- The role of the medical examiner
- Preparing a body for autopsy
- Autopsy procedures
- Determining the time and cause of death
- Identifying the victim

Even though he or she is a cop, not a doctor, an experienced criminal investigator picks up a lot of forensic medicine on the job and can, as we saw in the preceding chapter, tell a great deal from a fairly quick examination of a victim's body.

But all unexplained deaths must be given more than a once-over. In virtually all jurisdictions, the medical examiner is called in and an autopsy is performed. You learned a bit about what the medical examiner does in the previous chapter; now let's explore that role in more detail.

Meet the ME

The medical examiner (ME) is a physician who specializes in pathology and, in most cases, has received additional training in forensic pathology. This means that a qualified medical examiner is an M.D. who has completed medical school as well as at least four years of postgraduate training in pathology and related disciplines *before* entering a year-long forensic pathology residency program. Such programs are usually offered by large urban medical examiner offices, which are affiliated with a medical school. In the entire United States, there are only about 40 such programs.

The extensive knowledge, skill, and training are only part of what it takes to be a medical examiner. Also required is an insatiable curiosity, acute powers of observation, and the emotional stamina to work with human tragedy and the results of human behavior at its most terribly violent and profoundly disturbing.

Dead Men and the Tales They Tell

The motto of the seagoing pirates of old was "dead men tell no tales," and, driven by this sentiment, they seldom left any living victims behind to betray them. Doubtless many of today's murderers believe much the same thing. They are, however, mistaken. To the medical examiner, the dead speak volumes.

Preparing for Autopsy

Both at the crime scene and in the morgue, the medical examiner searches the body for trace evidence. The ME records any available particulars concerning the circumstances of death, along with any available information identifying the deceased. The ME also notes physical characteristics, such as height and weight.

By the Numbers

In a typical year, the New York City Medical Examiner's Office uses 8,000 body bags for the transportation of remains to and from autopsy.

The body is handled carefully, in the knowledge that careless lifting or carrying may compromise important evidence, such as the trajectory path of a bullet. At this preliminary stage, the ME also remains alert for anything unusual. For instance, certain poisons leave telltale odors. (As any reader of old-fashioned murder mysteries knows, cyanide smells like bitter almonds.)

Once the body arrives at the morgue, a toe tag—an identification card with the victim's name (if known) and other basic information—is attached with a loop of string or wire around the toe of the cadaver. The body is then photographed. If it has been found fully or partially clothed, the body is photographed that way first. Then it is undressed and photographed again.

After photography, the body is x-rayed from head to foot. It is also weighed and measured. All distinguishing marks, such as birthmarks, tattoos, scars, and other evidence of injuries new and old, are carefully recorded. Another examination is performed to recover trace evidence. Hair, fibers, and dirt are collected from the body and from under the fingernails. Usually, the nails are clipped and the parings collected for analysis. The victim is also fingerprinted, and, if suicide by gunshot is suspected, the hands are chemically swabbed to detect the presence of nitrate (gunpowder residue). In cases of suspected rape, the genital area is swabbed for evidence.

Any clothing associated with the body—or, if the body was found naked, the wrapping sheet used by the ME office—is sent to the laboratory for examination.

def•i•ni•tion

An **autopsy** is a medical examination of the internal organs, including the brain, of the deceased in order to determine the cause of death and other circumstances relating to the death.

The Cutting

The *autopsy* proper is an examination of the internal organs. The body is rinsed clean, then laid out on its back on a stainless steel table. A stabilizing block is placed under the head.

The ME begins with a "Y" incision, cutting into the body from each shoulder and meeting at the breast bone (sternum), then continuing down the abdomen and into the pelvis. This efficiently exposes all of the internal organs.

Next, the ME uses a saw to cut through the ribs and collarbone, so that the rib cage can be lifted away from the organs in one piece. In the case of death by gunshot, the ME uses the x-rays that have been taken to help locate bullets and trace their trajectories. The ME also needs to avoid cutting into—and thereby compromising or destroying—any wound evidence.

Using the x-ray information for guidance, the ME begins to remove the individual organs and weighs them. Blood samples, tissue samples, and other fluid samples are taken from the organs. The stomach and intestines are opened to examine the contents. This can provide information as to when, what, and perhaps even where the victim last ate before he or she was killed.

After examining the viscera, the ME begins examining the head. First, the whites of the eyes are probed for minute hemorrhages known as petichiae, which indicate death by strangulation. Of course, the head is also thoroughly examined for contusions and other wounds.

When the external examination of the head is complete, an incision is made in the scalp at the back of the head, and the skin is peeled forward, over the face, exposing the skull. The ME opens the skull with a high-speed oscillating power saw, then applies a chisel to pry off the skullcap. This exposes the brain so that it can be lifted out, weighed, and examined.

Brain tissue and other organ tissue samples are sent to the lab for additional analysis (see the next chapter). Any organs the ME believes should be investigated further are preserved. The rest are returned to the body cavity.

Death: How?

In the best case, the work of the ME provides clues to the identity of the victim's assailant and produces evidence that helps secure a conviction. At the very least, however, the ME can usually determine, with precision, the cause of death.

Natural or Unnatural

In many instances, determining whether the cause of death was natural, the result of an accident, or a homicide is straightforward. Sometimes, however, the cause becomes apparent only after careful postmortem examination, including an autopsy and, perhaps, toxicological studies.

However simple or difficult, it is crucially important to determine whether or not a crime has been committed.

Shooting

The analysis of gunshot wounds is discussed in some detail in Chapter 9. The ME is in a position to confirm, amplify, or correct many of the observations a police investigator has made at the scene.

The analysis of entrance wounds and exit wounds is typically very important, because the trajectory of the bullet can be calculated using this relationship. With trajectory information, it becomes possible to infer the location of the assailant in relation to the victim. This information may support or refute statements from the suspect. For example, a suspect may claim that he shot the victim in self-defense, whereas wound analysis reveals that the victim was shot at close range, in the back of the head, execution style. The information is also frequently valuable for ruling in or out suicide or an accidental shooting.

Stabbing

As with gunshot wounds, stab and cutting wounds are discussed in Chapter 9; however, a full autopsy can reveal much more about stab wounds than an on-the-scene examination can. The extent of the injuries can be more precisely assessed, as can the angle at which the blade entered the victim. In the autopsy room, a suspect weapon can be more accurately matched to a wound than it can be in the field.

Beating

The extent of injury caused by blows with a blunt object is often apparent only upon autopsy. With autopsy, it is usually possible to demonstrate that certain injuries are consistent with a suspect weapon by showing how the size and shape of the weapon compares with the size, shape, and extent of the injury or injuries inflicted.

Investigation of child battery is greatly aided by autopsy, which can often reveal prior broken bones and internal injuries, thereby demonstrating a history of abuse.

Sworn Statement

We had a patient [at Bellevue Hospital] who was a heroin addict who had an infection of the heart …. We treated him and he survived, which was a real triumph. Then when I came down that weekend, there he was, dead on the autopsy table.…We'd treated his infection but not his addiction. That made me think I could contribute more to society by looking at people on the autopsy table and feeding back the findings so that lots of people could benefit, rather than just treating patients one at a time. So I stayed in pathology.

—Dr. Michael Baden, famed former New York City medical examiner, quoted in Katherine Ramsland's, "Crime Investigation Through Autopsy: Dr. Michael Baden," at www.crimelibrary.com/forensics2/autopsy

Asphyxia

Asphyxiation is a common method of homicide as well as suicide and accidental death. It occurs when the brain and other body tissues receive insufficient oxygen to support the oxygen-carrying red blood cells and is caused by anything that seriously interferes with breathing or the respiration process.

In cases of suspected asphyxiation, the ME looks for a blue or purple coloration around the lips, fingernails, and toenails. Then the ME looks beyond this sign in an effort to determine the cause of asphyxiation.

Did the victim choke? The presence of a foreign body in the trachea indicates this. Choking is almost always accidental.

Did the victim drown? The circumstances of how and where the body was found provide the most important clues. Most drownings are accidental; however, the ME's examination will reveal if an already dead person had been placed in water to make it appear as if the victim had drowned.

Was the victim smothered? Despite what mystery movies and crime novels portray, few murderers smother their victims, and most deaths by smothering are, in fact, accidental. The ME's examination can sometimes determine if a struggle was associated with the smothering, which would indicate foul play.

By the Numbers

A bizarre form of unintentional suicide by hanging is known as autoerotic asphyxiation, in which sexual gratification is sought by placing a rope around the neck and tightening it, often by hanging, in order to induce semiconsciousness. If this extremely hazardous sexual experimentation goes too far, asphyxiation and death can result; 500 to 1,000 people die from autoerotic asphyxiation each year.

Hanging is almost always a means of suicide, not murder, but for that very reason, murderers have used hanging in an attempt to disguise their crime. The ME's examination reveals whether hanging was the cause of death or whether the victim was hanged after death.

Death by strangulation is almost always homicide. The ME looks for evenly grooved, horizontal ligature marks on the victim's neck, in contrast to the type of ligature marks found on the neck of a victim of hanging. In hanging, the ligature marks are not horizontal, but start from below the chin and travel *up* to a point just below the ears. Manual strangulation—choking with the hands—often leaves signs of hand pressure, even long after death.

A number of chemicals, including chloroform and ammonia, can induce asphyxiation, as can an overdose of sleeping pills or the combination of narcotic and alcohol use. In cases of chemically induced and drug-induced asphyxia, there are signs of paralysis of the air passages. Depending on the chemical involved, death may be interpreted as an accident, suicide, or homicide.

Death: When?

In Chapter 9 we discussed how rigor mortis and postmortem lividity serve as important indicators of time of death. The ME also uses four additional factors to help determine how long the victim has been dead.

Temperature

In and of itself, body temperature is a very crude indicator of time of death, but it can be helpful when considered along with other indicators. Body temperature declines 2 to 3 degrees in the first hour after death, then 1 to 1.5 degrees for each subsequent hour, up to 18 hours.

Eyes

After death, there is a dramatic reduction and eventual disappearance of tone in the eye muscles, so that the pupils dilate. After about seven hours, the pupil begins partially to contract. After 12 hours, the cornea clouds over.

In addition to examining the appearance of the eyes, the ME may withdraw fluid from the eyeball to determine the level of potassium present. This level rises after death at a predictable rate so that, based on the potassium level, an estimate of the time of death can be made.

Stomach

If investigators on the scene can determine when the victim last ate, an examination of the stomach contents at autopsy can serve as a gauge to the time of death. Digestion proceeds at a reasonably uniform rate in all people. Because digestion ceases at death, it is possible to estimate the time of death based on the degree of digestion evident in the stomach contents. It is also true that food remains in the stomach for one to two hours after eating, and then is emptied into the small intestine. A full stomach places the time of death within one or two hours after eating. If the stomach is relatively empty and the small intestine full, death most likely occurred four to six hours after eating. After four hours, the contents of the small intestine begin to pass into the large intestine. If the large intestine is empty, at least 12 hours have passed between the victim's last meal and the time of death.

Decomposition

Few sights are as inherently repulsive as the decomposing body of what had once been a living, breathing, sentient human being. Yet, to the ME, decomposition is not a source of disgust, but valuable evidence to be studied. Based on the state of decomposition, it is possible to estimate the time of death.

The first signs of decomposition are a distended stomach and abdomen, the result of internal gases created by the decomposition process. *Adipocere*, hardening of fatty tissue, creates a soapy appearance that develops if the body is in a relatively hot and moist location. It may take as long as three months for this condition to develop extensively. After about a year, if the body has been in a warm, dry area, *mummification*, the complete dehydration of all body parts, will be apparent.

def•i•ni•tion

Adipocere is a postmortem hardening of fatty body tissue, which creates a soapy appearance that develops if the corpse is in a relatively hot and moist location. **Mummification** is the complete dehydration of all body parts; it develops months or years after death.

Typically, decomposing bodies are attacked by insects (and, often, other animals as well). In this case, the ME may call in a forensic entomologist, whose work is discussed in Chapter 13.

Bodies recovered from water typically undergo changes that are strongly indicative of the time of death. In warm water, a dead body sinks, remains underwater for 8 to 10 days, and then, because of the buoyancy of gases formed during decomposition, rises. In cold water, a body may remain immersed for two to three weeks before rising.

The ME carefully examines the skin of any body that has been recovered from water. Outer skin loosens after five or six days of immersion, and the nails separate in two to three weeks. By looking for the presence of water in the lungs, the ME can determine whether the person drowned or was killed and then thrown into the water to dispose of the body or to make the death look like accidental drowning.

Death by Poisoning: Forensic Toxicology

Poisoning is a sufficiently common cause of death that the medical examiner's office of most large jurisdictions employs a full-time forensic toxicologist—a specialist trained in the study of poisons, their detection, their use in homicide, and their effect on the human body—to determine if poisoning occurred and what substance or substances caused death. Forensic toxicology is the subject of the next chapter.

Identification

Most people carry with them some form of identification, usually a driver's license. Identifying a corpse is frequently as simple as examining the contents of a wallet. In other cases, neighbors or witnesses can provide identification.

But not infrequently, a body is found without any identification at all and is associated with no friends, neighbors, or witnesses. In these cases, the ME and other forensics experts work from the evidence at hand to make an identification.

They begin with the obvious: the overall appearance of the individual. This information is compared to missing persons reports that are on file. If a match is found, relatives are contacted to make a positive identification.

Fingerprinting

The next obvious step is to compare fingerprints taken from the body with local and federal fingerprint files. If a match is found, the body has an identity.

Forensic Odontology

Forensic odontology is a highly specialized field of dentistry that uses dental evidence to determine identity. Teeth are among the very last parts of a body to decompose. Mummified remains thousands of years old often retain teeth. From the size, condition, and number of teeth, odontologists can tell much about the age and even the sex of fully decomposed remains or partial remains. Moreover, because most of us make or have made fairly regular visits to the dentist, the forensic odontologist notes the presence of any dental work (fillings, crowns, and so on), as well as missing or broken teeth, and compares this data to the files in the dental offices of a particular area. Forensic odontology is discussed in Chapter 12.

Forensic Anthropology

Most physical anthropologists study ancient mummified or fossilized human remains to learn about the evolution of our species, *Homo sapiens*. Forensic anthropology applies physical anthropology to the legal process. Specialists in this field examine skeletal or badly decomposed human remains for the purpose of making an identification. Frequently, forensic anthropologists work in conjunction with forensic pathologists, odontologists, and homicide investigators. Forensic anthropology is discussed in Chapter 12.

The Bug Detectives

Insects occupy a key niche in any ecosystem because they thrive on decay and decomposition. Sooner or later, a dead body attracts insects. To some extent, this destroys evidence, but the presence of insects, larvae, and eggs also provides clues to time and place of death. Locating and evaluating this evidence requires the expertise of the forensic entomologist (FE)—a biologist who specializes in the study of insect evidence as it relates to criminal investigation and the legal process. The work of this expert is discussed in Chapter 13.

Talking Plants

Blind, deaf, and mute, plant life hardly seems a likely choice as a witness to crime. Yet anyone who has taken a walk in the woods or even through an overgrown vacant lot knows that plants do interact with the animal and human life around them. Plant parts break off and adhere to clothing, the seeds of certain plants stick to anything or anyone who passes by, microscopic pollens and spores get on the skin or in the mucous membranes. Murder someone, dump him in a remote field, and chances are you carry a part of that field with you. Detecting, identifying, and analyzing plant materials in the context of criminal investigation is the job of another highly specialized scientist, the forensic botanist. This job is discussed in Chapter 13.

The Least You Need to Know

♦ Forensic autopsies are performed by a medical examiner, a physician who has specialized in pathology and who has additional specific training in forensic pathology.

♦ After all possible information has been gathered from external observation of the body, the internal organs, including the brain, are examined by surgical removal. This is the main part of the autopsy.

♦ The purpose of the autopsy is to determine, at minimum, the cause and time of death; in addition, the ME looks for clues as to the circumstances of death (including the identity of the perpetrator) and, if unknown, the identity of the body.

♦ Other specialists who may be called on to collaborate with the ME include a forensic toxicologist (an expert on poisons), a forensic anthropologist (who principally analyzes skeletal evidence), a forensic entomologist (an expert on insects), and a forensic botanist.

Chapter 11

Death by Poisoning

In This Chapter

- The job of the forensic toxicologist
- The Markov case
- Poisons, drugs, and narcotics defined
- Pharmacodynamics: how toxins work
- Toxicology procedures

Accidental poisoning is distressingly common, especially among children, who put just about anything in their mouths; and the elderly and disabled, who sometimes accidentally take dangerous overdoses of medication. But poisoning is also one of the oldest methods of murder.

A forensic toxicologist is a forensic scientist who specializes in the study of drugs and poisons as they relate to the fields of criminal justice and public safety.

Job Description

In most jurisdictions, forensic toxicologists are professional forensic scientists who hold at least a baccalaureate degree (many have doctorates in analytical chemistry) and have undergone specific training in general forensic science as well as forensic toxicology. Various organizations offer certification of forensic toxicologists in any or all of three areas:

◆ Certified Forensic Toxicologist: A forensic scientist who has successfully passed a process of peer review and has been formally examined in the field of forensic toxicology.

◆ Certified Forensic Alcohol Toxicologist: A forensic scientist specializing in the analysis of specimens for the presence of ethanol (potable alcohol) and related substances; like the Certified Forensic Toxicologist, this specialist has successfully undergone a prescribed evaluation and examination process.

◆ Certified Forensic Drug Toxicologist: A forensic scientist specializing in the analysis of biological specimens for drugs; he or she has successfully undergone peer review and examination in the specialty.

On a day-to-day basis, the forensic toxicologist runs chemical tests on body fluids, blood, and some organs to identify the presence of poisons. Some agents, such as arsenic, accumulate over time in the hair and fingernails. In cases of suspected arsenic poisoning, these are always tested. Traces of arsenic remain in hair and fingernails indefinitely and, if necessary, a body can be exhumed for examination many years after death.

The forensic toxicologist can test for blood alcohol level, to determine if the victim had been intoxicated at the time of death and perhaps sufficiently so to cause death. The toxicologist also has the ability to test for the presence of a wide variety of illicit drugs that are often abused, including amphetamines, barbiturates, powdered cocaine and crack cocaine, marijuana, and opiates such as codeine and morphine.

Legitimate therapeutic drugs are sometimes taken in deliberate or accidental overdoses. The toxicologist tests for the presence of acetaminophen, anticonvulsants, tranquilizers, and aspirin products.

Beyond drugs both legal and illegal, many common substances are highly toxic and can cause accidental poisoning or be used to commit murder. Tests have been developed for most of these, including arsenic, benzene, bromide, butyl nitrite, cyanide, strychnine, and warfarin (a common rat poison).

Case in Point

Perhaps the most famous "cold case" (a crime that has gone unsolved for many months or even years) in history is the death of Napoleon. The former French emperor died on May 5, 1821, in British custody while exiled to the island of St. Helena. The official cause of death was stomach cancer, but many—in the nineteenth century and today—believe he was poisoned with arsenic, perhaps killed by his British captors, by a traitor within the small circle of Frenchmen attending him during his exile, or by a conspiracy between the two.

Ben Weider, a retired Canadian physician and amateur student of Napoleon, advanced the murder conspiracy theory, which most academic historians reject. In 2001, Weider commissioned French forensic toxicologist Pascal Kintz to analyze five samples of Napoleon's hair preserved since his death in 1821. Kintz reported to the Reuters news service: "The analysis showed there was major exposure, and I stress 'major,' to arsenic." In addition, Paul Fornes, a forensic pathologist collaborating with Kintz, reviewed the original diagnosis of stomach cancer and said that it was not supported by the autopsy performed on Napoleon a day after his death. According to Fornes, "The lesions to the stomach described by Francesco Antommarchi [the doctor who performed the autopsy in 1821] were not the cause of death."

Napoleonic hair samples had been analyzed in the past and had been found to contain arsenic; however, these findings were not widely accepted as proof of homicide because, in the early nineteenth century, arsenic was a common ingredient in medicines as well as in pigments used to color cups and plates and even in paints and wallpapers. Most historians believed that the arsenic found in Napoleon's hair was the result of medication or even environmental exposure. After the 2001 testing, however, Kintz explained to Reuters that the natural upper limit of arsenic concentration in hair is one nanogram per milligram of hair, whereas one of Napoleon's hair samples showed a concentration of 38 nanograms, which Kintz concluded was evidence of deliberate poisoning—homicide.

Ben Weider theorized that the British governor of St. Helena conspired with French count Charles de Montholon to assassinate Napoleon to prevent his escape and return to France. In order to avoid making a martyr of the former emperor by simply assassinating him, they used a method of murder that mimicked death from natural causes.

Although a number of historians have been swayed by the new findings, some have disputed the authenticity of the hair samples. An undaunted Ben Weider responded to this by seeking permission from the French government to open Napoleon's tomb to recover DNA for purposes of comparison to the hair samples. As of 2007, that permission has not been forthcoming.

The Society of Forensic Toxicology (SOFT) recognizes three major branches of the field:

- Postmortem forensic toxicology: This branch determines the absence or presence of drugs and their metabolites (a term explained later in the chapter) and toxins in human fluids and tissues; it evaluates the role of these substances in the cause or manner of death.

- Human-performance forensic toxicology: This branch works with the living rather than the dead and determines the absence or presence of alcohol, drugs, and other chemicals in blood, breath, and other specimens; it evaluates the role of such substances in affecting performance and behavior.

- Forensic urine drug testing: As with human-performance forensic toxicology, this branch works with living persons and determines the absence or presence of drugs and their metabolites in urine with the object of demonstrating prior use or abuse.

The Case of the Lethal Umbrella

On September 7, 1979, 49-year-old writer Georgi Markov was admitted to a hospital in London with a high fever and violent vomiting. He pointed out to his doctors an area of inflammation surrounding a tiny puncture wound on his right thigh. The day before, while he was crossing Waterloo Bridge, Markov had felt a sharp poke there and turned around just in time to see behind him a man with a tightly furled umbrella. In a thick Eastern European accent, the stranger mumbled an apology and walked on.

Infections are common, and the doctors dealt with Markov's condition by administering large amounts of antibiotics. But no matter what they did, his temperature rose while his blood pressure fell, even as his pulse raced above 160 beats per minute. Markov's white blood cell count skyrocketed to more than three times normal. Injured on Thursday, he fell ill on Friday; by the weekend, he was delirious, and on Monday, dead.

Toxicologist on the Case

In an era before the science of forensic toxicology, such a death would undoubtedly have been ascribed to natural causes. But in 1978, in Great Britain, no suspicious death was allowed to go unexamined—and Markov's identity as an anticommunist writer who had defected from Bulgaria in 1971 and who, for the past seven years, had been making international radio broadcasts against what was then Bulgaria's Communist regime, automatically made his death suspicious.

An autopsy was inconclusive until the section of skin containing the umbrella puncture wound was examined by Dr. David Gall, one of Britain's top toxicologists. Gall examined the tissue microscopically and discovered a tiny metal pellet, just 1.5 millimeters in diameter. Into this miniscule sphere two holes had been drilled at right angles to one another.

The pellet was analyzed and found to be of very sophisticated material, an alloy of platinum and iridium, which made it both impervious to corrosion and virtually undetectable by x-ray. Gall reasoned that the tiny holes had been packed with some sort of poison, and that the pellet had been fired into Markov's thigh by a gas gun disguised as an umbrella. Presumably, the assassin—a man with a heavy Eastern European accent—was an agent of the Bulgarian government.

Case Closed?

In the cloak-and-dagger world of the Cold War era, the idea that Markov had been assassinated with a poison umbrella seemed quite plausible. Yet the case was far from closed.

Typically, the forensic toxicologist must find traces of a poison or its byproducts in body tissue in order to conclude that poisoning had taken place. But if Markov had indeed been killed by a substance sufficiently minute to be stuffed into a hole drilled into a 1.5-millimeter pellet, there was virtually no chance of finding any trace of it in his body tissues. Unable to find a suspicious substance, Gall and his team began a process of elimination by asking what poisons would produce Markov's symptoms *and* be powerful enough to do so even in such a small quantity?

They were left with only one: ricin, a derivative of the humble castor bean, yet some 500 times deadlier than cyanide.

To test their conclusion empirically, Gall and his team injected a pig with a miniscule dose of ricin. The animal was dead in a day, and, on autopsy, its organs exhibited precisely the same kinds of damage as those of Georgi Markov: ricin causes red blood cells to clump together (agglutinate), then destroys other body cells.

By the Numbers

The average lethal dose of ricin in human beings is 0.2 milligrams ($1/5{,}000$th of a gram). There is no antidote for exposure.

The human-pig analogy was compelling, but was still circumstantial rather than definitive evidence of homicide by ricin poisoning. Ordinarily, definitive proof would require a trace of the substance in Markov's tissue, yet the very absence of ricin—or any other toxin—in Markov's remains was itself a strong argument for ricin poisoning. Not only was the quantity of poison probably too small to leave a recoverable trace, it is the nature of ricin that the process by which body cells make protein completely breaks the poison down—albeit not before the substance has done its lethal damage. By the time the damage has been done, all trace of the ricin is gone.

Although British authorities concluded, on the basis of forensic toxicology, that Georgi Markov had been murdered, the identity of his assassin was never determined. After the fall of communism throughout Eastern Europe, the democratic government of Bulgaria admitted that the Communist regime had authorized the assassination of a number of defectors, including Markov. Bulgarian officials did not volunteer information concerning the agent or agents who carried out these deadly missions.

Poison World

How many poisons are known to humankind? The medieval Swiss alchemist and physician Paracelsus, called the father of toxicology, declared "Everything is poison, there is poison in everything. Only the dose makes a thing not a poison."

In investigating a homicide, the forensic toxicologist potentially has an almost limitless list of candidate toxins to search for. In practice, however, there is a far more limited range of substances involved in accidental deaths or deliberately used in homicides.

By the Numbers _____

America's poison centers handle one poison exposure every 14 seconds—about 2 million per year. Most poisonings involve common household items such as cleaning supplies and medicines, and 89 percent of all poison exposures occur in the home. Most exposures—92 percent—involve only one substance, and 86.7 percent of exposures are unintentional.

Poison? Drug? Narcotic?

In the toxicologist's view, a poison is a substance that, in relatively small amounts, causes harm or death to an organism. Although when misused, a drug may also cause harm or death, it is intended to serve as a remedy or medicine. A narcotic is a kind of drug that causes sedation, dulls the senses, or even brings about unconsciousness or sleep. Applied to human beings, poisons have no legitimate purpose. Both drugs and narcotics can be beneficial, but both categories of substance are also subject to abuse, including criminal abuse.

Death by Substance

Some *poisons*, *drugs*, and *narcotics* can cause death quickly through a single dose. This is called *acute toxicity*. With some substances, death or harm can also eventually result from repeated non-lethal doses; however, in the case of certain drugs and narcotics, such does produce *intoxication*, often accompanied by some euphoric sensation. For this reason, various drugs and narcotics are actively sought after, even though their use may be illegal and dangerous. Depending on the substance involved, the desire to obtain and use the drug or narcotic is driven by a desire to produce euphoria. With some substances, however, the drive is a physiologically or chemically based addiction. The user physically craves the substance and may even feel that he cannot live without it. Being deprived of the substance may produce dramatic symptoms termed *withdrawal*.

def•i•ni•tion

As defined by forensic toxicologists, a **poison** is a substance that, in relatively small amounts, causes harm or death. A **drug** is intended as a remedy or medicine, but may cause harm or death if misused or abused. A **narcotic** is a drug that causes sedation, dulls the senses, or induces unconsciousness.

Acute toxicity is the term applied to the effect of ingesting substances that cause more or less rapid death with a single dose. **Intoxication** describes the effect of certain substances that do not cause acute toxicity, but have a lesser effect, sometimes harmful, sometimes euphoric, and sometimes both harmful and euphoric. In the case of some substances that cause euphoric intoxication (such as certain narcotics and, in some cases, alcohol), deprivation of the substance may produce an acute, painful, and sometimes harmful constellation of symptoms termed **withdrawal**.

Even drugs and narcotics that do not cause death directly may be responsible for death indirectly. Under the influence of drugs, narcotics, or alcohol, the driver of an automobile may cause a fatal accident. Or compelled by a need for cash in order to obtain a drug, an addict may resort to criminal behavior, including murder.

A Dynamic Situation

Typically, a true poison is sufficiently lethal to bring death quite abruptly by creating an effect so devastating to cells and organ systems that the body's natural defenses are simply overwhelmed. In some cases of homicide by poison, the job of the forensic toxicologist is simply to find traces of the lethal substance and identify it in order to prove that the death in question is a homicide.

Often, however, the forensic toxicologist faces the more complex task of determining if a substance found on autopsy was the true cause of death. Or he or she may be asked to attempt to estimate, given the time of death, the probable time at which a potentially deadly substance was administered—and in what dose.

To answer such questions requires a knowledge of *pharmacodynamics*, the study of what a particular substance, in a particular quantity and over a particular span of time, does to the body. In conducting a pharmacodynamic study, the toxicologist may chemically compare the quantity of *parent* (as the poison, drug, or narcotic is called in its original form) to the quantity of *metabolites* present in a victim's body tissue. Metabolites are compounds created (generally by the liver) as the body works to detoxify the invading substance.

A pharmacodynamic study also calls for knowledge of the duration of a substance's activity. In the case of drugs and narcotics, this is termed the "half-life" of the substance. The time required for the total amount of drug, as measured by the level of the drug present in the blood, to be reduced by 50 percent is that drug's half-life.

Finally, in addition to measuring the comparative quantities of parent and metabolites in the victim's blood, the forensic toxicologist may also consider the condition of certain organs, assessing them for degree of damage.

def•i•ni•tion

Pharmacodynamics is the study of the effect on the human body of a particular substance in a particular quantity and over a particular span of time.

A **parent** substance is a poison or drug in its original chemical form. A **metabolite** is a compound created (generally by the liver) as the body works to detoxify the invading parent substance.

The evidence at the crime scene—needle tracks on a victim's arm and drug paraphernalia nearby—strongly suggests death by drug overdose. A toxicological analysis will confirm this and also determine the type and quantity of drug or drugs involved.

(Photo courtesy of Bobby Tribble, Clarke County [Georgia] Coroner)

Scorecards

As with any scientific field, it is a goal of forensic toxicology to replace guesswork and speculation with accurate assessment and analysis. Fortunately, the toxicologist has the benefit of centuries of accumulated human experience with poisons, drugs, and narcotics, including, in relatively recent years, careful observation and study of effects and relative toxicity.

Except in instances of monstrously aberrant civilizations—Nazi Germany, for example—extensive experimentation to determine the toxic levels of various substances has been carried out on laboratory animals rather than human beings. The results obtained through animal experimentation are readily extrapolated to human beings by calculating the relative weight of the experimental animal versus that of the average person.

The substance in question is administered to experimental animals in carefully measured quantities. Any dose that kills at least one animal is deemed the minimal lethal dose. A dose that kills 50 percent of the test subjects is termed "lethal dose-50 (LD 50)." The results of these studies are tabulated to give a picture of the toxicity of the substance.

Togetherness—Not Always a Good Thing

Toxicity is not always a simple matter of dosage, however. Some substances interact with one another, either increasing or decreasing the toxicity of a given dose.

- If substance A reduces the toxicity of substance B, it is said to have an antagonistic effect on B.

- If substance A tends to increase the toxicity of substance B, it is said to have an additive effect on B.

- If substance A increases the toxicity of substance B even as the presence of substance B increases its own level of toxicity, the combination of A and B are said to have a *synergistic* effect.

def•i•ni•tion

Drug **synergy** results when two ingested toxins (or drugs) mutually enhance their effects.

Drug synergies lead to numerous accidental poisonings. Washing down a Phenobarbital-based narcotic with a few shots of vodka (ethanol), for example, can be fatal.

Popularity Contest

Various scientific publications provide the toxicologist with information on the relative frequency with which a variety of toxic or potentially toxic substances are commonly used—for example, in industrial applications, in cleaning products, or in pesticides. The U.S. Drug Enforcement Administration (DEA) publishes reports and factsheets tracking the popularity of illegal drugs and narcotics. Data such as this often helps forensic toxicologists and other criminal investigators focus their investigation of deaths in which drugs, narcotics, or poisons are suspected.

What Do You Expect?

In addition to tables of toxicity, toxicologists also consult clinical and anecdotal reports on the physiological and behavioral effect of drugs and narcotics. Such information can be very helpful to criminal profilers and to victimologists, because people who abuse one type of drug—amphetamines, for example—behave differently from those who primarily abuse another type, such as barbiturates. That is, for forensic purposes, it is often as important to understand the effects of a drug as it is to understand its chemical composition and the chemical changes it causes within the body.

From the Autopsy Table

In his book about forensics, *Crime Scene*, author Larry Ragle calls toxicologists "a special breed, [who] work with an array of body parts and coroner's samples that under the best of circumstances are disgusting just to think about."

Working a typical case, the forensic toxicologist is presented with samples of body fluids, stomach contents, and organ parts. In addition, he or she is also given full access to the coroner's report, which includes postmortem observations, some of the circumstances of death, the circumstances in which the body was found, and, sometimes, the signs and symptoms that preceded death.

The toxicologist approaches the analytical task with a thorough understanding of how the body metabolizes poisons, drugs, and narcotics. He or she realizes that the "parent" substance may be found, but it is also quite possible that the only substances left in the specimens he examines will be metabolites.

> **Sworn Statement**
>
> Toxicologists wash their hands before going to the bathroom.
>
> —Response of a forensic toxicologist to the question "What makes your job different from other people's?" quoted in Larry Ragle, *Crime Scene* (2002)

Acid or Base?

Usually, the first step in the chemical analysis of body fluids is to divide specimens into acidic and basic fractions. The reason for this preliminary division is that most drugs and many poisons are either acids or bases (as opposed to a salt, which is the product of a chemical reaction between an acid and a base). Acid drugs (such as barbiturates) are extracted from the specimen fluid using an acid reagent, whereas base drugs (such as amphetamines) are extracted with a base reagent.

From Fluid Sample to Drug Sample

Once extracted by an acid-base procedure, the fluid specimen is now an actual drug sample and is subjected first to screening tests and then to confirmation testing.

Screening tests provide quick indications of what sort of drug or toxin exists in the sample. Methods of screening include:

- ◆ Physical tests—to determine boiling point, melting point, density, and refractive index

- ◆ Crystal tests—the use of various reagents to produce crystals that are characteristic of various substances

- ◆ Chemical spot tests—the use of various reagents that produce color changes indicating the presence of specific categories of drugs or toxins

- ◆ Chromatography—a method of separating the components of a mixture

After screening tests produce a positive result, mass spectrometry is used as a confirmation test. In a mass spectrometer, each drug or toxin yields a known mass spectra, which is the "fingerprint" of that substance. The results of this test are generally considered infallible proof of the existence of a given substance.

Even the Toxicologist Has Limits

Although some forensic toxicologists have sufficient training in physiology to render an expert opinion on whether toxin levels found in a victim's body were sufficient to cause death, most of the time it is a physician—a pathologist—who uses the toxicologist's report to make this determination. Indeed, questions of what constitutes a lethal level in a given case are often subjects of intense dispute and wrangling between prosecutors and defense attorneys.

Because forensic toxicology is such a vast field, many toxicologists specialize in a toxicological subfield. Three of the most important subfields include:

1. Drug Recognition Experts (DRE)

2. Experts in alcohol intoxication measurement

3. Experts in carbon monoxide poisoning

The Future

Demand for forensic experts, including forensic toxicologists, by police agencies, prosecutors, and defense attorneys has dramatically increased in recent years and is likely to continue. The increase is not due to a spike in homicide by poison, but to increased and more complex patterns of drug and narcotics abuse as well as emerging problems of environmental industrial contamination, which have brought with them an increase in the volume of lawsuits involving toxic substances.

In recent years, the field of forensic toxicology has become more complex, as toxicologists are called on to testify concerning the health effects of various substances. It is likely that more and broader training will be required to obtain certification as a general forensic toxicologist. It is also likely that toxicologists will increasingly benefit from ever more sophisticated computer-based analytical equipment, which will not only speed their work, but increase the detail with which they can provide answers to medical and criminal investigators.

The Least You Need to Know

♦ Poison is one of the oldest of murder weapons; however, most poisonings are unintentional, resulting either from accidental exposure to a toxin or through drug and narcotic use and abuse.

♦ A forensic toxicologist specializes in the study of drugs and poisons as they relate to the fields of criminal justice and public safety.

♦ Forensic toxicologists analyze specimens from the living as well as the dead.

♦ Although it is the job of the forensic toxicologist to identify and analyze toxic substances in human fluid and tissue specimens, the final determination of whether a given substance actually caused death is usually made by or in consultation with a forensic pathologist.

12

Of Teeth and Bones

In This Chapter

- ◆ Forensic odontology
- ◆ Dental identification
- ◆ Bite-mark evidence
- ◆ Forensic anthropology
- ◆ Bone evidence
- ◆ Facial reconstruction

The work of the medical examiner makes a lie of the old pirate maxim, "Dead men tell no tales." But what happens when there's almost nothing left of the "dead man"?

Most human tissue is fragile. It can be consumed by fire, by the action of animals and insects, and by time itself. At many homicide or suspected homicide scenes, precious little is left, except for teeth and bones or bone fragments. Thanks to two forensic specialties, the forensic odontologist and the forensic anthropologist, these meager remains are often just enough to catch a killer.

The Dentist Is in (No Appointment Necessary)

Forensic dentists play two major roles in criminal investigation. They use dental remains to identify the dead, and they also analyze dental evidence left on crime victims or, for that matter, on any other object associated with a crime scene: *bite marks*.

In effect, at their most basic, both jobs boil down to matching teeth to existing dental records and matching teeth to bite marks.

def•i•ni•tion

In forensics, a **bite mark** is a tooth pattern found on the skin of a crime victim or on other objects associated with a crime scene. The forensic odontologist tries to match the bite-mark evidence to the teeth (or bite pattern) of a suspect.

Better than DNA?

Normally, there are 32 teeth in the mouth of an adult human being. The shape of the teeth and their arrangement in the mouth (the "bite") vary greatly from individual to individual. Wear and tear, decay, and violence usually reduces this number through life, and most people make regular—or at least repeated—trips to the dentist to repair or remove damaged or ailing teeth. Dentists take x-rays and keep records of therapeutic work done.

Just by examining a single tooth, a forensic dentist can draw conclusions about the late owner's age, health, and even socio-economic status. The so-called "Gustafson method" enumerates six signs of tooth wear, rating them numerically and coordinating these ratings with age ranges. Another method, the "Lamendin system," which is often used in conjunction with the Gustafson method when tooth roots are still intact, gauges the degree of root transparency. Transparency changes with age; at an early age, the roots of teeth become increasingly transparent at their tips, the transparency progressing toward the crown as one ages.

In some cases, the hard outer covering of a tooth sufficiently preserves the soft inner tissue, or pulp, so that mitochondrial DNA specimens (see Chapter 14) can be extracted.

If more than a single tooth is recovered from human remains, the forensic odontologist can begin the process of comparing the teeth to existing dental records. In cases where genetic material is so badly decomposed that DNA testing is difficult, inconclusive, or impossible, dental identification can be better—more conclusive—than DNA identification.

In examining dental evidence from human remains, the forensic odontologist takes an impression of the teeth as they exist in the upper and lower jaws. He also x-rays the teeth, noting all evidence of decay and disease, twisted teeth, malformed teeth, broken teeth, and missing teeth as well as fillings and other dental work. He may then put this information in a bulletin sent to perhaps thousands of dentists, focusing on those practicing in the locality associated with the victim. Although there is no dental equivalent to the databases law enforcement agencies maintain to compare fingerprint and DNA evidence, all dentists use the so-called "Universal System" to chart human teeth, so it is quite easy for the forensic odontologist to communicate information to his colleagues in the dental community.

> **Sworn Statement**
>
> Teeth are terrific. Give us one tooth and we just might be able to make an identification. Give us a mouthful, and we can often match suspects to victims, unknowns to names—even evidence items to victims and suspects. They last almost forever. They're well-documented in most cases. They're about the toughest biological evidence available.
>
> —Forensic odontologist James Berry, quoted in N. E. Genge, *The Forensic Casebook* (2002)

The work of forensic odontologists is especially valuable in instances of mass disaster, as in the terrorist attacks on the World Trade Center in New York and the Pentagon in Washington, D.C., on September 11, 2001. In such cases, human remains are often fragmentary, and the numerous victims are separated from any form of identification (such as driver's licenses). Under these chaotic circumstances, dental evidence may be the only reliable means to obtain a positive identification.

A Bite Out of Crime

The forensic odontologist is also an expert examiner of bite-mark evidence. Some murderers bite their victims, perhaps in the course of a struggle, perhaps for sadistic or sexually deviant motives. To the odontologist, the bite mark is nothing less than an impression of the perpetrator's teeth. From this evidence, the odontologist may be able to advise police as to whether they should look for a large or small person. Even more important, it is often possible to match a suspect's teeth to a bite mark found on the victim.

All human beings are animals, but violent criminals can behave like beasts. Many violent attacks include biting, and biting leaves an impression of the assailant's teeth. Some crime scenes also include other items into which the perpetrator has bitten, such as food, some of which retains bite marks. In some cases, bite-mark evidence is found on the suspect rather than the victim. For example, in defending herself against an attempted rape, a woman may bite her assailant, leaving a characteristic imprint. In all cases, the objective of the forensic odontologist is to match the bite evidence to a set of teeth.

In most cases, the forensic odontologist takes a series of photographs of the bite-mark evidence, using various combinations of lighting and photographic techniques to create the clearest image possible. Often, photographs will be taken over a period of time because changes in the tissue of a dead person, including lividity, blanching, and other postmortem processes, may actually reveal more detail in the bite mark. Ultraviolet (UV) photography may be used to bring out maximum detail at the tips of tooth penetration in a bite mark, and infrared (IR) photography may be used to get a more accurate picture of bleeding and damage below the skin surface. All bite-mark photographs include a ruler in the image, to insure that prints made from the photograph are precisely life size.

The forensic odontologist takes an impression of the suspect's teeth, upper and lower, then uses this to make a cast of the bite. He may then simply lay the cast on top of a life-size photograph of the bite mark, showing how the teeth match the mark. Another method of matching uses computer graphics programs to overlay an image of the suspect's bite onto the bite-mark evidence.

At times, comparison is straightforward—especially if the bite mark is clear and the suspect has such dental distinctions as a crooked tooth or a gap in his bite, which show up in the bite mark. In some cases, however, tissue damage and decay and overlapping bite marks—from multiple bites—complicate identification and require very careful analysis.

In addition to matching bite marks with the teeth of suspects, forensic odontologists may also provide an analysis of bite evidence that speaks to the nature of the crime. For example, they note four degrees of a biting attack:

1. Clear: The result of significant bite pressure

2. Obvious: "First-degree pressure"

3. Noticeable: The result of violent pressure

4. Lacerated: A bite in which flesh is torn from the body

Case in Point

Theodore Robert "Ted" Bundy was probably the most notorious serial killer in American history. Although he confessed to more than 30 murders, most authorities believe he killed even more. It was bite-mark evidence that finally brought Bundy down, leading to his conviction and execution.

On January 15, 1978, Bundy strangled and clubbed to death Lisa Levy and Martha Bowman in the same room in the Chi Omega sorority house at Tallahassee's Florida State University. In the attack, he also raped Levy, then he went on to murder two other girls in the sorority house. He attacked a fifth victim, who survived.

No fingerprints were found at the crime scene, but there was a bite mark on the left buttock of Lisa Levy. Crime scene investigators photographed the mark, and later, when Bundy was arrested on suspicion of having committed the murders, investigators obtained a search warrant allowing them to make an impression of Bundy's teeth. Forensic odontologist Dr. Richard Souviron took the impression, noting the uneven pattern of the teeth, which he said would make identification easier.

Although the tissue from Levy's buttock had been destroyed in the process of analysis, the photograph was preserved, and, testifying before a jury, Souviron pointed out the unique features of the bite mark, demonstrating how these features matched the dental impressions of Bundy's teeth. Key features of the match were the structure of alignment, chips, the size of the teeth, and the relative sharpness of the bicuspids, lateral, and incisor teeth. Finally, Souviron displayed an enlarged photo of the bite-mark and overlaid it with a transparent enlargement of Bundy's teeth. The overlay matched perfectly.

Souviron was able to describe the bite attack in detail, showing how the evidence was actually a double bite, Bundy having bitten once, then turned sideways to bite again.

This was the first case in Florida's legal history that relied on bite-mark testimony, and it was sufficient to convict Bundy on July 31, 1979. After multiple appeals, he was executed a decade later, on January 24, 1989.

The Bone Detectives

Like teeth, bones long outlast fleshy tissues, and from even partial and fragmentary skeletal remains, the forensic anthropologist is able to suggest the age, sex, ancestry, stature, and other unique features of a decedent. This specialist can also distinguish between a skeleton that may be decades old or even older and one that is of more recent origin. Skeletal remains often reveal the results of injury, and the forensic anthropologist can help other investigators determine if the injury was likely the result of homicide.

Although the primary task of most forensic anthropologists involves the analysis of skeletal remains, their work is not limited to this evidence. Much as traditional anthropologists excavate a site to recover evidence of an ancient civilization, forensic anthropologists may use the techniques of archaeological excavation to recover skeletal remains as well as other evidence, including (according to the *FBI Law Enforcement Bulletin* of July 1990) "hair, insects, plant materials and foot prints." In addition, forensic anthropologists may employ "facial reproduction" techniques to image fleshy tissue that no longer exists, in effect "building" the face of the deceased, so that relatives or friends may be able to make an identification. Forensic anthropologists also note evidence of past injury and medical treatment, which may provide clues to the identity of the deceased.

By the Numbers

Most anatomists agree that the skeleton of an adult human being consists of 206 bones. But this is only an average, since the number of bones varies slightly from individual to individual. Human beings are born with about 300 bones, some of which fuse together in the process of growth, yielding the smaller adult number.

Hidden Crime Scene

When a forensic anthropologist is called to excavate an area of interest to police, he or she goes about the work in much the same way as a traditional archaeologist excavates a historic or prehistoric site—which is itself very similar to the way in which criminal investigators examine any crime scene.

Each step of the excavation is precisely recorded using words, drawings, and photographs. The area excavated is staked out with a grid of twine, and this is represented on a graph-paper sketch. The position of everything uncovered in the excavation is precisely recorded on this graph. It is also photographed and perhaps sketched before it is bagged for further examination in the laboratory. Archaeological anthropologists are trained to look for detail, for minutiae; it is a characteristic they share with any good crime scene investigator. The object is not only to recover relevant evidence—weapons, cigarette butts, articles of clothing, skeletal remains—but to get an accurate picture of the physical relationships these objects bear to one another. For it is such relationships that speak volumes about whatever drama deposited the objects there in the first place.

Bone Story

The bones speak. That may sound like the title of a horror movie, but it is the leading principle of forensic anthropology.

The forensic anthropologist begins by recovering as much of the skeleton as possible. He then lays out the bones to reconstruct the skeleton. From this, it is possible to judge the height and basic body type of the deceased. Even if few bones are recovered, measurement of the long bones, especially those of the legs, can serve as the basis for a quite accurate estimate of height. By examining the position, size, and type of muscle attachments to the bones, the forensic anthropologist can estimate weight as well as muscularity. He or she may even be able to hazard a guess as to the type of activity the deceased was involved in: someone who did a lot of heavy lifting, for example, as opposed to a white-collar worker.

Gender is evident from skeletal remains. In women, the pelvic bones are lower and wider than in men. The appearance of the pelvic bones also enable the forensic anthropologist to say whether or not a woman has given birth. Other bones—including those of the base of the skull, the forehead, and the jaw—bear sex-specific characteristics.

Because bones grow and otherwise change throughout life, they provide ample evidence as to age at the time of death. The bones of the skull "knit together" at their suture points most obviously as an infant matures, but this process of closure continues more subtly throughout life. Skull sutures therefore reveal much about age. Generally speaking, the smoother the skull, the older the person. Other clues to age include joint condition and wear, particularly in the bones of the spine.

Remarkably, race and even ethnicity may be at least somewhat evident in bone structure—although this remains a gray area, subject to a certain amount of educated guess work. Much easier is the determination as to whether a person was right- or left-handed. There is more muscle attachment on the wrist bones of the dominant side.

Beyond issues of identity, skeletal remains say something about the range of time in which death occurred. Even hard bone tissue, after all, is subject to environmental wear. The bones also reveal evidence of violence, which says something about the nature of the crime committed or may even help investigators determine whether death was caused by a crime or was accidental.

> **Sworn Statement**
>
> That's how I feel about the skeletons in my laboratory. These have tales to tell us, even though they are dead. It is up to me, the forensic anthropologist, to catch their mute cries and whispers, and to interpret them for the living, as long as I am able.
>
> —Forensic anthropologist William R. Maples, in his book *Dead Men Do Tell Tales* (1994)

Bringing the Dead to Life

Skillfully interpreted as evidence, bones may indeed speak for the dead. Yet they remain the very symbol of death. Even a victim's closest friends and relatives would not recognize him from the skeleton alone. Remarkably—almost miraculously—forensic anthropology has found ways to put flesh back on the bones.

Facial reconstruction is a set of techniques that enables investigators and family members to identify remains when all other methods of identification have failed. Reconstruction is conjecture and approximation, but it may provide the stimulus that leads to positive identification of crime victims who otherwise would remain entirely unknown.

def•i•ni•tion

Facial reconstruction is a set of scientific and artistic techniques, sometimes computer-aided, that enables investigators and family members to identify remains when all other methods of identification have failed.

Two-Dimensional Methods

Specially trained forensic artists, whose experience includes a knowledge of forensic anthropology, may reconstruct a face through hand-drawn portraits based on x-rays, the actual skull, and—if a candidate for identity is available—photographs of that candidate. Often, a forensic artist works in collaboration with a forensic anthropologist to make this kind of reconstruction.

In recent years, computer software programs have been developed to aid in creating two-dimensional facial approximations. These may be easily altered and manipulated until a plausible likeness is achieved.

The Third Dimension

Again, working together, an artist and a forensic anthropologist may model a facial reconstruction in clay or using sophisticated 3D computer modeling programs.

For clay reconstructions, a cast of the actual skull is used as the armature or foundation on which the clay is applied. A sculptor with a thorough knowledge of skeletal anatomy may be able to make a close approximation of the likely structure of the flesh on the bone. Typically, the finished clay model is painted to enhance the approximation. Glass eyes may be included, along with hair.

Three-dimensional computer programs create reconstructions based on digitally scanned photographs of the unidentified cranial remains, which are combined with stock photographs of facial features and other data.

Forensic Superimposition

In cases where investigators have some theory as to the identity of the skeletal remains, a forensic superimposition may be created to test the identity theory. The photograph of a person suspected of belonging to the skeletal remains in question is superimposed over an x-ray of the unidentified skull. If the anatomical features correctly align, it is reasonable to assume that the remains are those of the individual in the photograph.

A Little Background

Although sophisticated computer graphics programs especially designed for forensic facial reconstruction are recent and still emerging developments, the basic techniques of facial reconstruction date back to the late nineteenth century, when anatomical researchers produced the first data on average facial tissue thickness. It was not until 1962, however, that the American anthropologist Wilton M. Krogman presented a cogent method for facial reconstruction and introduced it into the field of forensics. His 1986 book *The Human Skeleton in Forensic Medicine* is the most comprehensive work on the subject.

Not Quite a Miracle

As stunning as the results of modern facial reconstruction can be, the method has many limitations. The major problem is the limited nature of data available on average facial tissue thickness. Although much work has been done in this field, the range of variation related to age, sex, and body build is far greater than the range of available data. The gap between the data and these ranges is bridged by the subjective judgment of the forensic artist or anthropologist.

Another area in which subjectivity plays a major role is the method of reconstruction. Drawing and sculpture, even with the aid of computer programs, is at best a synthesis of science and art—with art often predominating. It is inexact. There are no standard methods for approximating facial features and individuating characteristics, let alone any one official method.

Inadmissible

The gold standard of forensic science is to achieve *positive identification*, which is established when a unique set of biological characteristics of an individual are matched with a set of skeletal remains. Positive identification occurs when skeletal or dental remains correspond precisely with medical or dental records, or when evidence of some unique characteristic (such as evidence of a very specific wound) can be found in the remains and in the ante-mortem (pre-death) records of the individual. DNA analysis, when possible, is another means of making a positive identification.

When positive identification is not possible, the next best thing is *circumstantial identification*. This is established when an individual seems to fit the general biological profile indicated by skeletal evidence. Identity is suggested, but not proved. After all, more than one individual may fit the same biological profile.

Positive identification is always compelling evidence in an investigation and in a courtroom. Circumstantial identification can be extremely helpful in an investigation, but it is less compelling in a courtroom—and may even be inadmissible.

In 1993, the U.S. Supreme Court established the Daubert Standard, a legal precedent regarding the admissibility of expert witness testimony during legal proceedings. The standard is intended to ensure that expert witness testimony:

◆ Is based upon adequate facts or data

◆ Is the product of proven principles and investigative methods

◆ Is the product of principles and methods that have been applied reliably to the facts of the case in question

def•i•ni•tion

In forensics, **positive identification** is established when a unique set of biological characteristics of an individual are uniquely matched with a set of skeletal remains. Positive identification evidence is almost always admissible in court.

In forensics, **circumstantial identification** is made when an individual seems to fit the general biological profile indicated by skeletal evidence. Circumstantial identification evidence is often inadmissible in court, but may nevertheless be valuable in criminal investigation.

In facial reconstruction, no two forensic anthropologists or artists produce identical approximations for a given set of skeletal remains. Moreover, the data on which the approximations are based are incomplete. For these two reasons alone, facial reconstruction does not meet the requirements of the Daubert Standard and is therefore not recognized in any American courtroom as a means of positive identification. Even as circumstantial identification, it is inadmissible, and forensic artists are not called on as expert witnesses. Facial reconstruction is currently limited to investigative work, as a last resort for identification when all else has failed.

More Evidence

As the July 1990 *FBI Law Enforcement Bulletin* states, forensic anthropology includes, in addition to bone analysis and facial reconstruction, the recovery, identification, and analysis of several other kinds of evidence, the most important of which are the "examination of … insects [and] plant materials." These are the province of specialized forensic scientists, the forensic entomologist and the forensic botanist, and are the subject of the next chapter.

The Least You Need to Know

- Teeth and bones greatly outlast soft body tissues and are therefore often the only remains criminal investigators encounter at a suspected crime scene.

- Forensic odontologists are dentists who specialize in matching dental evidence recovered from crime scenes—including teeth and bite marks—with suspects and victims.

- Forensic anthropologists use the methods of traditional archaeological anthropology to excavate suspected crime scenes in order to recover and analyze evidence.

- The chief form of evidence forensic anthropologists examine is human skeletal remains, mainly for purposes of identification, but also for what the condition of the bones reveal about the nature of a violent crime.

- Facial reconstruction is a specialized branch of forensic anthropology that attempts to build or visualize a "flesh" identity using a skull recovered from a suspected crime scene.

Chapter 13

Of Bugs and Botany

In This Chapter

- Using forensic entomology to determine time of death and link suspects to crime scenes
- The many branches of forensic botany
- Finding clandestine graves
- Diatom evidence
- Botany and a victim's last meal
- Introduction to forensic geology

Despite their often primitive behavior, human beings are at the top of the evolutionary pyramid, but they still have to share the world with a lot of so-called "lower" life forms, including insects (and other arthropods) and plants. Both before and after death, people interact with bugs, bushes, and the like, creating—quite unintentionally—a record of that contact. In conjunction with a corpse, suspect, or crime scene, that bio-environmental record may speak volumes to criminal investigators.

Time of Death

The field of forensic entomology did not become widely recognized in criminal investigation until the mid-1980s, but its earliest history may actually be traced to thirteenth-century China, when the detective-jurist Sung Tz'u described his investigation of the case of a stabbing near a rice field. Just one day after the murder, Sung Tz'u went to the rice field and ordered all workers to put down their sickles. Immediately, traces of blood, though invisible, attracted blowflies to one sickle. Sung Tz'u confronted the owner of the implement, who instantly confessed.

In its early days in law enforcement, forensic entomology was used strictly to determine *post-mortem interval* (*PMI*)—the time of death. From the presence of insect eggs or of the insects themselves at various stages of development, the forensic entomologist (FE) can estimate PMI because insects and other *arthropods* inhabit and often mature in decomposing bodies. The forensic entomologist collects whatever insects have infested a corpse, identifies their species, then notes the life-cycle stage at which the specimens were recovered. Since insects of a given species under a given set of climatological conditions (such as temperature and humidity) mature at regular rates, it is possible to gauge the length of time the specimen has inhabited the body in question and, therefore, estimate the PMI.

def•i•ni•tion

Post-mortem interval (PMI) is the span of time between the discovery of a body and the time of death.

Arthropods are members of the phylum Arthropoda, which includes lobsters, crabs, beetles, spiders, insects, centipedes, and millipedes.

The Blowfly Bears Witness

When any animal dies in the open, the blowflies know it. They lay their eggs in carrion—decaying flesh—and that becomes the environment in which the eggs hatch into larvae, which go through regular, recognizable stages of maturation until they become adult flies.

The blowfly egg hatches into a maggot, a larval stage known as the first instar, which feeds on the decay around it until it grows from about 2 millimeters to 5 millimeters, whereupon it ruptures through its skin, leaves the old skin behind, and emerges as a second instar. That larger maggot continues eating, growing from about 6 millimeters to 9 millimeters in length. At this point, it sheds for a second time, leaving the old skin behind and becoming a third instar, growing from 10 to 13 millimeters. In this third instar phase, the skin no longer resembles that of a maggot, but darkens, grows thicker, and becomes tougher. At the point when this third instar stops eating but still moves about in search of a place to continue its maturation, the insect is called a prepupa. Its thickened skin further hardens into a puparium—similar to a butterfly's cocoon or a moth's chrysalis—within which the prepupa matures into a pupa, which continues to develop entirely within the puparium until that structure splits, and a fully formed adult fly emerges.

Entomologists have closely studied and documented the time a blowfly spends in each stage of its metamorphosis, carefully noting how these spans of time vary with temperature and available moisture. Observations in the field have been extensively supplemented by controlled laboratory experiment. For the forensic entomologist, this knowledge transforms the blowfly into a reliable yardstick for measuring PMI.

The Clock Starts

It is all well and good to know the amount of time required for the blowfly to pass from one state of maturity to the next, but this information is useless for gauging PMI if you don't also know when the biological "clock" started. Fortunately, there is ample entomological data on this subject as well. The FE knows that blowflies prefer to lay their eggs approximately two days after death. Therefore, if third instar maggots are recovered from a corpse and under the prevailing conditions of temperature and moisture it is known that the third instar appears eight days after eggs are laid, it is reasonable to place the time of death at 10 days prior to discovery (and examination) of the body.

Blowfly Alternatives

Blowflies are not found in all locations, climates, and seasons; however, many other insect and other arthropod species mature in carrion, and entomologists have studied them all. Many can be used—beetles are especially popular—to determine PMI.

Indeed, even when blowflies are plentiful, the FE collects all insects and arthropods found on and in a body. This is because a decaying corpse becomes not only part of the ecosystem surrounding it, but is itself an ecosystem for various life forms that live off decay. Forensic entomologists understand that some species feed directly off decaying flesh, whereas others feed off the molds that grow on that flesh. Still other species feed on the insects that feed on the flesh. The FE collects all the insect "waves" (as they are called) present in the body, knowing that one species succeeds another in a predictable pattern.

By the Numbers

A square yard of moist soil contains 500 to 2,000 insects, or about 4,000,000 insects per acre.

The succession of waves is another means of creating a timeline that points to the PMI. This succession may also provide another important piece of the history of the body in question.

Most of us think of decay as a disgusting and chaotic process. Disgusting it may be, but in fact, the process is quite orderly. Under most circumstances, there are five distinct phases of bodily decay:

1. *Initial decay:* From the outside, the body does not appear greatly changed, but has begun to break down internally due to microorganisms present within the body when it was alive.

2. *Putrefaction:* As internal microorganisms break down the body, gases are formed. The putrefying body swells, and a "putrid" odor is produced.

3. *Black putrefaction:* At this stage, the flesh darkens—sometimes to black, but often to purple, brown, blue, green, or a combination of these. The swelling due to gas subsides and recedes as the gas leaks out; however, the odor of putrefaction intensifies.

4. *Butyric fermentation:* At this stage, tissues and organs have liquefied and escaped from the body, which becomes desiccated (dried out). Externally, the body is usually covered with mold, and a new, less intense odor is produced.

5. *Dry rot:* More slowly than the progression of the previous four stages, the body continues to rot and dry, ultimately skeletonizing.

The FE associates the stage of decay with the kind of insect found in the body. For example, blowflies infest bodies during the putrefaction stage (stage 2). Let's say a body is discovered deep in the stage of butyric fermentation (stage 4), but the FE finds no sign of there having ever been blowfly infestation. Depending on other circumstances (such as season and temperature), this may suggest that the body was elsewhere during putrefaction, somewhere effectively sealed off from blowflies, and was moved later.

Sworn Statement

Nick [Polchak] is an amalgam of the real-life forensic entomologists I've interviewed. They're brilliant people, with remarkable memories and an eye for the smallest detail. They're also eccentric people; after all, these are people who decided to get a Ph.D. in bugs! They're not policemen, they're not investigators, they're not even pathologists—and that means they don't exactly "fit" in a traditional crime investigation.

—Tim Downs, author of the "Bug Man" novels, *Chop Shop* and *Shoofly Pie*, featuring forensic entomologist Nick Polchak

A Matter of Protocol

Collection of entomological evidence requires great care and the strict observance of orderly protocols:

First, the FE takes careful note of the location of the body in relation to climate, season, surrounding vegetation, and conditions of sun or shade. If the body is discovered indoors, the investigator notes the proximity of the body to open windows, doors, or other points of access to the outside.

The FE also meticulously documents the locations of insect infestations on or within the body and, of course, makes a thorough record of what species and stages of insects are observed. Other notes include evidence of insect waves, such as fire ants, which prey upon blowfly eggs and larvae. Certain vertebrate animals also scavenge insect infestations.

Next, the FE collects climatologic data prevailing at the scene, including ambient air temperature; the temperature of the maggot mass—obtained by placing the thermometer directly into the larval mass center; the temperature at ground surface; the temperature at the point where body and ground contact one another; and soil temperature directly under the body—taken immediately after the body has been removed. In addition, weather data is obtained for the period spanning one or two weeks prior to the disappearance of the victim to three to five days after discovery of the body.

In actually collecting the insects from the body and the scene, the FE first attempts to recover adult flies and beetles. The reason is simple: these insects move quickly and, once disturbed, they may "flee" the scene of crime. Some specimens are simultaneously killed and preserved (usually by immersion in alcohol) and some are trapped live.

Each set of specimens is carefully labeled with geographical location, date and hour of collection, case number, location on the body from which the specimens were recovered, and the name of the collector.

After the fast-moving adults have been collected, the FE recovers larval and egg specimens. Usually, he or she begins by searching for eggs—a process that must be conducted scrupulously, since tiny, semitransparent eggs are easily overlooked.

Next, the larvae are collected, with emphasis on recovering the largest. A sample of 50 to 60 specimens from the maggot mass is also collected. Some of the eggs and larvae collected are immediately killed and preserved, and some are collected alive, so that maturation rates can be measured under controlled laboratory conditions.

Beyond PMI

While determining time of death remains the most important of the FE's jobs, entomological evidence can also tell much more. The FE can use the type of insects or insect eggs found on the body to tie that body to a specific geographical area. This can be especially revealing if it is suspected that a body has been transported a considerable distance.

The FE may also look for insect evidence on nonbody evidence associated with a crime scene. For example, as every road tripper knows, the radiator grille of an automobile collects whatever insects happen to collide with the car. This collection of corpses can serve as a road map, revealing every place the vehicle has traveled. If that vehicle belongs to a criminal suspect, the information can confirm or destroy an alibi.

Case in Point

In one case, a body was discovered in a coastal area, about 100 miles from where the chief suspect lived. The suspect denied ever having been in the remote area where the body was found. An FE was called in to examine insects found on the suspect's car. Among these he identified a species of mayfly that is found only in the area from which the body was recovered. Moreover, this species of mayfly was known to be active at a particular stage of its development only during a limited time. The ME determined that the time of death was consistent with the period in which the mayflies were active. This fact, coupled with the presence of the insects on the suspect's car, was sufficient to warrant an indictment.

Sometimes the failure to recover insects from where they are expected is in itself revealing. For example, in 1943, the body of a child was discovered nine days after death. Insect infestation was present in all the usual areas—except for the mouth. Back then, the specialty of forensic entomology did not exist, but the medical examiner on the case had a hunch that some substance—perhaps a poison ingested orally—had kept the insects away from the mouth. Although he could not find the poison through toxicology—after nine days, all traces of the substance had broken down—when a suspect was presented with the entomological evidence, he readily confessed to having poisoned the child.

Other esoteric applications of forensic entomology include the investigation of certain cases of abuse in children and neglect of the elderly. Cases have been investigated in which parents meted out bizarrely abusive punishment to their children by intentionally using wasps and bees to sting them. In cases of elder abuse, entomological evidence has been introduced to demonstrate neglect and lack of proper wound care, both in home and institutional environments.

Forensic entomologists have been called on to provide evidence in certain car accidents for which no definitive cause could be found. They have sometimes been able to prove that a driver was stung by a bee or another insect. In several automobile accident cases, FEs have been consulted to identify the fragmentary remains of insects lodged in the radiator grille or impacted against the windshield of an automobile in order to determine the probable path of the vehicle through certain areas.

By the Numbers

According to some studies insect bites and stings are among the top 20 causes of automobile accidents.

Insects have even been implicated in airplane crashes. Entomological evidence has suggested that errant bugs obstructed cockpit instrumentation or even blocked fuel lines, causing engine failure.

Blood splatter experts (see Chapter 9) have sometimes consulted forensic entomologists when they suspect that odd blood pattern evidence might be caused by cockroaches walking through pooled or splattered blood, creating strange tracks. Insects may carry blood evidence to strange places—such as the ceiling—leading crime scene investigators to misinterpret splatter evidence.

Forensic Science Turns Over a New Leaf

It was called the "Crime of the Century." On March 1, 1932, Charles A. Lindbergh Jr.—infant son of the first man to fly the Atlantic solo and his wife, Anne Morrow Lindbergh—was abducted from the Lindberghs' New Jersey home and subsequently murdered. After many months of investigation, suspicion finally fell upon Bruno Richard Hauptmann, a German immigrant with a criminal record, who was arrested in 1934. His sensational trial included the first botanical testimony to be heard in a North American courtroom, as the jury listened to expert testimony concerning the wood grain of the crude homemade ladder that had been used to enter the baby's second-story room. According to the expert, the grain matched wood in Hauptmann's home, and this evidence surely helped to convict him.

Modern forensic botany is based on the Exchange Principle or *Principle of Contact Traces*, which was first articulated in 1910 by a criminal investigator named Edmond Locard. The principle is this: a criminal always leaves something at the crime scene and/or takes something away. In many cases, especially when the crime occurs outdoors, trace botanical evidence can be used to link an object or a suspect to a crime scene. Conversely, this kind of evidence may also rule out a suspect or support his alibi.

def•i•ni•tion

The **Principle of Contact Traces** states that a criminal always leaves something at the crime scene and/or takes something away.

The forensic botanist (FB) is an expert in identifying plant anatomy and ecological requirements and assigning these to specific species and varieties of plants, which may be associated with certain locations. By identifying a plant fragment found on the clothing of a suspect, for example, and matching this fragment to a plant present at the crime scene, the FB links the suspect to the scene and, therefore, to the crime.

Pollen Police

Palynology is the study of pollen grains and spores, as well as certain other acid-resistant microorganisms. The FB may recover pollen or spores from a suspect or from objects belonging to a suspect and compare these microscopically with pollen found at a crime scene. If the "pollen rain" (the types of pollen that fall on a given geographical area) for the crime scene is known, then it may be assumed that anyone or anything associated with that scene may carry traces of the same pollen.

Ecological Investigation

A forensic botanist must have a thorough ecological knowledge of plant species so he can determine whether plant fragments recovered from a victim or object came from where that victim or object was actually found or from some other location. Similarly, plant fragments recovered from a suspect or objects associated with the suspect may link him or her to a crime scene.

One of the more macabre tasks of the FB is to locate hidden or clandestine graves. Any burial disturbs the soil, but such a site does not long remain bare. So-called pioneer species soon appear, followed by later-succession species, and then climax species. Because this species succession is predictable in at least some geographical locations, any site showing a successional stage different from the surrounding area suggests soil disturbance and, possibly, a burial site. Such successional variations may persist for as much as 20 years.

Written in Water

Bodies are not always discovered on dry land. Forensic botanists with a specialized knowledge of *limnology*, the study of freshwater ecology, may be called on to identify evidence linking suspects and victims to crime scenes in or around fresh water. Algae, especially the diatoms, often provide such evidence.

Diatoms are aquatic plant organisms that have uniquely characteristic cell shapes and cells with high silica content, which gives them a crystalline appearance. Diatoms may be recovered from the tissues of suspected drowning victims and from bodies dumped in the water. Diatom tests are often used to diagnose drowning and to estimate PMI.

def•i•ni•tion

Limnology is the study of freshwater ecology and can be very useful when investigating bodies recovered from water.

In decomposed bodies recovered from water, it is difficult to diagnose drowning because the process of decomposition destroys the usual physiological indications of drowning; however, the presence of diatoms in body tissues is a highly reliable indicator of a freshwater drowning. Even in skeletal remains, diatoms may be recovered from bone marrow, thereby indicating death by drowning.

Diatom and other algal evidence can be used to determine time of death. The growth pattern and diversity of the algal types that colonize a body recovered from fresh water provide a useful means of assessing the amount of time the body has been submerged.

Case in Point

In July 1991, two boys were attacked by several persons while fishing in a Connecticut pond. The boys were bound with duct tape, beaten with a baseball bat, and thrown in the pond to drown. Remarkably, one of the boys managed to free himself and saved his friend. Later, three suspects were arrested.

Investigators collected mud samples from the pond, which were compared to mud from the sneakers of the victims as well as the suspects. The samples all contained diatoms and another type of silica-producing algae called scaled chrysophytes. A forensic botanist isolated 15 genera of algae 14 of which were common to all samples. A scaled chrysophyte species identified as Mallomonas caudate was the most numerous species recovered in all of the samples. It is found only in ponds and lakes—not in flowing water—and is the dominant algal species in the ponds and lakes of the northeastern United States.

In addition, the forensic botanist identified and analyzed three species of the Eunotia algae found in all the samples. This diatom is common in freshwater, but it is very rare for the population ratios of species from the same genus to be similar in communities that come from different habitats. In other words, statistical analysis strongly suggested that all of the samples came from the same habitat—namely the crime scene pond. The prospect of the victims' testimony, together with the findings of the forensic botanist, prompted all three suspects to plead guilty.

Bone Dating

An FB can assist a forensic archaeologist in estimating the age of skeletal remains recovered from crime scenes. Plant roots are often found with exposed or shallowly buried bodies. An FB may examine root development after the root has been damaged, assuming that the damage was caused by the digging of a grave. Like tree trunks, the cross-section of a root exhibits annual growth rings. Careful examination can differentiate between the number of rings laid down before the root was damaged and the number laid down after it. The second count is the number of years since the damage occurred, which corresponds to the number of years since the body was buried.

A forensic botanist may also examine roots that are in direct contact with the remains, actually growing *through* them or through some article of clothing associated with them. Such roots can be cross-sectioned precisely at the point of penetration through the body or clothing and the annual rings counted from this point to establish a minimum frame for time since death.

Finally, the FB may analyze linear root branch growth. It is possible to estimate annual root growth and to determine a time frame based on the length of a root from its point of contact with the body to the tip of the root.

Last Meal

Medical examiners routinely analyze the stomach contents of bodies under autopsy in an effort to determine PMI and perhaps even where the victim ate his or her last meal. The medical examiner may consult a forensic botanist to help identify cell types from food plants in order to determine the victim's whereabouts just prior to death. Such cell types as sclereids (pears), starch grains (potatoes and other tubers), raphide crystals (pineapple), druse crystals (citrus, beets, spinach), and silica bodies (cereal grasses and bamboos) are among the most commonly identified.

Tree Ring Circus

A *dendrochronologist* is a botanist who specializes in the study of tree rings. The number of rings accurately gives the age of the tree, and variations in the width of the rings indicate changes in environmental conditions. In forensics, dendrochronology can be used to date wooden objects and match them with a crime scene, as was done in the case of Bruno Hauptmann's ladder.

Evidence provided by tree ring analysis is often used to date and to authenticate the antiquity of wooden art objects. An unscrupulous dealer in musical instruments may demand millions of dollars for what he claims is a seventeenth-century Stradivarius violin. If the forgery is a good one, it may

def•i•ni•tion

A **dendrochronologist** is a botanist who specializes in the study of tree rings.

be impossible to distinguish a modern fake from a genuine instrument on the basis of aesthetics alone. However, by x-raying the wood, it is possible to compare the tree ring evidence to standard curves for spruce from the Alps of northern Italy, the wood Stradivarius used. If such comparison indicates a provenance (date of creation) less than about 400 years old, the violin in question could not have been made by the Italian master.

Rock Patrol

Somewhat less established and less widely used than forensic entomology and forensic botany is the field of forensic geology, which applies the principles of geology to the identification and analysis of geologic materials involved in criminal as well as civil matters of law.

Forensic geologists may be presented with rocks and soil samples associated with a crime scene, suspect, or victim, as well as objects associated with any of these, and asked to identify the material and to determine its origin. The object of such identification is to determine if the material in question is unique to a crime scene or to circumstances under which a crime was committed.

The geologist may also be consulted in the identification and investigation of clandestine burials. Most frequently, however, the geologist uses his or her expertise to match rock and soil traces associated with a victim or suspect to the rocks and soil found at a crime scene. In this respect, geological evidence typically plays the same linking role that some entomological and botanical evidence plays, connecting suspects with victims and linking both to a particular place and time.

The Least You Need to Know

♦ The forensic entomologist analyzes insects (and other arthropods) found on and in corpses to determine post-mortem interval (PMI) or to link a victim, suspect, and crime scene.

♦ The forensic botanist analyzes plants and plant fragments to link victims and suspects and to connect both with a crime scene; he or she can also use plant evidence to determine PMI and to discover clandestine graves.

♦ The forensic geologist matches rock and soil samples found on suspects, victims, and articles associated with a crime to a crime scene.

♦ The work of forensic entomologists, botanists, and geologists is largely based on the investigative Principle of Contact Traces, which holds that a criminal always leaves something at the crime scene and/or takes something away.

14

DNA Evidence: The "Smoking Gun"?

In This Chapter

- ◆ Using DNA "fingerprinting"
- ◆ Obtaining and analyzing DNA evidence
- ◆ Analytical techniques for difficult cases
- ◆ Reliability and validity of DNA evidence
- ◆ Using DNA evidence to exonerate the innocent
- ◆ The DNA database controversy

Investigators and, in the end, juries evaluate evidence. Such evaluation determines, step by step, the further course of the investigation or the final verdict in a criminal case. Ideally, the evidence presented is straightforward and clear cut, the proverbial "smoking gun" that pretty much proves guilt or innocence.

But crime is a human activity, and evidence, the product of human activity, is usually far from straightforward and clear cut. Often, the prosecution has only a few precious pieces of physical evidence—a fragment of fiber, a few strands of hair, a trace of blood—to link the accused to a crime. Analyzed properly and presented persuasively, such evidence may point to the defendant, but traditionally, material like this has rarely been sufficient to secure a conviction—a verdict, beyond a reasonable doubt, of guilty.

What if there were an ironclad way to link such trace evidence, beyond any reasonable doubt, to a particular person? Until recently, this was idle speculation, nothing more. But with the discovery of the role DNA plays in heredity and the development of methods to extract and to analyze the DNA in most tissue and tissue traces, it has become reality. A very short time ago, DNA evidence represented the extreme cutting edge of forensic science. Today, while still involving technologically advanced and demanding laboratory procedures, it has entered the mainstream of criminal investigation, as we'll see in this chapter.

The Double Helix

The field of genetics was revolutionized beginning in 1953, when two biochemists, James D. Watson and Francis H. C. Crick, described the structure of the deoxyribonucleic acid (*DNA*) molecule, which is found in the cells of all living things (and in some viruses, too). DNA was discovered back in 1869, but Watson and Crick demonstrated that, structurally, the DNA molecule consists of two nucleotide chains that twist around one another to form a double helix, rather like a spirally twisted ladder. The curved sides of this ladder consist of alternate phosphate-sugar groups, while the rungs of the ladder are protein bases joined by weak hydrogen bonds.

def•i•ni•tion

DNA, or deoxyribonucleic acid, carries the genetic information of the cell and is uniquely capable of replicating itself and synthesizing RNA (ribonucleic acid), which, like a chemical messenger, transmits the genetic information.

This unique structure enables DNA to replicate itself—something it does prior to cellular reproduction. When a cell divides to form two new cells, the double-stranded helix "unzips," and each "unzipped" strand picks up complementary nucleotides, which, incorporated into the unzipped strands, create two new DNA molecules that are identical to each other as well as to the original molecule. The DNA molecule carries chemically coded genetic information for the transmission of inherited traits. When the double helix "unzips," the coded information is passed on.

Biological Barcode

The function of DNA is double-edged. The process of replication during reproduction ensures that a baby born to a human mother and a human father will be a human being as opposed to, say, a kumquat. The genetic information coded in the DNA signals the pattern for human development. It also ensures that the baby will inherit certain genetic traits from the mother and father. That is, thanks to DNA, the newborn will not be a new species or totally different from its parents. Yet even as DNA transmits characteristics in common with one's species and one's parents, it also ensures that each individual is unique. Except for identical twins, each person, at the molecular level of the DNA contained in the nuclei of each cell, is unique.

Human beings have 23 pairs of chromosomes containing the full DNA code that serves as the blueprint for everything needed to build the individual and the molecular instructions for how to run him or her once he or she has been built. One member of each chromosomal pair is inherited from the mother, and one from the father. The unique DNA pattern that results is copied in each and every cell of the body.

DNA Fingerprinting

Most of the structure of DNA doesn't differ much from one person to another. That makes sense, if you consider that, viewed as organisms, human beings have more in common with one another than differences from one another: they all have two legs, two arms, two eyes, the ability to walk upright, the capacity to learn and use speech, and so on. In fact, only about 0.10 percent of the base pairs of human DNA differs from person to person. This is a very small percentage of difference, but it nevertheless represents differences in about 3 million base pairs of DNA. That is, there are some 3 million molecular elements in each of us that can be mixed and matched in different ways to produce a unique human being.

The range of possible combinations among 3 million of anything is virtually infinite. Therefore, if we focus on the DNA in chromosomal regions that do differ, we can identify a unique *DNA fingerprint* for each individual in the human population.

How can criminal investigators make use of this kind of "fingerprint"? The key to using DNA evidence is to identify the unique features of DNA taken from a suspect's tissue with DNA left at the scene of a crime.

def•i•ni•tion

Some professionals and laypersons alike speak of the **DNA fingerprint,** which refers to how the structure of certain parts of the DNA molecule uniquely marks and identifies each individual, much as an actual fingerprint is unique to each person.

Step by Step

Obtaining and analyzing DNA evidence is a complex, time-consuming, and exacting procedure, which must be carried out step by step, with scrupulous care to ensure scientific accuracy that will produce valid probative evidence. While the principles of DNA profiling are extremely reliable and well established, the practices of individual investigators, technicians, and laboratories must be closely monitored and questioned, because they can produce misleading results.

Obtaining the Specimen

The first step is obtaining the specimen. Getting DNA from a suspect is easy. A sample can be obtained from saliva by means of a simple, quick, and painless swab of the mouth.

> **Sworn Statement**
>
> Every year since 1989, in about 25 percent of the sexual assault cases referred to the FBI where [DNA] results could be obtained ... the primary suspect has been excluded by forensic DNA testing.
>
> —Barry C. Scheck, attorney and professor of law and director of clinical education, Benjamin N. Cardozo School of Law New York, New York

Isolating DNA from material at a crime scene can be much trickier. DNA is found in blood, saliva, semen, hair, and other bodily fluids and tissues. Whichever of these substances are available, investigators collect.

Often, laboratory specialists not only must isolate the DNA, they have to clean it up, because at the crime scene it is typically contaminated by dirt and other debris. Very frequently, DNA must be isolated from substances that are little more than stains—for example, dried blood on a carpet or article of clothing. The process of extracting the sample safely from the fabric is painstaking and sometimes risky. If the sample is very small, a botched attempt at extraction can end up destroying the evidence altogether.

Getting at the Good Stuff

As hard as it can be to obtain the DNA sample, it is only after it's been isolated that things get *really* complicated. There are two kinds of "polymorphic regions"—areas where there is a lot of DNA diversity—in the genome, or genetic material, of a person: sequence polymorphisms and length polymorphisms.

Sequence polymorphisms are simple substitutions of one or two bases in the genes themselves. These aren't very useful for DNA fingerprinting in criminal cases.

Now, the number of tandem repeats at specific places—called loci—on chromosomes varies between individuals. For any given *VNTR* locus in an individual's DNA, there is a certain number of identifiable repeats. Each individual inherits one copy of each chromosome from his or her mother and father. Therefore, each individual has two copies of each VNTR locus (just as each person has two copies of real genes).

def•i•ni•tion

> **VNTRs** (variable number tandem repeats) are short, identical repeat sequences of DNA molecules in length polymorphisms that may be readily compared. If the VNTRs of one DNA sample match those of another, it is highly likely that both samples came from the same individual. Length polymorphisms are nothing more than variations in the length of the DNA molecule. It is a special kind of length polymorphism that is used in DNA evidence. Investigators look for special variations that come from series of short, identical repeat sequences of DNA molecules. A given sequence may be repeated from 1 to 30 times in a row. For this reason, these DNA regions are called variable number tandem repeats, or VNTRs.

To arrive at an individual's unique DNA profile, the investigator determines the number of VNTRs at several distinctive loci. This procedure is called restriction fragment length polymorphism (RFLP) analysis, and it is one of the two most widely used processes by which the DNA analyst identifies the specific features that mark the individual's DNA as distinctive to that individual.

Just as an analyst of actual fingerprints focuses on a limited catalog of specific features to identify the uniqueness of a fingerprint (see Chapter 7), so the DNA investigator, through RFLP analysis, identifies only the specific features that mark the individual's DNA as distinctive to that individual. This makes comparing a sample from a suspect with a sample from the crime scene manageable. To compare hundreds of millions of molecular features would consume many lifetimes and require an army of analysts. To compare a relatively small number of nevertheless unique markers can be done in a far more timely and practical fashion.

Let It Gel

After the DNA is isolated, special enzymes are used to cut it up into fragments containing known VNTR loci. The next step in the analysis is to sort these DNA fragments by size. This is done by gel electrophoresis, a process in which the DNA sample is loaded into a slab of a gel called agarose. An electric current is passed through the agarose. Because the DNA is negatively charged, it is pulled through the gel toward the positively charged electrode. Larger fragments move more slowly than smaller ones, so that it is possible to determine the relative size of each fragment based on how far it has moved.

Preserving the DNA

At this point, the DNA fragments in the gel are quite unstable and will disintegrate within a day or two. To preserve the evidence permanently, it is transferred by an electrochemical process to a nylon membrane, which not only keeps the evidence from simply vanishing, but prepares it for the next step.

Conducting the Probe

This next step actually determines which fragments of DNA contain a particular VNTR locus and then marks them so that the fragments of the sample from the suspect can be compared to the corresponding fragments from the crime scene.

As Watson and Crick demonstrated in 1953, DNA occurs as a double-stranded molecule, a structure held together by weak chemical bonding between nucleotides (the basic constituents of DNA) on opposing strands. Only certain pairs of nucleotides form bonds with each other; these are called complementary. To locate a specific VNTR sequence on a single-stranded DNA fragment, the analyst employs a "DNA probe" using a DNA sequence complementary to that of a VNTR locus. This probe is tagged with a radioactive compound and allowed to bind with the sample DNA.

> **Sworn Statement**
>
> One thing is very clear, DNA works. DNA is perhaps our most powerful tool in law enforcement to come along since the fingerprint.
>
> —Christopher H. Asplen, Executive Director, National Commission on the Future of DNA Evidence

Next, the sample—preserved in its nylon membrane and now having been probed and radioactively tagged—is placed on a sheet of special x-ray film. The radioactive tag reacts with the film just as visible light reacts with ordinary photographic film. That is, it produces an image. In this case, it is an image of the places on the membrane where the probe has bound to DNA containing the VNTR sequence. The image appears as a pattern of darkened bands. The pattern produced by the DNA sample from the suspect may easily be compared to the sample taken from the crime scene.

In the following example of VNTR sequence analysis, the three columns marked "L" are markers (called allele ladders), which are used as a scale to show the position of the DNA evidence samples. The column marked "E" is from the DNA of a murder victim. The column marked "F" is from the DNA obtained from under the fingernails of the victim; presumably, this material contains skin cells from the murderer, because the victim scratched at her assailant in self-defense. The column marked "G" is from DNA taken from Suspect #1, "H" is from Suspect #2, and "I" from Suspect #3. The analyst concluded that columns "F" and "G" match, indicating that Suspect #1 is the possible donor of the skin cells beneath the victim's fingernails. (More VNTR sequences would need to be examined in order to make a definitive match.)

An example of VNTR sequence analysis.

(Image from crimescene.com)

Hard Cases

RFLP-based DNA analysis works best when investigators have a good, fresh specimen to analyze—fresh saliva, blood, or other tissue. Many times, however, fluid and tissue samples are tiny, old, or degraded. For example, trace evidence may consist of nothing more than a single shaft of human hair with its root or perhaps the long-dried saliva on the flap of an envelope. In cases such as this, investigators rely on OCR-based technology or mitochondrial DNA typing.

PCR: A Biological Xerox Machine

PCR stands for polymerase chain reaction. It is DNA technology that copies very short segments of DNA many millions of times in a process that mimics the way in which DNA replicates itself naturally. Some have dubbed the PCR process a "biological Xerox machine."

Using PCR technology—or a refinement of it, which combines PCR with RFLP and is called the short tandem repeat (STR) method—the DNA in miniscule or degraded specimens can be "amplified" sufficiently to enable analysis.

The Mitochondrial Method

RFLP and PCR technologies analyze DNA taken from the nuclei of cells; however, DNA is also found in cell mitochondria, organelles (cell constituents) that are found in the cellular cytoplasm surrounding the nucleus. Mitochondrial DNA (mt-DNA) differs from nuclear DNA in that it is a smaller molecule, is inherited only maternally (not from both mother and father), and is present within the cell in multiple copies. The reason for this third difference is that, whereas each cell has only a single nucleus, each cell has numerous mitochondria.

Mitochondrial DNA typing is useful in missing persons cases, because the questioned DNA sample can be compared to samples from a mother or sibling (any maternal relative). A match indicates that the donor of the questioned sample is related to the known donor.

Mitochondrial DNA typing is also used to analyze DNA material that is very badly degraded or to analyze trace evidence or tissue (shed hairs, for instance) that contains very little DNA. Because mitochondrial DNA is more plentiful than nuclear DNA, there is a better chance of obtaining a useful analytical result from a degraded or small mt-DNA sample than from a degraded or small nuclear DNA sample.

Playing the Numbers and Making the ID

When a fingerprint found at a crime scene is compared to a print taken from a suspect, it is hardly sufficient to compare just one or two features of each print. Analysts look for a pattern of matching features at specifically defined points. Similarly, it is not sufficient to compare the results from one VNTR locus. The key to identifying a DNA match beyond a reasonable doubt is combined analysis of several VNTR loci on different chromosomes. In practice, the forensic DNA profile is built up from the results of four or five probes, each of which targets a different VNTR locus.

Consider what happens when four probes are used. Immediately, you get eight pieces of information about the individual in question, since each person has two separate copies of each VNTR region (two times four is eight). Moreover, each VNTR locus has about 30 different length variants (called alleles). Each allele occurs at a certain known frequency in a population. To arrive at the probability that a given eight-band profile will occur, it is necessary to multiply together the eight different allele frequencies, each of which, remember, presents about 30 possibilities. Thus, using just four loci, the probability of finding any given allele combination in the general population is about 1 in 5,000,000.

If two DNA samples match at four loci, there is only 1 in 5,000,000 chance that the match is a coincidence, an error. However, the FBI insists on using not 4, but 13 loci to build its profiles. This means that not 8, but 26 different bands are studied, making the chance of an erroneous match (that is, finding two unrelated individuals with the same DNA profile) 1 in 100 billion.

By the Numbers

Using FBI analytical standards, you are 2,000 times more likely to win the Publisher's Clearinghouse sweepstakes (odds are 1 in 50,000,000) than to emerge with a DNA profile that matches anyone who is not your identical twin.

DNA Evidence in the Courts

DNA evidence was first admitted into a United States courtroom in 1985. In 1988, a person was convicted in large part on the evidence of a DNA profile. Today, DNA evidence is generally accepted by the law enforcement community, judges, juries, and lawyers—at least in principle. As with any other form of evidence and analysis, however, validity of principle is not enough. The procedure and process by which the evidence is actually collected, handled, analyzed, and interpreted is critical and always open to close scrutiny in a court of law.

In *principle*, DNA evidence can be used to establish identity to an extraordinarily high degree of certainty. In *practice*, however, much can go wrong.

A marvelous feature of DNA evidence is that while it can be used to identify and convict the guilty, it can also serve to defend the innocent and exonerate the wrongfully convicted. In recent years, dozens of persons jailed or even slated for execution for violent crimes, including murder and rape, have been freed because DNA evidence analyzed with techniques unavailable at the time of the original trial and conviction ruled out the prisoner as perpetrator.

> ### Case in Point
>
> On the evening of April 27, 1990, a woman was attacked in her home by a man who came at her from behind, placed a pillow over her head, sexually assaulted her, then fled. Even though the victim could not meaningfully describe the man, she picked out Gilbert Alejandro from a photograph in a police mug book. Alejandro was convicted and sentenced to 12 years in prison. The prosecution based its case on the victim's identification of Alejandro, but the smoking gun was the testimony of a DNA expert. A subsequent investigation revealed that the expert, Fred Zain, had falsified results and lied about his credentials. As part of an appeal, a new DNA analyst testified that at least one other DNA test performed had excluded Alejandro. He also said that the test to which Zain had testified was inconclusive. Alejandro's conviction was overturned.

The Future of DNA Identification

DNA analysis is likely to figure more and more prominently in criminal prosecutions, both as inculpatory (guilt-proving) and exculpatory (innocence-proving) evidence. Laboratory methods are continually being streamlined and refined. There is a trend toward developing the ability to analyze smaller and smaller samples, so that even the most minute trace of blood, semen, or saliva may be made to yield sufficient DNA for accurate analysis.

The FBI currently maintains the Combined DNA Index System (CODIS), a DNA profile database of convicted felons. Each state also maintains its own database of convicted felons, and an FBI initiative proposes to link these networks with its own, thereby creating one vast national DNA database.

The idea is to make it possible to match, rapidly and with a very high degree of certainty, DNA evidence recovered from crime scenes with individuals represented in the database.

As thrilling as this prospect is for criminal investigators, many believe such databases challenge one of the most basic rights of our democracy: the legal presumption of innocence. The technology to create and effectively use such databases exists today. The moral and political questions they raise have yet to be resolved.

The Least You Need to Know

- ◆ DNA contains features unique to each individual; therefore, properly analyzed, DNA evidence can be used as a molecular "fingerprint," to identify individuals to an extremely high degree of certainty.

- ◆ The basic procedure for linking a suspect to a crime using DNA is to collect DNA evidence from the crime scene or victim, collect DNA from the suspect, and, through laboratory analysis, compare the two.

- ◆ Matching the DNA recovered from a crime scene or crime victim to a DNA sample taken from a suspect requires identifying specific features that may be meaningfully compared and that yield unambiguous conclusions.

- ◆ DNA evidence can be inculpatory, pointing to the guilt of a suspect, or exculpatory, excluding a suspect from having committed the crime in question.

- ◆ Technically, it is now feasible to create a national database of DNA information for the general U.S. population. Legally, however, this may constitute a violation of the presumption of innocence.

Part 4

The Long Arm

This is the report from the trenches—the streets and the highways, the big cities and the remote villages—that are the front lines of society's struggle with crime: everyday police work.

We begin with the origin of professional policing in classical Rome and in eighteenth-century London, and we survey the development of policing in Europe and the United States. Then we look at the typical police force of today and how cops gather and manage information and harness technology to get at the facts of a case. We end with a look at the fringes of police work, the use of "truth serum," hypnosis, and even "psychic detectives."

15

Policing: The Way It Was

In This Chapter

- ◆ Origins of policing
- ◆ The police of ancient Rome
- ◆ London: evolution of the modern police force
- ◆ The birth of Scotland Yard
- ◆ Terrorism and Jack the Ripper
- ◆ London police innovations

Police have been a part of civilization for a very long time, at least since the days of Babylon under the lawgiver Hammurabi, nearly 4,000 years ago.

The modern police force, a civil agency answerable, ultimately, to the people, was a long time in coming, however. This chapter covers a portion of the evolution of the police forces familiar to us today, with particular focus on the first modern force, London's Metropolitan Police.

The First Cops

The first cops were specially designated members of religious, military, or political forces who were given the responsibility of enforcing religious, military, or political law and order. The earliest identifiable police forces developed from the corps of personal bodyguards and palace guards maintained by kings and warlords. Their responsibilities expanded from providing immediate protection of the ruler to extending the ruler's reach into the general population by executing and enforcing the laws he imposed.

> **Sworn Statement**
>
> Policemen are soldiers who act alone; soldiers are policemen who act together.
>
> —Herbert Spencer, *Social Statics* (1851)

Some early forces were highly organized. In Rome, the emperor Caesar Augustus (63 B.C.E.–14 C.E.) saw a need to bring order to the often violent and anarchic streets of a capital populated by nearly a million people. Using personnel from the Roman legions, Augustus decreed three distinct orders of police. These units were removed from military command and placed directly under the urban prefect. At the discretion of the commanders of this police force, assistance could be secured immediately from the Praetorian Guard, the emperor's personal bodyguard.

The organization and discipline of the great military legions demonstrated the administrative skill with which Rome built its military. Augustus applied similar acumen in deploying his urban police force. He divided the city of Rome into 14 wards, or *regiones*, then subdivided the wards into precincts (*vici*). To each precinct, Augustus assigned a corps of *vigilies*—"vigilant ones"—each corps consisting of seven squads. Each squad mustered 1,000 freedmen, who reported to a precinct captain, or *vicimagistor*.

By day, the squads stood ready to respond to crime, to quell civil disturbances, and to fight fires—which were frequent and very hazardous occurrences in the old city. By night, they took a more proactive approach and ventured out to patrol the city streets.

Through much of history, quasi-military, quasi-civil police forces were active in many parts of the world. The shoguns (hereditary military rulers) of renaissance Japan created elaborate police forces with specially designated samurai warriors, called *yoriki* and *doshin*, who patrolled the streets and reported to a samurai magistrate.

Elsewhere, the police took on a more sinister role, developing into enforcers of tyranny and terror. In prerevolutionary France, the Paris police were agents of the king and had almost unlimited power to regulate the day-to-day activities of the common people of the capital. In early twentieth-century Russia, the Bolshevik Revolution brought with it *secret police*, the Okhrana and Cheka, which evolved into the Soviet

NKVD and later the KGB. Japan, under the military dictatorship that prevailed during the first half of the twentieth century, had the Thought Police, and, during the 1950s into the 1970s, the shah of Iran maintained his power by means of the much-hated SAVAK.

Such agencies, associated with totalitarian governments in many parts of the world and at many times in history, represent the extreme of the police as a force of oppression and control. In modern democracies, such as the United States, the sworn function of the police is to "serve and protect" the citizens, but most police officers are well aware that, while those citizens gratefully welcome them in times of danger, they are also wary of the potential for abuses of police power. It is easy to be a cop in a dictatorship, quite difficult and demanding to occupy the same office in a democracy.

def•i•ni•tion

Secret police is a general term for political police forces whose power derives directly from a dictator or monarch and who have almost unlimited authority to monitor and regulate the day-to-day activities of the common people. Examples include the Soviet NKVD and KGB, the Thought Police of World War II–era Japan, and the SAVAK operating under the former shah of Iran.

Case Study: London

"When a man is tired of London," the great eighteenth-century English man of letters Samuel Johnson declared, "he is tired of life; for there is in London all that life can afford." By the 1700s, the bustling metropolis was one of the greatest cities in the world, brimming with life, with civilization, with opportunity—and with crime. The problem was how to cope with the crime without sacrificing the benefits of a free and vigorous society.

From Mr. Fielding's People to the Bow Street Runners

Lovers of British literature remember Sir Henry Fielding as the author of the sprawling and uproarious novel *Tom Jones*, but, from 1748 until his death in 1754, Fielding's day job was that of magistrate for the City of Westminster, one of London's great boroughs.

At the time of Fielding's appointment to this post, it was no great honor to serve as magistrate. The office was in deep disrepute—and for good reason. Fielding's predecessors had been little more than racketeers who sheltered and fostered the city's flourishing criminal element. Fielding took charge, determined to rid Bow Street (as the magistrate's headquarters was called) of corruption.

Instead of coddling crime, Fielding looked for ways to fight it. In 1752, he commenced publication of *The Covent-Garden Journal*, which publicized thefts and descriptions of criminals and generally sought to raise public awareness of crime. The following year, securing a modest grant from the government, Fielding recruited a force of a dozen men to investigate a series of murders in London. Dubbed "Mr. Fielding's People," they are considered the first designated police force in London.

On his death in 1754, Henry Fielding was succeeded in the magistrate's office by his half brother, Sir John Fielding. He transformed Mr. Fielding's People into the Bow Street Runners and the Bow Street magistrate's office into a genuine police headquarters. Within that headquarters, Bow Street Runners were continually on call. A pair of horses was kept at the ready just outside, so that Runners could instantly answer the call to pursue robbers and bandits.

> ### Case in Point
>
> Sir John Fielding transformed the city magistrate's office into something resembling a modern police department, a designated body of officers explicitly dedicated to fighting crime. He wanted to go even further, however, and repeatedly lobbied Parliament to finance a sufficiently large force to deploy on continuous routine patrol, so that the police would not merely chase wrongdoers, but proactively discourage and prevent crime. Although Parliament resisted, and Fielding's plans for an expanded, full-time force would not be implemented for another 50 years, Fielding himself was a relentless crime fighter. It was said that he could recognize and identify some 3,000 known criminals by nothing more than the sound of their voices. This founder of the first professional police force for London had developed a keen sense of hearing. He had to. He was totally blind.

The Peelers, 1829

Sir Robert Peel had a distinguished career in British politics. The founder of the Conservative Party, he served three terms as prime minister; before assuming this office, however, he was home secretary, the cabinet official responsible for the conduct of domestic affairs.

As home secretary, one of Peel's main goals was to reform the British judicial system, including the police. His great ambition was to create a single national force, but this proposal was met with the objection that it smacked of tyranny. He scaled down his ambition to creating a local force for London and environs. Crime had thoroughly overwhelmed the 350 to 400 "watchmen" (including the original Bow Street Runners) who constituted the city's only police agency.

Peel secured passage of the Metropolitan Police Act of June 19, 1829, creating a unified 1,000-man Metropolitan Police force for most of London, except for the central district (known as "The City"), which remained under the jurisdiction of the Bow Street Runners. The new officers were familiarly called "peelers" or "bobbies." Both nicknames are tributes to the father of the modern London police force, Sir Robert (Bobby) Peel.

Peel introduced a number of policing principles that laid the foundation for modern police forces throughout Europe as well as America. He put the police firmly under government control, not subject to the whim of some individual magistrate. He defined the mission of the police as, first and foremost, crime *prevention*, then, only secondarily, the pursuit of criminals and the investigation of crime. He established the principle that the success of a police force is directly dependent on the goodwill of the people served; accordingly, he instructed his police officers to be courteous, civil, helpful, and trustworthy.

Peel established the value of discipline, and he organized the police force along quasi-military lines, although the force was to be clearly distinct from the actual military. Peel saw the necessity of creating a force of professionals, who were specially trained and who were subject to an initial probationary period before being given full policing authority.

Under Sir Robert Peel's direction, police officers were deployed strategically in high-traffic and high-crime areas, where they were needed most. He instructed officers to prosecute their duties energetically, yet always with the minimum force necessary.

Sir Charles Rowan and Sir Richard Mayne were appointed justices of the peace, charged with the day-to-day administration of the new force.

Sworn Statement

The primary object of an efficient police is the prevention of crime: the next that of detection and punishment of offenders if crime is committed. To these ends all the efforts of police must be directed. The protection of life and property, the preservation of public tranquillity, and the absence of crime, will alone prove whether those efforts have been successful and whether the objects for which the police were appointed have been attained.

—Sir Richard Mayne, 1829

Officer Down, 1830

It was not long before the Metropolitan Police suffered its first casualty. In a riot at Somers Town, Euston, Police Constable Joseph Grantham became the first Metropolitan officer to be killed in the line of duty. His death shocked Londoners, and Parliament immediately voted to increase the ranks of the Metropolitan Police more than three-fold, to 3,300 men.

Metropolitan Police Expand

In 1836, the Metropolitan Police began a further expansion as the organization absorbed the Bow Street Horse Patrol. The next year, a Select Committee proposed that the City of London (central London) be placed under the control of the Metropolitan Police, and in 1838, the committee further recommended that the Marine Police (the department charged with patrolling the Thames River and the docks) and the Bow Street Runners be incorporated into the Metropolitan Police. These measures were carried out, and, by the Metropolitan Police Act of 1839, Rowan and Mayne were officially redesignated commissioners of the newly enlarged jurisdiction.

By the Numbers

In 1847, the Metropolitan Police of London recorded 14,091 robberies and took into custody 62,181 persons. Of this number, 24,689 were summarily dealt with by the police; 5,920 were remanded for trial; and 4,551 were convicted and sentenced; and 31,572 people were discharged by the magistrates. The population in London at this time was 2,473,758.

The First Detectives

Until 1842, all police constables were uniformed officers, charged primarily with stopping crimes in progress and apprehending wrongdoers. In 1842, a Detective Department was established within the Metropolitan Police, and in 1846, the duties of plain-clothes officers—detectives who wear no distinguishing uniform—were explicitly laid out. Two officers per division were to be employed on detective duty, and it was firmly established that police constables working in plain clothes must announce themselves as officers when making an arrest or otherwise intervening to restore order.

Headquarters: Scotland Yard

Despite its name, Great Scotland Yard was a tiny London street that ran east from the northern end of Whitehall, parallel with Whitehall Place. The office of the Metropolitan Police Commissioner, at No. 4 Whitehall Place, backed on to it, and in 1875, a new building on the street was acquired to house the Detective and Public Carriage Departments. From this point on, the growing detective division of the Metropolitan Police was referred to simply as "Scotland Yard."

The origin of the name remains a mystery. Some believe the location was once the site of a residence owned by the kings of Scotland before the political union of England and Scotland; the residence was occupied by the kings when they were visiting London. Others say the street name was derived from the name of the man who owned the property during the Middle Ages, a Mr. Scott.

Terrorism 1884: A New Police Challenge

We tend to think of terrorism as a plague of recent times, but Europe had known it far earlier. In the nineteenth century, the Fenians, militant Irish nationalists, staged periodic terror attacks against British targets, including the London neighborhood of Clerkenwell, where a Fenian bomb killed 12 and injured 126 in 1867.

Between 1883 and 1885, the Fenians conducted a veritable bombing terror campaign. In 1883, Scotland Yard received an anonymous letter threatening to "blow [Police] Superintendent Williamson off his stool" and to dynamite all the public buildings in London on May 30, 1884. True to their word, the Fenians detonated two bombs shortly before nine o'clock on the threatened night. Both targets were police facilities in Scotland Yard, including the superintendent's office, which was completely destroyed—but since the explosions came after hours, Williamson was not on his stool, and only one person was injured, a cabman who was hit by flying glass.

Elsewhere that night, bombs went off in two other locations, and an unexploded bomb was found at the foot of Nelson's Column in Trafalgar Square.

The failure of Scotland Yard to protect its own offices caused a great public crisis in confidence. This was intensified by subsequent detonations under London Bridge, in the Tower of London, and in the House of Commons, all in 1885.

In response to the Fenian bombings, the Metropolitan Police created the Special Branch, and thus police jurisdiction was expanded to combating the political crime of terrorism.

Jack the Ripper and After

As shocking as the police failure was in the Fenian cases, even more scandalous was the inability of London detectives to solve what is surely among the most famous crime sprees in history.

Shortly before 4 A.M., Friday, August 31, 1888, Charles Cross walked through Buck's Row in the London slum of Whitechapel. Through the foggy morning gloom he saw what he thought was a tarpaulin on the ground in front of a stable yard. He approached it and discovered that it was a woman, lying on her back, skirts lifted almost to her waist.

When Cross saw another man, he called to him: "Come and look over here." Assuming she was a drunk or the victim of an assault—typical Whitechapel scenarios—the two passers-by pulled her aside, adjusted her skirt for the sake of modesty, and went to fetch a policeman. They didn't even notice three important things: the woman was horribly lacerated, she had been nearly decapitated, and she was quite dead.

> ### Sworn Statement
>
> I am down on whores and I shant quit ripping them till I do get buckled ....
>
> —Letter, signed "Jack the Ripper," sent to London's Central News Agency, September 25, 1888

Even before Cross and the other man could find a bobby, Police Constable John Neil discovered the body while he was walking his beat. An ambulance was summoned and the victim was transported to a morgue, where an autopsy revealed that her neck had been slashed twice, her windpipe and esophagus having been completely cut through; her left jaw was bruised; and her abdomen had sustained a long, deep jagged knife wound, along with several other cuts. She was later identified as Mary Ann Nichols, age 42, an alcoholic prostitute.

The horrific slaying of Nichols is generally considered the first of five murders committed by a man who would become known as Jack the Ripper because that's how he signed a taunting letter, dated September 25, 1888, received by the Central News Agency, and forwarded to the Metropolitan Police.

Each Ripper murder was covered by the press in lurid detail, and although the Metropolitan Police assigned a 25-year veteran inspector to the case, Frederick George Abberline, the identity of Jack the Ripper was never discovered, and confidence in the Metropolitan Police was badly shaken. The final Ripper murder, of Mary Jane Kelly, occurred on November 9, 1888.

Case in Point

Victorian London was often a violent place. During 1888 through 1891, there were a total of 11 slashing-style murders of women in Whitechapel, only 5 of which were attributed to Jack the Ripper. The most notorious of these "non-Ripper" slayings occurred on Monday, August 6, 1888, several weeks before Mary Ann Nichols's murder. Martha Tabram, a 39-year-old prostitute, was found dead in George Yard, stabbed 39 times on "body, neck and private parts with a knife or dagger" or, perhaps, a "bayonet." In addition, many other wounds had been inflicted with a penknife. The other five non-Ripper murders were similarly brutal, yet less attention was paid to these crimes, because they weren't attached to the much-publicized name of Jack the Ripper. Like the Ripper murders, none of these was ever solved.

Policing for a New Century, 1900

In the aftermath of the Ripper murders, the Metropolitan Police were subjected to intense public scrutiny, and the department adopted and adhered to an increasingly stringent code of ethics and professionalism. It also put greater emphasis on the systematic and scientific investigation of crime so that by the beginning of the twentieth century, Scotland Yard would set the investigative and forensic standard for police forces throughout the world.

Wireless Police Work: The Infamous Crippen Case

Among the many detectives who had participated in the failed investigation of the Jack the Ripper murders was Walter Dew, who became chief inspector of Scotland Yard's Criminal Investigation Department (CID) at the turn of the century. In 1910, Dew headed up a manhunt that was as successful as the Ripper case had been frustrating.

At two o'clock in the afternoon of June 30, 1910, John Edward Nash and his actress wife, Lil, reported to the police the disappearance of their friend Cora Crippen, a marginally successful singer whose stage name was Belle Elmore. The wife of a Dr. Peter Hawley Harvey Crippen of 29 Hilldrop Crescent, Camden Town, London, she had been missing since February. Nash and his wife had become suspicious of foul play when Crippen almost casually reported to them that his wife had died "while abroad."

"Where had she died?" the incredulous Nashes asked.

"Some little town near San Francisco, with a Spanish name, I think," Crippen replied. The doctor's evasiveness aroused their suspicions and sent them calling on the police.

Subsequent investigation at the Hilldrop Crescent house turned up a body buried in the cellar. It was headless and, even stranger, was missing its skeleton. Detectives described the remains as having been "filleted." In an early instance of forensic pathology, a physician traced an old surgical scar and some hair samples in order to identify the remains as those of Cora Crippen.

By the time the identification was made, Dr. Crippen and his secretary, Ethel Clara LeNeve, had disappeared. Police readily assumed that he was the murderer, and they theorized that he had used his medical knowledge to "fillet" the corpse so that it could more easily be incinerated in the cellar grate. With the police closing in, however, Crippen panicked, hastily buried the body, and made his escape.

Chief Inspector Dew launched a spectacular manhunt, using newspapers worldwide to publicize a description as well as photographs of both Crippen and LeNeve. The captain of the SS *Montrose*, bound for Canada, recognized the couple from a published photograph (even though LeNeve had disguised herself as a boy) and used the ship's radiotelegraph to alert Scotland Yard.

Dew took personal charge. He boarded a faster vessel and, all the while maintaining radio-telegraph contact with the *Montrose*'s skipper, overtook that ship at Father Point, off the Canadian coast. Boarding the vessel, he approached his man and calmly greeted him: "Good morning, Dr. Crippen. I am Chief Inspector Dew of Scotland Yard. I believe you know me."

For the first time in history, the mass media and the "wireless telegraph" had been used to extend the reach of the proverbial "long arm of the law." Crippen was returned to London, tried, and convicted of murder. He was hanged. LeNeve was cleared of complicity in the crime.

Women Join the Force, 1914

Four years after the technological triumph of the Crippen manhunt, the Metropolitan Police made an advance on the sociopolitical front by inaugurating the Women Police Service (WPS), primarily to deter pimps and to discourage girls and women from taking up lives as prostitutes. Within a year, the duties of the WPS were expanded to working with women and juvenile suspects and victims, and the female constables were given full arrest authority.

The "Police Box" Experiment, 1928

Since the early days of the Bow Street Runners, police leaders had appreciated the effectiveness of putting officers on routine street patrol, but the persistent problem was how to establish continuous, reliable communication between the patrol officer and headquarters.

In 1928, local police in the towns of Richmond and Barnes installed experimental police boxes. These were large blue outdoor kiosks topped by electric lights. Inside was a telephone wired directly to the local subdivisional police station. Officers on patrol could report their whereabouts, and the flashing light signaled a patrolling officer to make immediate contact with the station. Civilians could also use the boxes to make emergency calls to the police.

Installation of the boxes began in London in 1929, and by 1937, the city was thoroughly networked.

By the Numbers

The U.S. equivalent of Britain's 999 system, the 911 system, was not introduced until January 12, 1968. Why 911? AT&T, the principal telephone network operator at the time, gave no reason other than "a computer" had selected the numbers. More likely, the choice of 911 was probably based on a combination of the British 999 precedent and the ease with which two ones could be dialed on the rotary-dial phones then in general use.

Dial 999, 1937

Deployment of police boxes began a revolution in communication, which greatly increased the effectiveness of the police. The revolution was completed in 1937 with the introduction of the 999 system. A precursor of the 911 system familiar in the United States, the 999 system gave any telephone user instant emergency access to the police. With this innovation, the presence of the police was intimately woven into the fabric of daily life, establishing a relationship between law enforcement and the public so enduring that most of us today take it for granted.

The Least You Need to Know

- The idea of policing is probably as old as civilization, and the first police agencies were extensions of the political or religious ruler's personal bodyguard or palace guard forces.

- Rome's great emperor Caesar Augustus created the first thoroughly organized, formal police force for the bustling city of Rome at the start of the first century.

- Dictators and tyrants have little trouble creating a police force; establishing and maintaining a force in a free society, however, is far more complicated, since administrators and officers must enforce the law without compromising the principles of liberty.

- The evolution of a police force for London served as a model for police forces throughout Europe and, by the mid-nineteenth century, the United States.

Chapter 16

Policing America

In This Chapter

- The first American police force
- Policing old New York
- Teddy Roosevelt's police reforms
- A nation of lawbreakers: Prohibition and organized crime
- Policing goes national: the FBI

Like the British, nineteenth-century Americans largely opposed the creation of a standing police force—probably even more strongly than their trans-Atlantic cousins opposed it. After all, one of the causes of the American Revolution was outrage over the maintenance of a large standing army, which functioned chiefly to police the unruly colonists.

But by the early 1800s, American cities, like British ones, were burgeoning—and so were urban crime and disorder. New York was typical of American cities that, however reluctantly, decided to create police forces during the nineteenth century.

New York City Before 1895

In 1658, the Dutch settlers of New Amsterdam—as New York City was called before the English took it over on September 7, 1664—paid a band of eight night watchmen to look out for fires and Indian raiders. This "Burgher Guard" was the city's first police force.

By the Numbers

Both the New York night watch and the constables were kept very busy. By the 1780s, New York had a population of 25,000. The night watch consisted of 28 patrolman and one captain. It wasn't until 1800 that the constables and night watch were supplemented by 16 day patrolmen and some 40 marshals.

The English had been running the city for 67 years before they set up a watch service in 1731. The Montgomerie Charter not only established a night watch as a permanent policing body, but gave each constable the right to draft eight citizens for watch duty every night. In the eighteenth century, however, New York was not quite ready to be called the "city that never sleeps," and popular resistance to compulsory night watch duty prompted, in 1734, the replacement of the citizens' watch with a paid force of 3 to 12 men, expected to stand guard over a city of about 10,000. Just a year later, the citizens' watch was reinstated, and it wasn't replaced with another paid force until 1774, when 24 watchmen were hired.

Constable System

Only after the American Revolution had been fought and won did New Yorkers introduce an element of real professionalism into their police force by establishing, in 1784, a formal constabulary to supplement the night watch. While the night watch was paid a salary, the constables were compensated on a per-job basis. They were paid a set fee for serving a warrant, for issuing a fine, for making an arrest, and even for detaining prisoners.

Following the London Model

Beginning in 1801, John Hayes was appointed High Constable for New York, and for the next 50 years he single-handedly ran the city's small force.

New York eyes were turned toward London, however, where the Metropolitan Police was building a reputation for efficiency and effectiveness. In 1845, under Mayor William Havermayer, the New York City Council passed a Municipal Police Act, creating the first full-time professional force in the nation.

Small, poorly trained, badly led, and ill equipped, the New York City police force was hardly equal to the task of maintaining order in a bustling, rough-edged American metropolis. By 1850, the murder rate in New York City exceeded that of London.

Case in Point

The most stunning demonstration of the inadequacy of the department came with the Astor Place Riot on May 10, 1849. About 15,000 demonstrators swarmed outside the Astor Place Opera House to protest the appearance of the British Shakespearean actor, William Charles Macready. Macready was unapologetic in his snobbish advocacy of the British aristocracy and his criticism of Americans as uncultured boors. Meaning to give Macready his comeuppance, the crowd shouted their support of Edwin Forrest, a great *American* Shakespearean. They hurled paving stones and construction debris. The unarmed police were summoned, but the crowd overwhelmed them, injuring several. At last, the armed militia was called in. When it was over, 23 people lay dead or dying. More than 100 were wounded.

Rival Forces

Efforts were made to improve the police force, such as giving the officers uniforms in 1853. At last, in 1857, the state legislature created the Metropolitan Police for the city of New York, Brooklyn (at the time independent from New York), and Westchester County.

During this period, the state legislature was controlled by Republicans, whereas the mayor of New York was a colorful—indeed, thoroughly corrupt—Democrat, Fernando Wood. Although the Metropolitan Police was intended to replace the city's Municipal Police, Wood resisted and continued to back "his" force. The result was that, for nearly a year, two rival police departments existed in New York, the officers fighting with each other more often and with greater enthusiasm than they fought crime. Little wonder that, by 1860, 1 New Yorker in 10 had a criminal record!

Politics as Usual

By 1858, the state-mandated Metropolitan Police had finally supplanted and replaced Mayor Wood's Municipal Police force; however, the state exercised little direct control over the officers who actually patrolled the city's neighborhoods. Patrolmen tended to serve the local political machine, the neighborhood bosses.

Sworn Statement

Gentlemen, get the thing straight for once and for all. The policeman isn't there to create disorder; the policeman is there to preserve disorder.

—Chicago Mayor Richard M. Daley, 1968

These men encouraged the police to pursue some criminals—the casual burglar, the occasional street ruffian—and to overlook others: Irish gang members in an Irish neighborhood or the enforcers who provided the muscle for the local loan shark (especially if he also happened to be a precinct captain).

The City's Utility Men

From the decade before the Civil War until nearly the end of the nineteenth century, the police were more often political hacks than public servants. Nevertheless, while they enforced the law selectively at the whim and behest of local bosses, many of them did make a sincere effort to prevent crime and intervene when a crime occurred.

But they received precious little respect in return. And it was no wonder. The police were not perceived as gallant crime fighters, but as the utility men of the city, the guys who did the jobs no one else wanted to do. Yes, they tried to prevent crime. Yes, they chased after the bad guys. But they also hauled garbage, swept the streets, and ran menial errands for ward heelers and anyone else with a little political clout.

The Precinct: Sanctuary and Dungeon

If the neighborhood cop was there to do whatever had to be done (dirty work a specialty), the building he operated out of, the local *precinct* house—often simply called "the precinct"—was itself a kind of urban catchall.

def•i•ni•tion

In many urban jurisdictions, the **precinct** is the officially designated city district or subdivision assigned to a specific police unit. The word is also often applied to the police station house within the precinct.

The precinct was not only the place where officers got their marching orders, it was also headquarters for the local powers that be, the neighborhood politicos. And in bad weather some of the neighborhood homeless took refuge in the precinct. It was, therefore, a crowded and often disorderly place.

The central feature of the precinct was the holding facility for those arrested. Cells typically ranged from spartan to filthy, and somewhere in the back of the precinct was a room reserved for interrogation. It was a place where police might beat answers out of a suspect by applying "the third degree," which involved using intimidation and even torture. It was also a place where police sometimes administered a shorthand version of justice. Officers might decide that a legal trial for a habitual neighborhood troublemaker was just a waste of time. A summary sentence executed at the business end of a billy club might be just the thing to keep the neighborhood safe, orderly, and as the local precinct captain saw it, decent.

Enter Commissioner Roosevelt

Theodore Roosevelt was born in 1858 into a New York family whose money and pedigree were so old that they disdained the Vanderbilts and Rockefellers as rank upstarts. A frail and sickly child, Roosevelt grew into young manhood determined to strengthen his body, hone his mind, and generally make something very big of himself.

He entered Harvard, graduated in 1880, and went on to get a law degree before achieving election to the state assembly at the precocious age of 23. While serving in the state house in 1884, he headed up a special commission to investigate the long-notorious New York City police department.

Roosevelt was outraged by what he found: rampant corruption eclipsed only by incompetence and inefficiency. Officers were not only implicated in such fraudulent schemes as rigging elections, they were found to exercise brutality as a matter of casual routine.

Such findings were so much grist for Roosevelt's mill. A progressive reformer, he set about planning how to rebuild and reshape the New York police.

By the Numbers

While Roosevelt's reforms deprived some crooked men of power, they also rewarded and elevated the deserving. TR saw to the promotion of 130 honest, earnest officers, and he instituted a recruiting program to bring new blood into the organization. During his tenure, 1,700 rookies were inducted into the New York Police Department.

New Zeal, New Discipline

In 1889, Roosevelt was appointed one of four commissioners of the newly created Board of Commissioners, with a mandate to reform the police department.

Roosevelt descended on the department like a whirlwind. With intense vigor, he rooted out corruption and saw to its prosecution. Then, in 1894, the reform-minded William L. Strong was elected mayor of New York. Among his first acts was to appoint Roosevelt president of the Board of Commissioners. With his authority thus augmented, Roosevelt introduced a military-style discipline to the department. To loosen the grip of neighborhood political bosses, he consolidated control of operations and policy in a central headquarters, answerable directly to himself.

Thank You, M. Bertillon

While Roosevelt cleared away the cobwebs, he also encouraged the administration to modernize its investigative department. Under his leadership, the detective division became an elite unit to which the most ambitious and able officers aspired.

Roosevelt became highly interested in the innovations Alphonse Bertillon had introduced to the Paris police (see Chapter 7). He ordered the New York department to adopt Bertillon's techniques of suspect identification and classification, and in 1897, the New York Police Department (NYPD) for the first time began routinely photographing prisoners while also recording their Bertillon measurements. Soon the department had amassed a bulging but thoroughly documented file of offenders, which made it far easier to apprehend repeat and career criminals.

The First Bicycle Squad

It is no accident that the inventors of perhaps the greatest single advance in human transportation, the airplane, were Ohio bicycle mechanics and manufacturers. At the turn of the century, the bicycle was a cutting-edge vehicle, convenient, efficient, and fast. In 1895, at Roosevelt's direction, the New York Police Department fielded its first bicycle squad. Officers now had an unprecedented degree of mobility.

The fat, lazy denizens of the old-time precincts could not pedal a bicycle; they could hardly survive a few hours walking a beat. Commissioner Roosevelt, the delicate child who had built himself into a powerful man, an all-round advocate of what he liked to call "the strenuous life," introduced tough new standards of physical fitness for officers and officer recruits. He also instituted a carefully planned program of training, with special emphasis—for the first time in the history of any police department—on firearms training.

Honor and Morale

Of all the reforms Roosevelt introduced into the NYPD, none was more important than the sense of honor he revived within the hearts of the officers. By demanding excellence and by giving them his support, he lifted the morale of all policemen. Thanks in large part to Commissioner Roosevelt, the New York City police officer was transformed from a neighborhood errand boy and sometime bully into a true guardian of the public safety and welfare. Law enforcement became a noble calling—and the rest of the nation watched and learned.

A Nation of Immigrants

Despite his origin in old New York wealth, Theodore Roosevelt was keenly responsive to the everyday world of the ordinary New Yorker. And at the turn of the century, as likely as not, the "ordinary" New Yorker was a recent immigrant.

Many of the moneyed elite as well as the middle class shunned the immigrants, distrusting and even fearing them. What Roosevelt and other enlightened realists did was to acknowledge them as part and parcel of the new America.

> **Sworn Statement**
>
> For the middle class, the police protect property, give directions, and help old ladies. For the urban poor, the police are those who arrest you.
>
> —Michael Harrington, *The Other America: Poverty in the United States* (Macmillan, 1962)

Policing Diverse Populations

Among the 1,700 rookies Roosevelt recruited for the New York Police Department were members of ethnic minorities. Roosevelt met resistance to this policy; however, he believed that it was not only fair but, even more important, necessary to create effective policing. He reasoned that ethnic populations would respond more favorably to officers of their own background and heritage.

It was under Roosevelt's administration as well that more women were brought into the force. The number was still small—30 women working in all of the precincts by 1895—but this put New York far ahead of its London model. That city's Metropolitan Police would not take on women until 1914.

Prejudice and Racism

It was not Roosevelt, but the then-independent city of Brooklyn that hired the first African American officer in 1891. In an era of fully institutionalized racism, it was a bold step—and it failed. Officer Wiley G. Overton was refused a uniform, and he was universally shunned by his fellow cops. Under unremitting pressure, unable to perform his duties because he was prevented at every turn from doing so, Overton resigned after a year on the force.

By 1913, the NYPD had grown to 10,847 officers, 1 cop for every 463 New Yorkers. It was not until 1914 that Jesse Battle became the first African American hired by the NYPD. In 1920, Lawon R. Bruce became the first African American woman recruited by the department.

A Nation of Lawbreakers

By the turn of the century, the New York Police Department, as shaped by Theodore Roosevelt and other reformers, had clearly emerged as the model for the rest of the nation. But the police force of New York and departments in the rest of the nation were about to face their toughest law-enforcement challenge.

During the nineteenth century, a great national movement developed, mostly in Midwestern rural America, to combat what was seen as the evil of alcohol. By 1855, this "temperance movement" had succeeded in getting the manufacture, sale, and consumption of liquor banned in 13 of 31 states. The movement boldly soldiered on, and by 1916, 21 states outlawed saloons. In that year, voters sent a "dry" (anti-alcohol) majority to the United States Congress. Their mandate was clear: secure a constitutional amendment to prohibit the manufacture, sale, and consumption of alcohol in the United States.

Congress passed the Eighteenth Amendment in December 1917. They did so over the veto of President Woodrow Wilson. A strait-laced minister's son, Wilson was no lover of the bottle, but he believed that federally mandated prohibition would create, in his words, "a nation of lawbreakers."

And so it did.

Prohibition and Policing

Although the required two thirds of the states ratified the Eighteenth Amendment in 1919, and Prohibition went into effect the following year, the people of urban America were never behind it. Immediately, neighborhood folk defied the law, brewing up beer in cellars and making gin in bathtubs.

At first, people brewed and distilled only what they could themselves consume, but inevitably, they began to share with and sell to their friends and neighbors. Soon amateur brewers, winemakers, and distillers were marketing their goods to the corner grocer and pharmacist, as well as to local restaurateurs, who opened up *speakeasies.*

def•i•ni•tion

In the Roaring Twenties, **speakeasies,** illicit saloons and clubs that served liquor, were as common as legitimate teetotaling restaurants and coffee shops.

As for the cops, it was a hard thing to arrest the otherwise law-abiding people who daily greeted beat officers by name. Most neighborhood police looked the other way, and some did so for a price.

Organized Crime

For some time and in some places, violation of the Volstead Act—the law that enforced the Eighteenth Amendment—was certainly routine, but it was also almost innocent, the work not of hardened criminals, but of thirsty city dwellers.

Before too long, however, it became obvious that big money was to be made by trading in illegal liquor, either making and distributing it or smuggling and distributing it. Bootlegging became the province not of neighborhood entrepreneurs, but organized gangs.

Since at least the mid-nineteenth century, various ethnic immigrant groups, typically discriminated against by mainstream society, formed social and criminal gangs in the neighborhoods dominated by a particular ethnic minority. In New York, some of the toughest and most feared gangs were Irish.

During the 1920s, the Irish-based "White Hand" took over bootlegging in some parts of the city and began a fearsome war against the New York Police Department. Also rapidly on the rise were Italian gangs, many of them modeled on or directly related to the Mafia, the traditional criminal organization of Sicily, which for centuries had formed a kind of shadow government there.

By the Numbers

During the decade of the Roaring Twenties—the Prohibition era—57 NYPD officers were killed in the line of duty. This stands as the most NYPD officers to die in any decade—although the deaths of 23 NYPD officers in the terrorist attack on the World Trade Center on September 11, 2001, will tragically contribute to the final tally of the first decade of the twenty-first century.

The Evolution of the FBI

With the Roaring Twenties in full swing, it was no longer a question of city police departments turning a blind eye toward basement stills and neighborhood bootleggers. Prohibition had created not merely a nation of lawbreakers, but nothing less than organized crime—a system of gangs that ran their criminal enterprises like big business, pulling in millions of dollars and making big deals, not with a pen applied to a contract, but with a machine gun applied to rival gangsters, as well as law-abiding citizens and police officers. Police departments were overwhelmed, and many were also compromised, corrupted by organized crime money.

Tainted Bureau

Since the Eighteenth Amendment was national legislation, the federal government, recognizing that local police forces were inadequate to enforce the Volstead Act, assumed unprecedented policing authority. At first, special agents of the Department of the Treasury, "T-men," were the only federal force detailed to combat violations of the Volstead Act.

Case in Point

The most famous Prohibition-era government agent was Eliot Ness (1903–1957), who was appointed special agent for the Prohibition Bureau of the United States Department of Justice. Surrounded by corrupt colleagues, Ness gained approval of a plan to create a fresh squad of squeaky-clean agents. He wanted to call them the "Secret Six," but the press soon dubbed the incorruptible force "the Untouchables." Over the next six years, the Untouchables (grown from six to nine men) busted up stills and speakeasies, much to the amazement of bootleggers, whose police payoffs were suddenly useless. After the repeal of Prohibition, Ness moved to Cleveland, Ohio, to head the Treasury Department's Alcoholic Tax Unit, then, in 1935, became Cleveland's Director of Public Safety. Later, Ness wrote an account of his Chicago gangbusting days, which subsequently provided the basis for a popular television series called *The Untouchables*, which ran on ABC from 1959 to 1963.

It soon became apparent that more manpower was needed. There was another federal police agency, the Bureau of Investigation. But in the early 1920s, it was something of a bad joke. Created in 1908 by then Attorney General Charles J. Bonaparte, it immediately degenerated into what one congressman called a "bureaucratic bastard." Congress feared that a federal police agency would become a center for the abuse of power. Instead of supporting it as a genuine law-enforcement agency, the legislators used it as a dumping ground for political hacks seeking patronage jobs. The Bureau of Investigation was mostly useless and entirely corrupt.

During World War I, a use was at last found for the Bureau of Investigation—chasing draft evaders, suspected spies, and alien "radicals"—but it wasn't until after the war in 1920, when a zealous young Department of Justice lawyer, John Edgar Hoover, was named assistant director of the Bureau of Investigation that the agency began seriously to improve its reputation.

The Hoover Era Begins

Under Hoover and his boss, William J. Burns, the Bureau of Investigation continued to pursue individuals suspected of radical subversion until 1924, when Congress decided that prying into the lives and activities of such respected activists as Chicago social reformer Jane Addams and future New York Mayor Fiorello LaGuardia constituted an abuse of power.

Congress called for a shake-up in the bureau, and Burns was fired, leaving J. Edgar Hoover director of the agency. It was a post he would hold until his death in 1972.

Building a Rep, Setting a Standard

Hoover transformed the Bureau of Investigation into a high-profile crime-fighting organization. He changed its name to the more impressive *Federal* Bureau of Investigation, and he set about professionalizing the staff by creating a small, elite force of detective-level special agents who were not only trained in law enforcement and criminal investigation, but came to the FBI with law or accounting degrees (much of the crime the FBI fought was white-collar embezzlement and the like, calling for the trained eye of a skilled auditor).

The climate of organized crime created by Prohibition fostered the growth and enhanced the prestige of Hoover's FBI. Yet strangely enough, Hoover persisted in denying the existence of anything like organized crime in the United States, insisting that this was a fiction created mainly by a sensation-mongering popular press. Thus, during the waning years of Prohibition (the Nineteenth Amendment repealed the Eighteenth in 1933), the FBI dedicated itself to waging war not on organized crime, but on a handful of violent criminals who had become federal felons by virtue of interstate flight or by robbing federally insured banks.

J. Edgar Hoover was as keen on the brilliant use of publicity as he was on acquiring the latest in crime-fighting and investigative technology. While the local police and T-men continued to struggle against Prohibition-related crime, the FBI *G-men* tackled the likes of "Ma" Barker, her four career criminal sons and their associate Alvin "Creepy" Karpis, and John Dillinger. Criminals such as these who robbed banks, often with great violence, were dangerous to be sure, but Hoover elevated them to the status of "Public Enemies." He created a "Ten Most Wanted" list, which captivated

def•i•ni•tion

In 1930s parlance, **G-men** were "government men"; that is, federal law-enforcement officers, especially FBI agents.

public attention, and he topped this list with such men as Dillinger, identified not just as a public enemy, but as "Public Enemy Number One."

For all his grandstanding, and despite his misdirection of federal law enforcement energy away from organized crime, as well as his elevation of the FBI (and himself) to a status dangerously independent of executive, congressional, and even judicial oversight and supervision, Hoover did set the bar of law enforcement and criminal investigation to a lofty new height. Controversial though it was, the American FBI supplanted the British Scotland Yard as the world's premier crime-fighting and investigative agency.

At its best, the bureau coordinated effective nationwide police efforts; provided much-needed support, instruction, and assistance to local police agencies; developed sophisticated scientific methods of forensic analysis; compiled truly useful databases of crime and criminals; and advocated such proactive investigative approaches as criminal profiling, an attempt to do nothing less than get into the mind of the criminal and even anticipate his next move.

Imperfect as it was, the FBI brought police work to an unprecedented level of sophistication, efficiency, and respect.

The Least You Need to Know

- Until well into the nineteenth century, Americans were resistant to creating professional police departments, which they feared would be abused as instruments of tyranny and intimidation.

- Through most of the nineteenth century, New York's police department, although modeled after the efficient Metropolitan Police of London, was inefficient and corrupt; thanks to the work of Theodore Roosevelt and other reformers, it became a model for the rest of the nation by the turn of the century.

- Prohibition created an opportunity for large-scale organized crime to take root and grow, presenting an overwhelming challenge to local police and prompting the development of federal police agencies, including the FBI.

- J. Edgar Hoover transformed a corrupt and weak agency, the Bureau of Investigation, into the Federal Bureau of Investigation, regarded by many as the premier crime-fighting and investigative organization in the world.

Policing: The Way It Is

In This Chapter

- ◆ To serve and to protect: a police officer's sworn duty
- ◆ Organization of a typical department
- ◆ Police work: the routine risks and the emotional toll
- ◆ The police outgunned
- ◆ Modern police training
- ◆ The deadly force decision

For most of the time they have existed, police agencies have been fairly simple organizations. In the beginning, most had a single role: to pursue and apprehend criminals. Later, the more proactive mission of preventing crime was added, and police officers were sent out on routine street patrol. Later still, a third element was introduced: criminal investigation.

Even at this point, organization was minimal and tended to follow a military model: there were commanders (often called captains), subordinate commanders (lieutenants), supervisors or managers (sergeants), and the troops (patrol officers).

Today, the typical major-city police department is a complex bureaucracy—but not just for the sake of bureaucracy. If police agencies are complex, it is because the demands society puts on them are complex. Policing is no longer a relatively simple game of cops and robbers. Today's police force is an integral part of a criminal justice system, and officers are often called on to make the kind of judgments about constitutional law and departmental policy that judges and administrators make, yet they must do so not in the comfort of judicial chambers or a cozy corner office, but on the street and in life-and-death situations.

To Serve and to Protect

A police officer must serve many masters, but his or her *sworn* duty is to uphold the Constitution and to protect people and property. The twin missions—to serve and to protect—are emblazoned on the vehicles of most American police agencies. What those words say about the structure of the police department is this: no matter how complex the organization of the police force, ultimately the job comes down to how each officer functions in the field, how the officer relates to the people of the community, and how the officer serves and protects the citizen in peril or need.

> **Sworn Statement**
>
> The Delaware State Police recognizes cultural diversity as a fundamental characteristic of our society and, as a state institution, the Division of State Police is committed to providing effective police services that are appropriate, sensitive and equally responsive to all segments of our diverse society.
>
> —Diversity declaration of the state police of Delaware

Americans are accustomed to big government. They have accepted doing business with agencies many times the size of the typical police department. Yet when it comes to the police, no citizen can accept an impersonal bureaucracy. Whether the officer dispatched on a frantic 911 call is a rural sheriff or a big-city patrolman, the citizen in trouble expects effective, courageous, and, above all, human aid. In this, police departments are unique among government agencies. They may be the size of a small army, organized to fulfill many requirements and perform many functions, yet they must consistently present to the public a human face and an individual presence.

Typical Organization

There is probably no such thing as a "typical" police department. American cities vary greatly in size and extent. The two biggest, New York and Los Angeles, have comparable populations, but New Yorkers are massed densely together, while Angelinos are broadcast over a vast area. In New York City, the NYPD is by far the most extensive police presence, whereas in Los Angeles, the LAPD routinely coordinates its operations with those of the L.A. County Sheriff, the California Highway Patrol, and other agencies.

Then of course there is the great American array of smaller cities, towns, villages, and rural areas. Each has its own needs and its own resources (often limited) to finance those needs. We'll look at a department in a medium-size Midwestern city, the Cincinnati Police Division.

def•i•ni•tion

SWAT is an acronym for Special Weapons And Tactics, and a SWAT team is an elite special unit within a police force that uses assault weapons and guerrilla-style assault tactics to resolve such critical crises as hostage situations, mass shootings, terrorist threats, and any situation that calls for the application of superior firepower against suspects.

On the administrative level, a chief presides over an Office of Coordination, Planning, and Budget. On the operational level, that chief commands four bureaus:

- The **Operations Bureau** is subdivided into five police districts plus the Operational Support Section. The five districts represent geographical divisions within the city and address general criminal activities as well as community relations. These districts handle day-to-day patrol. The Operational Support Section covers the whole city and has units devoted to traffic, crime prevention, youth aid, alarm enforcement (responsible for programs to reduce the number of security-system false alarms that create a substantial drain on police resources), and a *SWAT* Coordination Unit.

- The **Investigative Bureau**—familiarly called the **IB**—is responsible for vice, drug, and criminal investigation. It carries out these missions through a number of sections, units, and squads:

  The IB's **Criminal Investigation Section** (**CIS**) comprises the …

  Youth Squad, which investigates child abuse, child neglect, and other situations involving endangerment of minors.

  Homicide Squad, charged with investigating homicides and all questionable deaths, in addition to aggravated assaults where death may occur and rape (when the victim is at least 18 years old); the squad may also investigate kidnapping and abductions, patient-abuse cases, and police-involved shootings.

  Robbery Unit, which investigates robberies of all kinds.

  Major Offender Project, which addresses cases that involve career or repeat offenders.

Criminalistics Squad, which handles crime-scene evidence gathering and processing.

Burglary and Auto Theft Unit, which takes charge of home and business burglaries, as well as "grand theft auto" and auto break-ins.

Pawn Shop Unit, which works with local pawnbrokers to identify stolen property.

Polygraph Unit, which specializes in the administration and interpretation of lie-detector examinations.

Fraud Unit, which is responsible for investigating a wide variety of so-called white-collar crimes.

The IB's **Central Vice Control Section** investigates criminal activity in the areas of prostitution, drugs, gambling, pornography, and liquor law violations.

The IB's **Intelligence Section** focuses on gang activity, cults, terrorists, and terrorist organizations. The section's mission is to develop information on such groups and individuals and, when appropriate, to initiate investigations. This section also conducts special in-service training for police personnel.

The IB's **Narcotics Liaison Section** works with county, state, and federal agencies in a coordinated program that targets illegal narcotics activities.

♦ The **Technical Services Bureau** consists of three sections, including …

Communications, which manages all aspects of police communications, including radio, telephone, 911 dispatch, and computer systems.

Equipment Management, which includes the Impoundment Unit, responsible for impounded vehicles; the Transportation Unit, which manages and maintains police vehicles; and the Supply Unit, which manages supplies and equipment.

Court/Records Services, which operates a Court Administration Unit, County Property Unit, Warrant/Identification Unit, and Records Unit.

♦ The **Personnel Resources Bureau** manages the Personnel Section, the Police Academy, the Inspection Section, and the Internal Investigations Section.

Every medium to large police department has an internal investigations section, sometimes called Internal Affairs, which is responsible for investigating police misconduct and corruption. In some departments, this section is independent of the department hierarchy and reports directly to a commissioner or civilian review board.

Community Emphasis

In that quasi-mythical time known only as "the good old days," the cop walking a beat—an old term for the area regularly assigned an officer for routine patrol—was a familiar neighborhood fixture, who was known to the locals by name and who, in turn, knew many of them. As cities grew and police resources grew proportionately thinner, the beat cop disappeared from the scene. It was, after all, much more efficient to put officers in patrol cars.

Then, during the turbulent 1960s, the gulf between the community and the cop widened dramatically. Many identified the police with "the Establishment" and saw them not as public servants and defenders, but as agents of official oppression. In many places, an adversarial relationship developed between the officers and those they were pledged to serve and protect.

But the 1960s also produced a new trend in policing, an approach that put the emphasis back on the community and sought to reestablish a cooperative relationship between the police and the neighborhood.

The trend toward community policing accompanied the rise of so-called "restorative justice" concepts in criminology, an emphasis on law enforcement as a socially healing ("restorative") process rather than an adversarial one.

Typically, community-based policing embodies some or all of the following principles, approaches, and features:

- Community policing programs start with and are maintained by close give-and-take communication between community members and the police.

- Community policing employs statistical analysis, so that crime trends and other needs of the community can be quantified and objectively identified as well as monitored.

- Community policing makes use of the media, communicating through press releases and public service announcements.

- Community policing involves citizens in crime prevention through Neighborhood Watch programs and the establishment of "safe houses" for children walking to and from school.

- Community policing often directs special attention to areas surrounding schools, watching for drug dealing, sex crimes, and alcohol-related abuses.

- Certain officers are specially trained as community policing officers (CPOs).

- CPOs get out of their patrol cars. They initiate contact with locals, especially merchants and school officials. They also establish liaisons with personnel involved in public works, the building department, animal control, the fire department, and area hospitals. These individuals are good sources for targeting community problems.

- CPOs may combine automobile, bicycle, and foot patrol. In some cases, they may also ride public transportation.

- CPOs monitor and review accident and traffic reports to identify issues that may be referred to public works or the department of transportation.

- CPOs don't go it alone; instead, they serve to coordinate the efforts of various police units so those units may better serve the community for which the CPOs are responsible.

Old Dangers, New Pressures

Police work has always been dangerous. After all, it is the business of the police to intervene in violent situations. The leading cause of death and injury among police officers is, not surprisingly, gunshots. During the twentieth century, almost 7,000 American police officers were shot to death in the line of duty, an end that accounts for 49 percent of all law enforcement fatalities during that 100-year period.

By the Numbers _____

Since the first recorded U.S. police death in 1794, more than 14,000 U.S. law enforcement officers have been killed in the line of duty. A total of 1,533 law enforcement officers died in the line of duty during the 1990s, an average of 1 death every 58 hours, or 153 per year. On average, more than 65,000 U.S. law enforcement officers are assaulted each year, and some 23,000 of these sustain serious injury.

From 1910 to 1939, when motorcycles were among the most common police patrol vehicles, 485 officers were killed in motorcycle wrecks, making it the second leading cause of officer death. By the end of the twentieth century, automobile accidents pulled ahead of motorcycle wrecks as the second leading cause of police fatalities; some 2,000 cops were killed in car wrecks during the twentieth century.

Other physical risks to cops include being struck by vehicles (16 officer deaths in 2005), job-related auto accidents (42 officer deaths in 2005), being killed in aircraft—typically helicopter—accidents (2 officer deaths), falling (3 officer deaths), drowning (4 officer deaths), stabbing (1 officer death), and being killed by bomb detonation (1 officer death).

Despite a general increase in violent crime during the second half of the twentieth century and, equally important, an increase in the violence of the individual criminal, officer deaths from gunshots actually declined during the last two decades of the twentieth century. The reason? Better training, the use of soft body armor (such as Kevlar vests or flak jackets), and better police equipment and weaponry. During the 1980s, an average of 187 U.S. officers were shot to death each year; during the 1990s, the annual average fell to 153. In 2005, 59 police officers were killed by gunshot.

Taking the Point

When a column or patrol of troops advances through hostile territory, one or more soldiers volunteer, or are assigned, to lead the way. As the G.I. says, they "take the point."

Today more than ever, the police officer "takes the point" for society. He or she is at the raw, ragged, and all too often bloody leading edge of modern civilization. The immediate physical dangers are ample, but it has been only in recent years that the emotional and delayed physical dangers of police work have been fully recognized.

Continual exposure to danger, to shocking or traumatic events, and to threats from suspects and prisoners can create tremendous emotional and physical stress. In addition, police officers often face conflicting demands—for example, to be aggressive, but never *too* aggressive, to finely hone one's instincts, but to think carefully before reacting—and they often carry a burdensome workload. Even the stress of testifying in court can take its toll when a successful prosecution may ride on what the arresting officer says and how he or she says it.

> **Sworn Statement**
>
> While the Vietnam veteran was at war for a minimum of nine months, police officers alternate between the violence of the street (e.g., shootings, witnessing death and mutilation, dealing with abused children) and the normalcy of civilian life on a daily basis.
>
> —J. Volanti, "Police Trauma: Psychological Impact of Civilian Combat," in *Police Trauma: Psychological Aftermath of Civilian Combat*, Charles C. Thomas, 1999

In the United States, about 16 of every 100,000 adults commit suicide annually—0.16 suicides per 1,000 adults. During 1984 through 1994, of the 30,000 cops of the NYPD, 63 committed suicide, making for a rate 31 percent higher than the average. More recent studies suggest that police suicides occur at two to seven times the rate in the general population. As of 2006, one American police officer commits suicide every 24 hours.

def•i•ni•tion

As defined by the National Institutes of Mental Health, **post-traumatic stress disorder (PTSD)** "is an anxiety disorder that can develop after exposure to a terrifying event or ordeal in which grave physical harm occurred or was threatened."

Police units or squads are typically close-knit groups, analogous to a family, and the injury or death of a fellow officer hits everyone very hard. Even compassion for victims can cause burnout, or compassion fatigue—a term some psychologists have used to describe the burnout suffered by police officers and other care givers who are continually exposed to the suffering of others.

Stress and burnout are characterized by physical and mental exhaustion. In the worst cases, *post-traumatic stress disorder* (PTSD) may occur, bringing flashbacks, nightmares, extreme anxiety, and/or severe depression. Officers may suffer precisely the kind of symptoms that characterize what was called "shell shock" in World War I and "battle fatigue" in World War II and after.

An Armed Camp

The AK-47, also known as the Kalashnikov assault rifle, has long been the workhorse of guerrillas and terrorists worldwide. Invented by a Russian soldier toward the end of World War II and now manufactured chiefly by the Chinese, the AK-47 is rugged, cheap, and powerful, capable of firing 100 rounds per minute in automatic mode or 40 rounds per minute in single-shot mode. Each of these rounds leaves the muzzle at the rate of 2,330 feet per second. Each is a 7.62-millimeter short bullet with a steel core and a hooked nose, which causes tumbling action and solid penetration.

On January 17, 1989, Patrick Edward Purdy carried his AKS rifle, a semiautomatic variant of the standard AK-47, into his childhood elementary school in Stockton, California. In the span of a single minute, Purdy squeezed off 100 rounds. Five children were killed and 30 others wounded before Purdy discharged the final shots into himself.

A shocking story? Perhaps the most shocking thing about it is that this horrific scene is hardly unique. Despite a 1994 federal ban on assault weapons and the presence, in some states, of even more stringent assault-weapon legislation, these deadly machines are still widely available, and on September 13, 2004, the 1994 Assault Weapons Ban expired. (Although President George W. Bush promised to sign a renewal of the ban, should Congress enact one, he did nothing to encourage such legislation. As of early 2007, there is no federal ban on assault weapons.)

Some anti-gun-control groups have pointed out that assault weapons account for only a small fraction of police-officer deaths, but the point is that, these days, officers are apt to walk into a situation in which they are woefully outgunned. A police service pistol cannot face down such weapons as the AK-47 assault rifle or the Uzi submachine gun, let alone an RPG, a rocket-propelled grenade launcher. All of these, and more, have been used in the United States in the commission of crimes.

Today's police departments must have training and equipment to fight what may amount to full-dress battles with truly formidable weapons. They must also possess the wisdom and restraint to refrain from employing such weapons and tactics except when absolutely necessary.

By the Numbers

The U.S. Department of Justice reported in 2004 that the impact of the 1994 Assault Weapons Ban "on gun violence is likely to be small at best, and perhaps too small for reliable measurement." In contrast, the Brady Center to Prevent Gun Violence—a gun control advocacy group—concluded in 2004 that, since the enactment of the Assault Weapons Ban, "assault weapons have made up only 1.61% of the guns ATF [Bureau of Alcohol, Tobacco, and Firearms] has traced to crime—a drop of 66% from the pre-ban rate." The Brady Center believes that the act prevented 60,000 assault weapon crimes.

Police Academy: The Latest Sequel

During the nineteenth and early twentieth centuries, what little training police officers received was on the job. Today, all major departments train recruits in police academies, and smaller departments make use of state-run academies for law-enforcement officers. All states have legal minimum training standards for sworn peace officers in state and local departments. These officers are officially designated, duly authorized law-enforcement officers, who have received legally mandated training and have taken a prescribed oath of office.

Guy Antinozzi demonstrates one of the most important lessons an officer must learn: taking advantage of cover while tactically approaching an offender's vehicle.

(Photo by Sgt. Connie Rembert, Agnes Scott College Police Department)

The typical police academy offers a demanding and extensive educational experience. The St. Louis Police Academy, for example, subjects recruits to a 23-week intensive program, in which classroom instruction is supplemented by practical application exercises, role playing, situational training, and ride-along observation. Eight hundred eighty training hours are committed to a comprehensive curriculum:

Behavioral Studies and Cultural Diversity: 10 hours

Human Behavior: 40 hours

Legal Studies:

      Law I—Constitutional Law: 57 hours

      Law II—Missouri Law: 48 hours

      Traffic I—Traffic Law: 28 hours

      Liability Issues: 2 hours

Skill Development:

    Computer Skills: 18 hours

    Defensive Tactics/Physical Training: 139 hours

    Driver Training: 16 hours

    Firearms: 109 hours

    Mobile Field Force: 16 hours

    Ride Along: 8 hours

Supplemental Program:

    Administrative Procedures: 18 hours

    Community-Oriented Policing: 20 hours

    Special Orders: 30 hours

Technical Studies:

    Criminal Investigation: 54 hours

    Domestic Violence: 32 hours

    First Aid: 42 hours

    Hazardous Materials: 8 hours

    Juvenile Procedures: 22 hours

    Patrol: 56 hours

    Report Writing: 64 hours

    Traffic II—DWI and Accident: 43 hours

The 2002 graduates of DeKalb County Sheriff's Office SWAT Training Class, including Special Investigator Guy Antinozzi, Sergeant David Aderhold (DeKalb County Sheriff's Office), and law enforcement officers from several agencies. SWAT training is no longer reserved exclusively for SWAT officers. Cross-training and joint training are increasingly essential training methods.

(Photo by Rod Huene, DeKalb County [Georgia] Sheriff's Office)

Deadly Force and Gentle Persuasion

In the terrorist attacks of September 11, 2001, police officers from several departments demonstrated heroic and relentless commitment "to serve and protect." Eighty-six officers of the NYPD, Port Authority, and other agencies lost their lives on that day.

def•i•ni•tion

The **Use of Force Continuum** is a conceptualization (often in the form of a schematic or chart) that illustrates the levels of force appropriate for police to use in meeting various levels of threat.

The tragic events of 9/11 showed us all just how much we count on our police. It was something victims of accident and crime already knew. And yet, in a nation that fought for its independence in part because of the British crown's oppressive laws and oppressive policies of law enforcement, we have always had a love-hate relationship with our cops. It is, after all, a solemn and profoundly disquieting thing to entrust any group with the authority to use deadly force on our behalf.

As much training as police receive in responding quickly and decisively to crime, they also learn to evaluate each situation, so that they may apply the least force possible that is consistent with their safety and the safety of others. State laws governing the use of force are typically quite broad and leave much to the discretion of the individual officer in a particular situation. Most police departments attempt to provide a clear policy statement on the use of force, and many employ the *Use of Force Continuum*, which prescribes a logical escalation of force.

In many cases, the mere appearance of an officer, in the uniform of authority, will secure cooperation and compliance from a suspect. This is Level 1 on the Use of Force Continuum. If this fails, the officer proceeds to Level 2, verbal communication. From here, Level 3 calls for control holds and restraints, including physically taking control of the suspect using various bare-handed defensive holds and then applying handcuffs. If Level 3 force is ineffective or impractical against a violent or threatening suspect, officers may use nonlethal weapons, such as pepper spray or tear gas. This represents escalation to Level 4.

The next level, Level 5, falls just short of deadly force. Against extremely violent suspects, it may be necessary to use a baton (popularly called a nightstick) or a stun gun or taser, which delivers a disabling electric shock. The object is to temporarily incapacitate the suspect, so that handcuffs or other restraints can be applied. The risk of doing serious injury or even killing the suspect is significant. A stun gun or taser may cause cardiac arrest, and even though officers are trained to use their batons to administer soft-tissue blows, rather than blows to the face or skull, any forceful blow can be lethal. Certain choke holds and martial arts holds that pinch off the carotid artery may incapacitate a suspect, but they may also result in death or permanent injury. Many departments explicitly outlaw such procedures.

The highest escalation in the continuum is Level 6, the use of deadly force. It is applied when the officer has reason to believe the danger of severe injury or death is imminent to him- or herself, or others. If possible, the officer must warn the suspect of the intent to shoot. However, once the officer fires his or her weapon at the suspect, the intent is to shoot to kill.

It is a testament to modern policing that most officers not only strive to resolve confrontations at the lowest possible continuum level, but that they deem it a mark of consummate professionalism to do so. Indeed, most officers look upon having to fire on a suspect as something of a professional failure.

The Least You Need to Know

♦ Large modern police departments are complex bureaucracies that must nevertheless deal directly, immediately, effectively, and compassionately with people in urgent need.

♦ Today's police forces are integral parts of the criminal justice system and often work closely with other social service agencies as well.

♦ The typical modern department is organized into units dedicated to specific categories of crime, yet these units must coordinate their actions with one another and with other public agencies.

◆ In many jurisdictions, modern police face daily urban combat, analogous to warfare, which creates great physical dangers and may take a heavy toll on the emotional health of officers.

◆ Police training today is extensive and comprehensive, as befits agencies whose members are authorized to use deadly force.

Chapter **18**

The Ultimate Weapon: Information

In This Chapter

- ◆ Information—and how police get it
- ◆ Problems with information from witnesses and victims
- ◆ Information obtained from suspects
- ◆ Use of confidential informants
- ◆ Undercover assignments: types and hazards
- ◆ How police share information

There are few professions that depend more on the flow of information than law enforcement. This is especially true in criminal investigation. A detective is first and foremost a good communicator. Seasoned, professional, and savvy, a detective above all knows how to tell a story and find good material.

But detectives are not the only police communicators. Dispatchers and 911 operators as well as the patrol officer all must gather, process, and transmit vital information quickly, clearly, and without possibly life-threatening error.

Sources of Information

Wheels spin and little is accomplished without good information. The criminal investigator needs to know who, what, when, where, and why. Beating the bushes, doing all the legwork required to get vital information, is glamorized on television, but in reality, it is just plain hard work. It is time-consuming work done in situations where time is almost always in short supply. The precinct detective who starts out with a thorough knowledge of the neighborhood has a major advantage over any outside investigator sent from "downtown" or another law enforcement agency.

Reports and Records

All police responses produce some kind of documented record. If any police action is taken, an *incident report* is prepared.

The incident report may be very simple or highly complex, depending on the officer and the incident. Most departments provide officers with some training and guidelines in report writing, but all good reports share certain characteristics:

- They are written from clear, well-organized notes made at the scene.

- They are factual, accurate, and objective.

- They show rather than tell; opinion is excluded.

- They are complete and thorough, but concise.

- They contain no internal contradictions.

- They are written in clear, standard English, without police jargon, street slang, grammatical errors, or misspellings.

def•i•ni•tion

An **incident report** is the responding officer's written account of the call to which he or she has responded. It is generally the first official record made of a crime or other incident.

Some departments have adopted computerized report-writing systems. These allow police officers to prepare incident reports using special software that provides preformatted screens and questions, which not only speed the report-writing process, but help to ensure that all relevant information is included and presented in a usefully organized form. Preparing reports on a computer also makes them more readily accessible to other investigators and to prosecutors.

Domestic violence incidents require a special domestic violence incident report, which typically is a form that asks for information about the physical condition and state of mind of both the victim and the suspect, the nature of the relationship between victim and suspect, what medical treatment the victim received (if any), and what physical evidence has been collected. On-the-spot photographs showing the victim's injuries are essential to domestic violence reports. Currently, most police agencies use Polaroid or Polaroid-type cameras for on-the-spot victim photography. Many courts hesitate to accept digital photography as evidence, because it is readily subject to alteration.

Most of the time, at the request of the reporting officer, the dispatcher assigns a unique case number to the incident, so that even if an incident report is not made, there is a record of the officer's actions in the form of a dispatch log.

When an officer is dispatched, the times of dispatch and arrival are recorded, as are the names of the personnel responding. If the response is self-initiated—the officer responded to something he sees, for example—it is protocol to call out the location and type of action over the radio. The dispatcher, monitoring this call, makes a record at this time. Such records can be very important later, when a follow-up investigation is conducted or a case is prosecuted in court.

In contrast to uniformed patrol officers, detectives are not expected to call out on the police radio their every move. Part of being a detective is accepting responsibility for greater independent action.

Victims

Victims would seem a natural and willing source of information, yet, often, this is not the case. In most crimes, the victim and perpetrator are not strangers to one another, and this relationship may prompt the victim to avoid cooperating in the investigation.

The best chance investigators have for obtaining the victim's help is at the scene of the crime, immediately after the incident has occurred. Fear and anger move many to cooperate, whereas the more time that passes, the less urgent the motive for cooperation becomes. Worse, in the many cases in which the victim and the perpetrator know one another, the perpetrator often

By the Numbers

Incorrect eyewitness identifications account for more convictions of innocent persons than all other causes combined. In a 1996 study by the Institute for Law and Justice, of 28 people released from long prison terms on the basis of DNA tests, 24 had been misidentified by eyewitnesses.

finds a way to intimidate or otherwise influence the victim. Victim and perpetrator may be wife and husband, for instance, or they may even be partners in some criminal enterprise.

Modern criminal investigation—particularly in domestic violence crimes—no longer centers on the cooperation of the victim. Responding officers are still trained to obtain as much information as possible from the victim at the scene of the incident, but the main emphasis is placed on gathering evidence that is separate and apart from anything the victim may say. Witnesses such as neighbors, family members, co-workers, and strangers are interviewed and always questioned independently.

Witnesses

Not surprisingly, witnesses are very important to a criminal investigation. Unfortunately, eyewitness accounts are notoriously unreliable. Police officers quickly become accustomed to the shock and frustration of hearing a dozen eyewitnesses to a crime give a dozen earnest, well-meaning, but entirely different accounts of the incident.

Because it is subject to so much distortion—the coloring of perception, the shading of emotion, the imperfection of memory—eyewitness testimony is not slam-dunk courtroom evidence. It is evidence, but it must be corroborated by other, more objective evidence. Most importantly, all eyewitness evidence must be obtained independently so that the recollection of one witness does not influence that of another.

Suspects

Willingly or unwillingly, suspects provide information in criminal investigations. Suspects can be tracked, their behavior observed, their patterns analyzed. In some cases, a search warrant may be issued to obtain blood, hair, or other items of evidence from a suspect. This can be analyzed and compared to an unknown sample found at the crime scene.

While the Fifth Amendment guarantees that a suspect cannot be forced to testify against himself, he may be compelled to provide the tissue evidence just described, and he may also be compelled to participate in a lineup in which the victim or other witnesses (usually shielded behind a one-way mirror) may identify him as he stands next to five other similarly featured men.

Undercover Work

Possibly the most misunderstood job in police work is the undercover investigation. The glamour portrayed on television and in the movies is, for the most part, missing from the real-life assignment.

Some investigators work undercover in a limited capacity and for a limited time. For example, they may pose as construction workers, taxi drivers, medical patients—whatever it takes to get close to people who have outstanding warrants against them and need to be taken into custody.

There are also investigators, typically in narcotics, who work undercover on a much more extended basis. They attempt to fit the image of a narcotics dealer or heavy user, and their goal is to infiltrate the drug world in order to develop a case and bring charges against the dealer or the dealer's suppliers or distributors.

That is a dangerous assignment, but even riskier are "deep undercover" investigations. In these, the investigator virtually assumes a new life and new identity to infiltrate a criminal enterprise so thoroughly as to become all but indistinguishable from those he or she is investigating. The physical risks of this work are obvious. More subtle are the psychological hazards of coming to identify oneself with the criminals under investigation.

Case in Point
Operation Drug Wheels was a major 1990 undercover "sting" operation in which federal undercover agents posing as narcotics dealers offered to purchase a fleet of cars for cash from an automobile dealership, which agreed to disguise the identity of the purchasers. The dealership also introduced the undercover agents to an insurance company, which agreed to furnish insurance on a fraudulent basis. Working undercover, the agents ultimately identified five New York dealerships and two insurance company agencies, which were charged with money laundering and cash reporting and mail fraud violations. Thirty-one new cars valued at $880,700 were seized by agents. Operation Drug Wheels is typical of undercover work on a large scale.

The Information File

Record keeping is essential to effective criminal investigation. The evidence must be kept secure after it is seized, the chain of custody maintained and the integrity of the evidence safeguarded. The narcotics, the bloodstained shirt, the gun, the knife, or other pieces of evidence seized at the crime scene must be the exact same items in the exact same condition when presented at the trial before the jury.

Cases must be preserved for many years. The trial process is long and the appeals process even longer. The file must be maintained and available. Witnesses need to be contacted and kept track of. All officers involved must ready themselves for trial—and keep themselves ready.

The Rat—a Necessary Evil

Who could be more despicable than someone willing to turn on his or her compatriots for money? Many juries answer this question with a resounding "no one," and they may discount or entirely reject information that has been bought and paid for.

The informant—also called by police a confidential informant (CI) and by the bad guys, a rat—is a special breed. This person's value as a witness increases as his or her value as a member of society decreases. That is, the more an informant is involved in criminal activity, the more valuable his or her testimony becomes.

The use of confidential informants in criminal investigations has become such an integral part of American law enforcement that it would be difficult to conduct an investigation without the use of such unsavory characters. But even here, there is a catch-22. For while intimate involvement in criminal enterprises makes the informant a valuable insider, the informant's criminality undercuts his or her credibility. The reliability of an informant is proportional to his or her involvement in criminal activity; as that increases, reliability increases because, in court, the informant can be shown to have adequate and personal knowledge of the criminal activity in question. At the same time, as involvement in crime increases, credibility decreases.

Informant testimony is always a precarious balancing act. The investigator pulls it off by using the totality of circumstances test—a package of facts and circumstances relating to a case and used to evaluate and corroborate informant information. If all the facts and circumstances, taken in their totality, support the informant's information, the information is considered probably reliable. The detective may also build up the credibility of the informant by stating that he or she has used the informant in the past to obtain information that led to arrests, seizures, and convictions.

> **Case in Point**
>
> All good police officers develop informants, people living or working in the areas under their responsibility who provide them with information. Some of these informants are citizens who simply want to make their community a better place. Some are criminals interested in ridding their turf of a competitor. The job of managing informants is a delicate and often dangerous one. The fact is this: all information is just that, information, not proof. Whatever the CI supplies must be verified by independent investigation.

A Question of Cash

Informants may be rewarded by being paid for the information they provide or pardoned for petty offenses. There is no general rule as to which type of incentive is better or more likely to produce reliable results. Cash payment does not necessarily compromise the information provided by the informant. Indeed, the informant may be more responsible and truthful because he or she is being "paid for the work." A tangible reward is a powerful motivator, and it is rare for a well-informed criminal to do anything out of a sense of social responsibility.

The Pitfalls

Obviously, there are drawbacks to using informants. If their reliability and credibility cannot be substantiated to a degree that meets judicial scrutiny, then the information they provide is useless. If they are relied on to the exclusion of other evidence or without proper independent investigation, their value is also very limited. Even more serious is the possibility that juries will simply tire of taking the word of one admitted criminal against another.

Police Networking

A well-known maker of computer systems used to employ as its corporate slogan this sentence: "The network is the computer." The message? Individual computers are fine and dandy, but the work of such a computer is made truly meaningful only when it is shared, combined with the work of other computers in a network.

Much the same can be said about the information police obtain. Scribbled in a detective's notebook or stored in a file drawer, information does little. Made accessible to other cops, harvested, winnowed, shared, and compared, information takes on enormous power.

Interpersonal Cooperation

Fighter pilots, alone in the cockpit—one pilot, one plane—are by nature independent sorts. But even the topmost top gun knows better than to try to go it alone. Fighters work in formations of two or more. Doing so multiplies their effectiveness far beyond the numbers involved. A formation of 2 planes is probably 10 times more effective than a solo flier.

Criminal investigators quickly learn much the same lesson. They eagerly take responsibility for a case, but they don't go it alone. They look at the files, they identify the cops who've worked on similar or perhaps related cases, and they talk to them—pump them for information.

Cops talk cases out. They network, both formally and informally. Grandstanders who jealously guard information relating to "their" case because they don't want to share the glory of solving the mystery are not likely to find any glory to share. They won't crack the case.

Like most professionals, cops form relationships with each other. Some find mentors among their colleagues, a veteran who's seen it all and has plenty of time-saving advice. Some find friendly adversaries—people to bounce ideas off of, people who won't pull punches concerning what's wrong with your theory.

Most seasoned investigators network both inside and outside of their department. A city cop may be well aware that his or her department does things a certain way and no other way. When that cop wants a fresh point of view, he or she contacts a friend in the rural county sheriff's office.

International Accord

Networking can be interpersonal, or it can be international. After World War I, an economically devastated Europe was swept by a great crime wave. In 1923, the head of the Viennese police department, Johann Schober, called for an international meeting of police agencies to create a network for cooperation among law enforcement officials across borders. The result, ultimately, was the International Criminal Police Organization, better known as Interpol.

Today, Interpol, with 125 member nations, is the chief organization by which criminal police forces cooperate worldwide to fight international crime. Each Interpol member maintains a domestic clearinghouse (the National Central Bureau), which acts as liaison between individual police forces and the police of other affiliated countries.

Interpol is not an international police agency, but a means of communication and coordination, a worldwide network that makes it much more difficult for criminals to find refuge in a foreign land.

The Least You Need to Know

- Information is the most valuable weapon in the police arsenal. Information sources include witnesses, victims, suspects, informants, and the officers themselves.

- Undercover work has been glamorized in film and fiction, but, in reality, is hard work that puts officers in physical and, often, psychological peril.

- The confidential informant—the "rat"—is the ultimate criminal insider, a criminal who agrees to provide the police with information concerning the criminal enterprises he or she is privy to.

- Police officers are inveterate networkers, sharing information both formally (from department to department and even from nation to nation) and informally, developing working relationships with mentors and colleagues.

Chapter 19

Lie Detectors

In This Chapter

- ◆ The polygraph: what it is and how it works
- ◆ Lie detector pioneers
- ◆ The polygraph examination
- ◆ How reliable is the polygraph?
- ◆ The polygraph and the courts
- ◆ Technological and human alternatives to the polygraph

At some point in the course of human evolution, hominids (our collective evolutionary precursors) discovered lying. And shortly after this time, they must have begun thinking up ways to find out who was lying and who wasn't.

At various times in history and among various cultures, methods have been devised and prescribed to test the truth. Some of these have been based on keen observation. For instance, the ancient Chinese understood that a dry mouth accompanies nervousness and nervousness accompanies lying, so they questioned a suspect as he chewed dry rice. After questioning, he was told to spit out the rice. If it came out nice and gooey, he was telling the truth; if dry, the suspect was caught in a lie.

Other methods have been less scientific. In Europe during the Middle Ages, if a woman suspected of witchcraft denied being a witch, her veracity could be tested by binding her hand and foot and tossing her in a pond. If she survived, she was a witch, because (as everyone knows) witches float; if she drowned, well then, she was (or, more accurately, *had been*) telling the truth.

Gooey gobs of rice or drowned innocents? By the twentieth century, law enforcement personnel decided there has *got* to be a better way.

The Polygraph

The truth (yes, the truth) is that perceptive questioners have always been able to gauge the trustworthiness of a source. Body language speaks loudly to those who can "hear" it. A liar rarely looks you in the eye, he puts his hand to his mouth, he shuffles his feet, he rubs the back of his neck, he shakes his head no while *saying* yes, his voice trembles, he sweats, he blushes.

The anxiety that accompanies lying often produces plainly visible physiological effects, but even when the effects are not clearly visible, they are almost always present—and measurable.

def•i•ni•tion

The **polygraph** is an assemblage of instruments (at minimum, a pneumograph, galvanograph, and cardiograph) that measure and record respiration rate and depth, electrical resistance of the skin, and blood pressure and pulse rate, which indicate the status of physiological processes commonly affected by the emotion of anxiety.

What It Is

The *polygraph*—commonly called a lie detector—is nothing more or less than an instrument that measures and graphically records the effects of several physiological processes.

Actually the polygraph is an assemblage of several instruments to measure several distinct processes:

 ◆ A pneumograph measures the rate of respiration and the depth of breathing.

 ◆ A galvanograph measures changes in the electrical resistance of the skin. Perspiration increases the skin's electrical conductivity.

♦ A cardiograph measures blood pressure and pulse rate.

Some polygraphs add another instrument, a plethysmograph, which attaches to a finger to measure peripheral blood flow.

How It Works

The premise on which the polygraph operates is simple, sound, and time tested. Socialized human beings lie, but they don't like to lie, because they've been conditioned to believe that lying is wrong. Therefore, lying produces nervousness and anxiety. Nervousness and anxiety, in turn, produce distinct—sometimes visible, almost always measurable—physiological effects, including …

♦ An increase in the rate of respiration and a decrease in the depth of the breaths taken (shallow breathing). The polygraph's pneumograph module measures these effects.

♦ An increase in perspiration. The galvanograph does not measure perspiration directly, but it does measure the difference in the electrical resistance of the skin produced when the subject perspires.

♦ Increases in pulse rate and blood pressure. The cardiograph measures these vital signs.

The polygraph machine records the measurements graphically. For some 50 years, polygraphs have traced out their measurements on moving rolls of chart paper, which is annotated by the polygraph examiner during the examination, then analyzed by the examiner later. In recent years, desktop computers and sophisticated computer programs have been married to the polygraph. These newer systems are paperless, graphing the data on a computer screen—and recording it digitally on disk so that it is storable and retrievable and, if desired, can be printed out on paper. An important feature of digital polygraph machines is the software, which includes complicated chart analysis formulas designed to aid the examiner in evaluating results.

We'll outline the examination procedure in just a moment, but the general idea is that the examiner asks questions, notes the verbal responses, and also notes the physiological response produced on the machine's graphical output. By analyzing variations in the physiological responses, the examiner can render an opinion as to the truthfulness of the verbal responses.

What It's Used For

Polygraphs are used in criminal as well as civil applications. In criminal investigations, polygraph examinations can reduce a large pool of suspects by eliminating people who seem clearly innocent. During interrogation of a suspect, the polygraph may be used to elicit a confession; however, the suspect must be fully advised of his rights.

Polygraph examination is also used to gauge the veracity of informant information, from a jailhouse snitch or a confidential informant (CI). (A CI is a civilian who is usually paid to provide information to the police regarding criminal activity; on the street, that person is usually called a snitch or a rat.) Key potential witnesses may also be screened by a polygraph examination.

Outside of the law-enforcement community, polygraph examination had been used for preemployment screening—formerly accounting for more than 80 percent of polygraph tests administered in the United States. Employers asked potential employees about past dishonesty and criminal behavior. However, in 1988, Congress passed the Employee Polygraph Protection Act (EPPA), which barred most preemployment polygraph examinations, except in the following cases: government jobs, companies that manufacture or dispense controlled substances (pharmaceutical drugs), and companies engaged in sensitive work on government contracts.

By the Numbers

The FBI administers about 5,000 polygraph examinations annually to persons entering sensitive government-related jobs. Each applicant is given two separate tests with different types of questions.

An employer may ask a *current* employee to take a polygraph examination only if the employer provides clear documentation of specific suspicions; however, the employee cannot be discharged solely on the basis of the polygraph results, nor can the employee be dismissed solely because he or she refused to submit to a polygraph examination.

In the civil arena—for example, in lawsuits involving personal injury, property damage, intentional misconduct, and breaking contracts—polygraphs may be used on witnesses and litigants, as long as rights under the Employee Polygraph Protection Act are not violated.

A Short History of the Lie Detector

Like many others, Boston attorney William M. Marston understood that liars paid a physiological price for their untruths. They blushed, they sweated, they breathed heavily. In 1917, he decided to use these physiological effects to make the detection of falsehood scientific. He designed a machine to continuously monitor systolic blood pressure (the pressure created during the contraction phase of the heartbeat; diastolic pressure is that created during the relaxation phase) and claimed that an increase in this pressure accompanied verbal falsehood.

Marston's Marvel

Marston's invention created a popular stir and began to be used by some law enforcement officials. In 1923, however, a federal appeals court issued a strong challenge to Marston's marvel.

Convicted of murder, James T. Frye appealed on the basis that the court had not permitted an examiner to testify about the results of a "systolic blood pressure deception test" he had taken and passed. The appellate court denied the appeal, introducing what came to be known as the "Frye Test." The essence of the Frye Test is this: the device or procedure on which any expert testimony is based must be "sufficiently established to have gained general acceptance in the particular field in which it belongs." In 1923, Marston's device was new and little tested, and the legal future of the "lie detector" was thereby put in doubt. The Frye Test or Frye Standard was generally accepted in American courts until it was superseded in 1975 by the Federal Rules of Evidence.

Larson's Refinements

Despite the blow Marston's machine had been dealt, many in the law enforcement community continued to be interested in the great potential of a lie detection device. Working independently of Marston, Dr. John A. Larson, a police officer turned educator and practicing psychiatrist, developed a true *poly*graph device (it measured pulse rate and respiratory changes in addition to blood pressure) in 1921. Unlike Marston,

Case in Point

During the 1930s and after, the law enforcement community embraced the polygraph, and Leonarde Keeler prospered after he established the first private lie detection agency in 1938. The enthusiasm was not entirely blind, but the fact is that not until 1950 was a series of objective scientific studies done to test the validity and reliability of the polygraph.

Larson was more cautious in introducing the device and, by the time he did, he had honed the machine and developed more solid procedures for using it.

Larson focused much attention on developing an interviewing technique, which he called the R/I procedure—the "R/I" standing for relevant/irrelevant. It worked like this: in the course of questioning, the examiner was to ask questions relevant to the crime ("Do you own a Glock handgun?") and questions that have nothing to do with the crime ("Do you live at 123 Felony Drive?"). Larson's assumption was that the innocent would exhibit a similar physiological response to both types of questions, whereas the guilty would react more strongly to the crime-relevant questions.

Keeler the Popularizer

There is no doubt that Larson improved the lie detector by inventing the true polygraph, measuring more physiological factors than just blood pressure and developing better methods of questioning. However, Larson failed to consider that innocent people, under police interrogation and suspected of a crime, might be quite nervous, perhaps even *more* nervous than a hardened criminal who was guilty.

Despite this, Larson's protégé, Leonarde Keeler, succeeded in popularizing the polygraph. He introduced refinements to the machine (obtaining a patent in 1931) as well as a greater degree of sophistication in the procedures for questioning, which addressed some of the shortcomings of the R/I approach. He based his work on an extensive study he carried out at the federal penitentiary at Joliet, Illinois, testing more than 500 inmates to develop reference points and baselines for analysis. Keeler compared police reports and court records against what inmates told him and was therefore able to obtain a range of real-world polygraph results in situations in which the truth was known. This allowed him to obtain a broad sample of truthful and untruthful responses, which provided an extensive opportunity for calibrating his equipment and for preparing polygraphers to interpret results accurately.

The Lindbergh Kidnapping

The popularity of the polygraph received its single greatest boost by its involvement—or, actually, high-profile noninvolvement—in the "crime of the century."

The time: night, March 1, 1932. The place: the Hopewell, New Jersey, home of aviation hero Charles A. Lindbergh and his wife, Anne Morrow Lindbergh. Someone snatches from his second-floor nursery the couple's 20-month-old son. As soon as the abduction is discovered, a network of roadblocks and a massive manhunt are put into place. There are clues: a homemade ladder, footprints, and a ransom note written in broken, German-accented English:

> Dear Sir!
>
> Have 50000$ redy with 25 000 $ in 20 $ bills 1.5000 $ in 10$ bills and 10000$ in 5 $ bills. After 2-4 days we will inform you were to deliver the Mony.
>
> We warn you for making anyding public or for notify the Police the child is in gut care.
>
> Indication for all letters are singnature and 3 holes.

A ransom payment with marked bills is prepared and delivered; as promised, directions to the baby are provided. Heartbreakingly, they prove false, and on May 12 a truck driver discovers a child's skull in a wooded area about four miles from the Lindbergh home. Police find a shallow grave—and, in it, the body of the Lindbergh baby.

In the aftermath of the tragedy, leads did emerge, only to result in one dead end after another. Strangest of all was the questioning of Violet Sharpe, a maid who worked for the Lindberghs' in-laws. Her stories were inconsistent through several interrogations—until, after one session with the cops, she gulped down silver polish and died minutes later. In desperation, investigators asked Lindbergh's permission to use Keeler's polygraph in questioning his own household staff. Flatly refusing to believe that anyone who worked for him could be guilty, Lindbergh withheld permission.

The investigation then stalled until, on September 15, 1934—more than two years after the murder—someone purchased 98 cents' worth of gas with a $10 gold certificate. In the depths of the Great Depression, this was a notable event, and the gas station owner scribbled down the license plate number on the certificate. He had spoken to the driver about the bill. He was a man with a German accent, who boasted that he had a lot more of these gold certificates at home.

The gas-station owner called the police, who traced the license plate to a carpenter, a German immigrant named Bruno Richard Hauptmann. A search of his house revealed more than $14,000 of the ransom money hidden away, and a missing rafter in Hauptmann's attic had been used in the construction of the homemade ladder found at the kidnap scene (as mentioned in Chapter 13, a fact established by the work of a pioneering forensic botanist).

Hauptmann certainly appeared guilty. He claimed that his former business partner had given him the money. The problem with this alibi? That man, Isador Fisch, had returned to Germany—and was now dead.

While in jail awaiting trial, Hauptmann learned about the "lie detector machine" and asked to be given the test. His request was denied. His defense attorney, a self-important incompetent who believed his client guilty, made little attempt to pursue the request, and FBI chief J. Edgar Hoover (it was discovered many years later) had issued a confidential memo: "Under no circumstances will we have anything to do with the [polygraph] test of Hauptmann."

In the "trial of the century" for the "crime of the century," Hauptmann was convicted and sentenced to death. While the public clamored for the speedy execution of a fiend, New Jersey's scrupulous and courageous governor, Harold G. Hoffman, wasn't so sure. He ordered a short reprieve for additional investigation and wanted Keeler to administer a polygraph examination. Keeler agreed to provide his services not only pro bono (at no charge), but in secret from the press.

That was key. Hoffman wanted no sensationalism. But Keeler, burning to promote his invention, broke his word and leaked the news. Instantly, he was off the case—and instead, his rival William Marston, equipped with his more simplistic blood-pressure machine, was called in to perform the test. The trial judge, however, would have none of it. He denied Marston access to Hauptmann, Governor Hoffman could not legally override the judge, and no lie detector was ever used in the Lindbergh kidnapping case. Hauptmann was executed, and debate over his guilt or innocence continues to this day.

And yet, the mere fact that the "lie detector" was *almost* used in this sensational, high-profile case enhanced its reputation probably far beyond what would have resulted had it *actually* been used. After all, experts and public alike were now forever free to speculate on how the machine *might have* solved the case.

The Polygraph in Action

Today, polygraph examinations are conducted systematically by trained, qualified, and certified examiners. Much of the work takes place before a single question is asked. The examiner begins by reviewing all the facts surrounding the case in question. Following this, the examiner reviews the facts with the subject before the test is conducted. Based on the view of the facts and the pretest interview, the examiner prepares specific test questions.

In the next step, the examiner explains the test process to the subject and, again before the test is administered, reads each question to the subject to ensure that all are easily understood. During the examination itself, the subject is not asked any surprise questions about the crime.

The subject is hooked up to the polygraph instrument and, in a neutral voice—without comment of any kind—the examiner reads the questions several times, noting the questions and answers on the resulting *polygram* (either in digital form or on paper, depending on whether the instrument used is digital or analog). No one other than the examiner and the subject is present at the interrogation (unless a translator is required). Interrogations are typically limited to no more than 90 minutes. If more time is required, additional examinations are scheduled.

def•i•ni•tion

The graphical readout or chart produced by a polygraph examination is called a **polygram**.

After the examination, the examiner analyzes the resulting polygrams and, using prescribed standards, develops a numerical score for the test, which results in a verbal conclusion of either "truthful," "deceptive," or "inconclusive." Results are typically furnished within 24 hours.

Polygraph examiners must design questions that can be answered *yes* or *no*. Nothing else is acceptable. Furthermore, the questions must have definitive, objective answers; they must not elicit mere opinion. Each question must bear on past events of a factual nature, and they must be worded without possibility of ambiguity. Here are some examples:

> *Unacceptable question:* "On April 5, 2002, were you thinking of robbing the convenience store at 234 Guilty Street?"

> *Acceptable question:* "On April 5, 2002, did you rob the convenience store at 234 Guilty Street?"

Unacceptable question: "Have you ever lied to the police?"

Acceptable question: "On April 5, 2002, did you rob the convenience store at 234 Guilty Street?"

Unacceptable question: "Are you a thief?"

Acceptable question: "On April 5, 2002, did you rob the convenience store at 234 Guilty Street?"

Questions asked in the same exam session must be related to one another. The examiner may ask the subject questions relating to the robbery at 234 Guilty Street, but not about (for example) illegal drug use. If the subject is suspected of illegal drug use, this issue must be addressed in a separate examination.

What Can Go Wrong?

Today, some champions of the polygraph claim accuracy rates as high as 99 percent. Critics disagree, arguing that examiners' techniques are based on some questionable psychological assumptions.

By the Numbers

A 1981 study of six polygraph interpreters revealed an error rate varying from 18 percent to 55 percent. Predictably, the most experienced examiners made the fewest errors.

While few question the accuracy of the polygraph instrument in registering the physiological changes it monitors, objective tests have found that many examiners are consistently more likely to label a truthful subject untruthful rather than an untruthful subject truthful. The physiological and mechanical principles on which the polygraph operates are considered quite sound, but there is significant variation in the quality and accuracy of interpretation.

False Confession

People fear polygraphs. The idea that the machine will absolutely determine the truth sometimes elicits confessions, including false confessions. False confessions, resulting from some deep-seated compulsion in the subject to confess, are not at all uncommon.

Beating the Machine

Certain deceptive subjects can defeat the examination by using cognitive or physiological countermeasures to gain control of their physiological responses. Moreover, people with antisocial personality disorder—a psychological condition that renders the individual incapable of feeling remorse—have reduced autonomic activity. That is, feeling no guilt, they exhibit few of the physiological effects that customarily accompany lying about a crime.

Guilt or Fear?

The polygraph registers heightened physiological responses, period. Such responses may be produced by fear, including the fear of being caught in a lie and punished, but they may also result from just plain fear. Fear is not always about deception. Indeed, an innocent, truthful person may be very fearful.

Inadmissible? The Courts and the Polygraph

The polygraph has traveled a rocky road through the nation's courts. Some courts allow the introduction of polygraph evidence, while others do not. Judges in many jurisdictions worry that polygraph evidence is given greater weight than other evidence and tends to sway a jury unduly. For this reason, in most cases, polygraph evidence is used during the maneuvering and negotiations that take place before a trial, rather than during the trial itself.

In 1993, the U.S. Supreme Court ruled in *Daubert* v. *Merrell Dow Pharmaceuticals, Inc.* (509 U.S. 579) that polygraph evidence does have a reliable scientific foundation and compares favorably with other such scientific evidence as fiber analysis, ballistics comparison, and blood analysis—all of which are routinely accepted by the courts. However, the Supreme Court's 1998 decision in *United States* v. *Scheffer* reduced the effect of the so-called *Daubert standard* by holding that any court can decide to exclude polygraph evidence per se (under any circumstances) or to evaluate it case by case. Thus, the admissibility of polygraph evidence depends on the discretion of the individual court.

def•i•ni•tion

The **Daubert standard,** based on the 1993 Supreme Court decision in *Daubert v. Merrell Dow Pharmaceuticals, Inc.* (509 U.S. 579), is often used to support the legal admissibility of polygraph evidence. The standard holds that courts may admit evidence based on tested, peer-reviewed scientific methods, which are widely accepted as valid in the scientific community.

Alternatives to the Polygraph

While the polygraph remains the most widely used and accepted technology for lie detection, two alternatives have emerged. The first began development in the 1970s as the psychological stress evaluator, or PSE, a device that measured stress in the "micro-tremors" of the human voice. By the early 1990s, the device was extensively refined as the computer voice stress analyzer (CVSA).

The principle behind the CVSA is that the voice involuntarily, if subtly, registers stress when the speaker is being deceptive. Experience and common sense support this assertion, of course; most people caught in a lie are unable to make themselves sound convincing.

CVSA equipment and training are considerably less expensive than traditional polygraph examination, and advocates claim an extraordinary 98 percent accuracy rate (versus the 45 percent to 85 percent claimed for the polygraph), but while numerous law enforcement agencies use the technology during interrogations and for pretrial negotiation of pleas, many courts do not admit CVSA results as evidence because of insufficient experience with the technology and a shortage of scientific tests.

Critics of the traditional polygraph find that CVSA suffers from the same major flaw that afflicts the polygraph: both technologies measure emotion rather than knowledge. But then, what technology could possibly look into a suspect's mind to measure his knowledge of a crime?

In the 1960s, researchers began studying what they called the p300 pattern of electrical activity in the brain. This is a "bump" in electrical activity that occurs from 300 to 800 milliseconds after a person receives a recognized stimulus (for example, is shown a familiar image). The electrical activity may be monitored via electrodes placed on the head and hooked up to amplifying and graphical recording devices.

def•i•ni•tion

Brain fingerprinting describes a new technology that monitors the brain for p300 electrical patterns, which appear when the subject is exposed to a familiar stimulus. The presence of the p300 pattern indicates the subject's knowledge of the stimulus. Some researchers have begun to apply the technology to lie detection.

In the 1980s and 1990s, a small group of researchers began developing this "brain wave" technology as *brain fingerprinting*, a more refined process for plotting p300 patterns in order to distinguish when a subject possesses or lacks knowledge about an event. In one experiment, Dr. Lawrence A. Farwell was able to identify 11 genuine FBI agents and 4 imposter agents by measuring brain wave responses to cues that would be familiar only to persons who had been trained in the FBI academy. These cues consisted of specific terms, acronyms, and images. Emotion played no part in the experiment. Simply, those who had the knowledge showed a p300 bump, while those who lacked the knowledge did not show such a pattern.

Brain fingerprinting is a very new technology that has yet to be extensively tested in the courts. However, *The New York Times* reported (October 9, 2001) that in 1998, Missouri police used the technology to generate evidence in support of a confession by James B. Grinder, who admitted to having participated in an unsolved 1984 rape and murder.

The new technology has critics, but even many of them believe that, with further development, brain fingerprinting may play a significant role in criminal investigation and even in prosecution.

Forensic Psychology and Deception Detection

Recent years have seen a trend away from sole reliance on technology to assess deception. The field of "deception detection" has increasingly emerged within the larger fields of forensic psychology and forensic psychiatry to develop data and methods designed to allow police interrogators and others to more effectively assess the veracity of witness, victim, and suspect statements.

Deception detection studies various aspects of deception, including verbal content and nonverbal behavior, as well as the use of the polygraph and other technologies. Those interested in the practice of deception detection become experts in reading the verbal and nonverbal signs of lying.

Body language consists of a usually unconscious and involuntary set of gestures and postures that accompany verbal expression. The body language of lies includes:

- Stiff physical expression. The deceptive individual may use few gestures. Arm movement, for example, is typically limited in range and stiff in execution. Hand, arm, and leg movements tend to be directed toward the body of the deceptive person, as if the liar unconsciously wishes to become less conspicuous by occupying less space.

- A person telling a lie tends to avoid making eye contact.

- The hands of a deceptive individual often touch the face, throat, and mouth. A person who is lying will often finger or scratch his nose or behind his ear. He does not touch his chest (heart) with an open hand.

- The liar often exhibits unnatural timing and duration of emotional gestures. The display of emotion may not seem spontaneous. It may be delayed, or it may be carried out longer than normal. Such displays also stop suddenly.

- The verbal expression of emotion and the gestures commonly accompanying that expression are separated when someone is lying. If you give a gift to a friend, and he exclaims "This is great!" then smiles several seconds after the verbal expression, chances are he really does not like the gift at all. In truthful expression, words and gestures coincide.

- Liars have trouble matching nonverbal with verbal expressions. "Did you take the money?" The suspect answers "No," even as he nods his head.

- Those who feign emotion usually express the emotion only with the mouth, whereas general emotion is expressed with the whole face.

- Most liars are defensive.

- Most liars are uncomfortable, so they tend to face away from a questioner.

- The deceptive person tends to put things—a coffee cup, a book, whatever is available—between himself and the questioner.

- Liars typically use the words of a question in their deceptive answer. "Did you steal the money?" The answer: "No I did not steal the money."

- Truthful responses tend to be more natural and casual than deceptive responses. Asked about Monica Lewinsky, President Bill Clinton did not say "I didn't have sex with her," but "I did not have sex with that woman." A statement using a contraction ("didn't") is more likely to be truthful than a statement that uses the complete words ("did not").

- Often, deception may be detected in the structure of the response. Liars may try to avoid lying by declining to make direct statements. Instead, they imply answers rather than denying something outright or directly.

- Deceptive people often talk too much, embroidering their lies with unnecessary detail. Above all, they want to avoid uncomfortable silences in the conversation.

- Deceptive speech is often monotonous and leaves out pronouns, whereas truthful discourse emphasizes pronouns.

- Liars often mumble, speak softly, trail off words; a liar's sentences will likely be muddled rather than emphasized.

- The liar relaxes when the subject is suddenly changed to something neutral.

Good cops have always been skilled human lie detectors. The scientific study of deception detection systematically compiles and analyzes data—the verbal and non-verbal cues of expression—in an effort to rationalize what seasoned interrogators learn by experience and common sense. Deception detection involves learning to ask questions most likely to provoke detectable lies, and it requires heightening ones sensitivity to subtle discrepancies between verbal and nonverbal expression as well as patterns of verbal expression that characterize truthful versus deceptive statements. Accurate deception detection can facilitate vital criminal investigations and increase their accuracy.

The Least You Need to Know

- In most people, lying produces significant physiological effects, some of which may be seen (blushing; sweating) and others measured (elevated blood pressure; rapid, shallow breathing; and decreased electrical resistance of the skin due to increased perspiration).

- The polygraph measures and records the physiological effects associated with anxiety, which, in turn, is associated with telling lies.

- The scientific basis of the polygraph is well established, but practical results depend on the skill and experience of the examiner, factors that introduce a significant element of subjectivity into the examination process.

- The polygraph is used extensively in law enforcement during criminal investigations, but it is often not admitted into evidence by the courts.

- Emerging alternatives to the traditional polygraph are the computer voice stress analyzer (which correlates voice stress with deception) and brain fingerprinting (which monitors the p300 brain wave patterns associated with recognition of a familiar stimulus).

- Most recently, forensic psychology has focused on the observational aspects of deception detection, which has reduced dependency on mechanical methods of "lie detection."

Chapter 20

Beyond the Fringe

In This Chapter

- ◆ The truth about the investigative use of "truth serum"
- ◆ Hypnosis in police work
- ◆ Problems with testimony under hypnosis
- ◆ Psychic detectives
- ◆ ESP: psychic ability or "cop sense"?

Criminal investigators share with the rest of humanity a basic reality and a common source of frustration. While we travel every which way through the dimension of space, in the dimension of time only one direction, forward, is possible. We cannot go backward to discover for certain what happened in the past.

Investigators have developed various means to compensate for the one-way street of time. In sensitive areas—banks, for example, or retail establishments—video cameras and video recorders make a copy of events. But visions of Big Brother notwithstanding, universal surveillance and recording are impossible. Plentiful as they may seem these days, cameras and recording devices are actually in very few places.

Over the years, law enforcement agencies have amassed an arsenal of techniques, each aimed at recovering the past in some measure. Fingerprint analysis, for instance, looks for traces of past presence and activity. The forensic autopsy attempts to read a victim's body as a record of past events. Polygraph technology likewise tries to resurrect elapsed events.

All of these techniques and technologies are conventional and widely used. Sometimes, however, the quest for bygone truth has led to unconventional, unusual, and even desperate avenues to the past.

"Truth Serum"

Of the many perils Agent 007 and his fictional ilk face—stretching on the rack, a searing slice up the midline with a laser beam—none is more dreaded than exposure to "truth serum." Why? The name says it all. *Truth serum.* Who can resist it? Get a dose of this, and you spill your guts. You can't help it. You have no choice. Or so goes the popular myth.

What Is It?

Actually, there is nothing miraculous—or irresistible—about "truth serum." Its chemical name is thiopental sodium, but it is better known as Sodium Pentothal, the name trademarked by its manufacturer, Abbott Laboratories.

def•i•ni•tion

Truth serum is the colloquial term for a class of sedatives that reduce inhibition and therefore tend to elicit verbal communication that might otherwise be self-censored or suppressed. The most common truth serum is thiopental sodium, better known by its brand name, Sodium Pentothal.

Physically, Sodium Pentothal is a yellow crystal that can be dissolved in water or alcohol. It has an alliaceous odor, which means it smells like a cross between onions and garlic.

Sodium Pentothal is a fast-acting barbiturate that produces short-term sedation. Thanks to its speed and the brief duration of its effect, it is commonly used as a surgical anesthetic. Within half a minute to a minute of injection into a vein, the patient is unconscious—albeit only for a few minutes. Therefore, the sedative is often used to induce initial unconsciousness to give slower but longer-acting anesthetics time to work. It's also the first drug administered in execution by lethal injection; the Sodium Pentothal is not itself delivered in a lethal dose, but it puts the condemned person into a deep sleep prior to the administration of a paralyzing agent (such as pancuronium bromide) and a toxic agent (potassium chloride, which induces cardiac arrest).

Sodium Pentothal is the most familiar "truth serum"; however, a related substance, sodium amytol, is also sometimes used. In the past, other sedatives—scopolamine and hyascine—were similarly employed to elicit verbal information.

Does It Work?

In lesser doses than those given to surgical patients, Sodium Pentothal slows the metabolism and minimizes stress but leaves the subject conscious. In reducing the level of stress, it also reduces the inhibitions that typically act as self-censors in most of us, holding us back from speaking our minds or revealing embarrassing (or potentially incriminating) truths.

There's a very old saying, *In vino veritas*—"In wine there is truth." And most of us are familiar with the bibulous friend who talks out of school when in his cups. Under the influence, many of us have, alas, said things we later regret having let slip. The action of Sodium Pentothal is similar to that of alcohol. A depressant, it acts first to depress the mechanisms of self-censorship and inhibition.

In psychotherapy, psychiatrists use Sodium Pentothal as a narcoanalysis agent, a drug to help elicit recall of events and facilitate the expression of feelings. In a criminal justice setting, just because the subject's inhibitions are neutralized does not mean that he will begin spewing out incriminating truths. Careful, focused questions must be asked—and even then, there's no guarantee that the forthcoming information will be useful or accurate.

Will the Courts Accept It?

In the end, Sodium Pentothal is just one more investigative tool, and, in fact, it's rarely used in law enforcement except as a last resort. Indeed, rather than administer Sodium Pentothal to a *suspect*, it's more likely that the *victim* of a violent crime who may be suffering some form of traumatic amnesia (a psychological process that may block out acutely painful memories) would be treated with the drug in the hope that it might enable him or her to recall relevant details of the crime and the perpetrator.

Sodium Pentothal is a powerful narcotic that must be administered by a physician (usually a psychiatrist), preferably in a hospital setting, so that the subject can be monitored. As with any strong sedative agent, there is danger of an adverse reaction, which may require prompt medical action.

As if this weren't problem enough for law enforcement, no American court officially recognizes the reliability of truth serums, and testimony or confession obtained under the influence of this (or any other) narcotic is inadmissible as evidence. The courts exclude all testimony, including confession, that is not the product of fully conscious free will.

You Are Getting Sleepy ...

Late in the nineteenth century, Sigmund Freud formulated his theory of the unconscious as the great repository of powerful motives that shape particular actions and even our entire lives, yet keeps these motives secret from our conscious awareness. Freud reasoned that if we could obtain conscious access to the realm of the unconscious, we would gain valuable insight into ourselves and, in cases of certain mental illnesses, even help effect a cure.

Eventually, Freud developed psychoanalysis, a method in which a patient, awake and alert but relaxed, lets his or her mind wander in free association and, sometimes prompted by the therapist, gains access to the unconscious mind. Freud arrived at this method first by way of hypnosis, which he saw used by the French psychiatrist Jean Martin Charcot (1825–1893) in an attempt to discover an organic basis for so-called hysterical illnesses.

def•i•ni•tion

Hypnosis can be described as a special psychological state that outwardly resembles sleep but is really an altered form of the ordinary conscious state. In hypnosis, the subject shows increased receptiveness and responsiveness, which raise inner perceptions to the same level as perceptions normally created only by external reality. Thus the hypnotized subject can be induced to imagine a reality that is as present and real to him as if it existed externally.

Hypnotic regression uses hypnosis to elicit recall of "lost" memories, memories typically repressed because the conscious mind finds them painful or traumatic.

Hypnotic Regression

Charcot didn't invent hypnosis, the origin of which is as ancient as sorcery, magic, and religious ritual. Scientific interest in hypnosis began toward the end of the eighteenth century with the work of the Viennese physician Franz Mesmer (from whose name the word *mesmerize* comes), but Charcot was the first to use it seriously and methodically in a medical context. In his early work, Freud and an associate, Josef Breuer, employed it specifically to help neurotic patients recover childhood memories that, because they were painful, had been totally repressed. Although forgotten by the conscious mind, the memories were still locked in the unconscious, where they caused mental illness, psychosomatic symptoms, or even motivated self-destructive acts.

In the early development of psychoanalysis, then, Freud and others practiced *hypnotic regression*, using hypnosis to, in effect, travel backward in time. More recently, hypnotic regression has appeared to some law enforcement professionals as a promising alternative to "truth serum," a way to induce recall of memories that, for some reason—typically because they are intensely painful—have been repressed.

Not an Option for Suspects

Hypnosis is used in law enforcement situations, but these days, less and less frequently. In contrast to truth serum, hypnosis is never used on suspects. Suspect testimony obtained under hypnosis is completely inadmissible in court and, indeed, may even taint other testimony, if a defense attorney can persuade a jury that his or her client had been unduly influenced by the hypnotist or even by the process of hypnosis itself.

However, hypnosis has been used on crime victims as well as witnesses to attempt to recover repressed memories and details of the crime and perpetrator. These individuals submit to hypnosis on a strictly voluntary basis, and the hypnosis, including the interrogation, is conducted by a medical specialist (usually a psychiatrist) trained in hypnotic technique. The session is usually recorded and videotaped.

Digression: A Story of Alien Abduction

Victims and witnesses have apparently recalled astonishing things under hypnosis, including the details of crimes and even the identity of perpetrators. Many law enforcement professionals and others have hailed hypnosis as a tool of extraordinary, even miraculous, utility.

But while undergoing hypnotic regression, some people have recalled events far more extraordinary than any crime. And this gives many police and judicial officials pause. Take the case of Betty and Barney Hill.

On the night of September 19, 1961, the Hills were returning to their Portsmouth, New Hampshire, home after a visit to Niagara Falls. They were driving south on Route 3 through the White Mountains, when at 10 P.M., near Groveton, some 70 miles south of the Canadian border, Betty noticed a bright star or planet just below the moon. An hour later, when the Hills were just south of Lancaster, a companion object appeared near the planet.

The Hills stopped their car and observed the object through binoculars. It had red, amber, green, and blue flashing lights. It appeared to have a fuselage shape, but no wings, and it flew in what Barney Hill described as a "steplike flight pattern, dropping vertically, leveling off, then tilting upward again." It was absolutely silent.

By the Numbers

A number of studies, most recently one conducted at Ohio State University and released in August 2001, suggest that hypnosis cannot help the subject to recover lost memories, but does tend to make the subject more confident in the validity of false memories—including memories that are entirely fabricated by the unconscious mind and bear little or no relation to external events.

The Hills resumed driving, and the object kept pace with their car. South of Indian Head, the object moved closer, and Betty saw a change to a steady white glow in the pattern of the flashing multicolored lights. When the object stopped to hover about 100 feet above the ground, the Hills stopped their car. Barney got out and approached the object, which now appeared to be a huge glowing disc with a double row of windows curved around its perimeter. Fifty feet from the object, using his binoculars, he could see eight to eleven humanlike creatures through the windows. They stood still at first, then began to scurry about within the ship, apparently manipulating controls on the wall. One of the figures remained at the window, gazing at Barney Hill.

At this point, two finlike projections, a red light on the tip of each, slid out of the sides of the ship as Betty, waiting in the car, heard Barney yell, "I don't believe it … I don't believe it …. This is ridiculous."

Barney ran back to the car, shouting that they were going to be captured. He put the car into gear, stepped on the gas, and took off down the highway. Strange beeping sounds, apparently coming from behind the car, made the vehicle vibrate. Both Betty and Barney Hill were overcome by a peculiar sensation of "tingling drowsiness." A while later, the beeps resumed. Then the Hills continued home without further incident—except that they arrived at 5 A.M., about two hours later than they should have. They had lost two hours out of their lives—two hours of which they had no conscious memory.

In the days, weeks, and months that followed, both of the Hills were plagued by nightmares, unbearable feelings of anxiety, insomnia, and in Barney's case, the development of duodenal ulcers. They sought psychiatric help and were given regressive hypnosis therapy, during which they apparently recovered the two missing hours.

Under hypnosis, Betty related how a group of humanoid beings approached their stopped car, opened the door of the vehicle, and pointed a small device at her. ("It could have been a pencil," she reported.) Independently, both of the Hills described being taken aboard an alien ship and given quasi-medical physical examinations. Betty recalled:

> Most of the men are my height …. None is as tall as Barney, so I would judge them to be 5' to 5'4". Their chests are larger than ours; their noses were larger than the average size although I have seen people with noses like theirs—like Jimmy Durante. Their complexions were of a gray tone; like gray paint with a black base; their lips were of a bluish tint. Hair and eyes were very dark, possibly black.
>
> In a sense, they looked like mongoloids …. This sort of round face and broad forehead, along with a certain type of coarseness. The surface of their skin seemed to be a bluish gray, but probably whiter than that. Their eyes moved, and they had pupils. Somehow, I had the feeling they were more like cats' eyes.

Barney Hill's description differed in some significant details, particularly concerning the hair and nose of the extraterrestrials:

> The men had rather odd-shaped heads, with a large cranium, diminishing in size as it got toward the chin. And the eyes continued around to the sides of their heads, so that it appeared that they could see several degrees beyond the lateral extent of our vision. This was startling to me …. [The mouth] was much like when you draw one horizontal line with a short perpendicular line on each end. The horizontal line would represent lips without the muscle we have. And it would part slightly as they made this mumumumummming sound. The texture of the skin, as I remember it from this quick glance, was grayish, almost metallic looking. I didn't notice any hair—or headgear for that matter. I didn't notice any proboscis, there just seemed to be two slits that represented the nostrils.

The beings, according to the Hills, communicated among themselves through audible language ("mumumumumming sound"), yet communicated with the Hills through telepathy in English (according to Betty, "with an accent"). "I did not hear an actual voice," Barney Hill reported. "But in my mind, I knew what he was saying. It wasn't as if he were talking to me with my eyes open, and he was sitting across the room from me. It was more as if the words were there, a part of me, and he was outside the actual creation of the words themselves."

Following six months of this regressive hypnosis therapy, the emotional state of both Betty and Barney Hill improved markedly.

Case in Point

In a 2001 study, Professor Joseph Green of Ohio State University questioned 96 college students about the date of certain historical events. Half of this group answered the questions under hypnosis, while the other half answered after performing a relaxation exercise. After the test, the students were asked to rate their confidence in their answers. Regardless of whether they were right or wrong, all subjects were told they had given at least one wrong answer. They were allowed to change their answers and to rank their confidence in the revised answers. Green found no difference in the accuracy of the hypnotized students versus the other group; however, the hypnotized subjects changed significantly fewer responses. Green concluded: "While hypnosis does not enhance the reliability of memory, there is some evidence that hypnosis leads to increased confidence in memories."

Those who believe the earth is regularly visited by extraterrestrials point to the regressive hypnosis of Betty and Barney Hill as compelling evidence in support of their belief. Those who are skeptical about "close encounters of the third kind" suggest that Betty and Barney Hill were victims of the inadequacies of regressive hypnosis. Subjected to it, critics say, people "recall" all sorts of peculiar things.

What the Courts Say

Testimony obtained from victims and witnesses under hypnosis was newsworthy but not rare in American courtrooms during the 1970s and again during the early to mid-1990s. As it became increasingly apparent, however, that much of this testimony was contradicted by attempts to corroborate it independently, law enforcement and legal professionals began to conclude that hypnotic regression was unreliable. Defense attorneys now turn to recent studies, including the one conducted at Ohio State University in 2001, for powerful ammunition to demolish incriminating victim and witness testimony obtained under hypnosis.

Psychic Hotline

Psychic detectives (or PDs) are civilians who claim psychic power and offer to use it to help law enforcement agencies solve crimes. In desperation, numerous police agencies have called on PDs; indeed, there is a sufficient body of psychic detective cases to support a popular "reality-based" television series, *Psychic Detectives*, which premiered in 2004 on the Court TV cable network. (Broadcast television's NBC offers a fictional series, *Medium*, which premiered in 2005.)

When the work of the psychic apparently leads to the solution of a seemingly hopeless case, tabloid magazines and tabloid TV shows rush in with ample coverage. In contrast, the failures and the outright phonies receive little if any media notice. Let's look at a few documented examples of psychic detectives helping to solve crimes.

Dauphine, France, 1662

One day, Jacques Aymar, a "water witch"—a person who claims to be able to locate sources of underground water with a divining rod—finds not water, but the severed head of a woman. The dead woman's face is recognized by a villager, and her head is brought back in a sack to her husband. Approaching the man's house, Aymar feels his divining rod vibrate. As the widower approaches, the rod vibrates so strongly that the man, seeing it, suddenly flees—and is later apprehended, charged, and convicted of his wife's murder. Subsequently, local police call on Aymar to solve other crimes.

Manville, Alberta, 1928

A famed Austrian medium, Maximilien Langsner, is invited by Canadian police to work on an apparently unsolvable multiple murder case. A woman, her son, and two workers are found dead on a Manville farm. Vernon Booher, the only surviving son, claims he discovered the bodies after returning home. The murder weapon, a rifle, belongs to a neighbor, Charles Stephenson, who says the weapon had been stolen from his home the week before the murders. Police detain Booher in a holding cell. Langsner sits outside of the cell and claims to read Booher's thoughts. The psychic reports that Booher had slipped out of church and had stolen the rifle. According to Langsner, Booher wanted to marry a girl of whom his mother disapproved. A quarrel ensued over this, and it ended with Booher killing everyone in the house. Confronted with this psychic report, Booher breaks down, confesses, and is tried and hanged.

Williston, Florida, 1997

On March 24, 1994, 76-year-old Norman Lewis goes missing in Williston, Florida, and stays missing for two years. His family asks local police to consult a psychic. Investigator Brian Hewitt is acquainted with Noreen Reiner, a self-proclaimed psychic who performs a reading in the case. She says that Lewis had traveled in his pickup truck east from his home to a place "where there is ... water in something like a pit." Reiner reports seeing Lewis surrounded by metal. She sees a cliff wall, loose bricks, a railroad track, and a bridge. She also sees the numbers "45" and "21."

After several searches of local bodies of water prove fruitless, police call in U.S. Navy divers to search a flooded limestone quarry. They locate the missing truck and the skeleton of Norman Lewis.

The story of Reiner's "reading" is widely reported and apparently inspires a spate of psychic readings, one of which persuades authorities in Graniteville, Missouri, to drain a three-million-gallon quarry in search of a girl missing for seven years. She is not found.

Intuition on Steroids

The list of apparently psychic solutions to mysteries unsolved by conventional police work goes on and on. Fortunately for the authors, a book on criminal investigation is not the place to debate the nature and validity of psychic insight or extrasensory perception (ESP) and its possible value in criminal investigation. Those interested in obtaining a quick but balanced assessment of Noreen Reiner, perhaps the best-known recent psychic detective, might look up Gary Posner's article, "A Not-So-Psychic Detective? A Case Study of Noreen Reiner's Latest and Greatest 'Success' Story," in *Skeptic* magazine (Vol. 5, No. 4, 1997).

> **Sworn Statement**
>
> Psychics claim their instinctual feelings come from special powers within; detectives say their gut feelings and hunches emanate from years of experience, that they have developed a "cop's sense."
>
> —Harvey Rachlin, "Psychics and Police Work" (*Law and Order* [professional law enforcement journal], June 1995)

Doubtless, some so-called psychics are well-meaning but deluded individuals, while others are out-and-out frauds. Yet some do seem to hit the proverbial nail on the head. Are these individuals possessed of a psychic gift or extrasensory power? Or, as some cops believe, are these civilians no more or less psychic than a really good detective? Perhaps the psychic, like the detective, merely combines keen powers of observation, years of experience, a savvy sense of human behavior, and a talent for putting two and two together to identify and track the most productive clues. Perhaps psychic detectives are just very capable detectives, people who, like any veteran criminal investigator, have extensively developed their intuition—have figuratively put their gut instincts on steroids, as it were, pumped them up, and become acutely sensitive and always attentive to what their intuition tells them.

The Least You Need to Know

- Sodium Pentothal is a narcotic that lowers inhibitions and, therefore, may loosen the tongue; despite its popular name, however, it is far from being an infallible truth serum and is rarely used by law enforcement agencies.

- In the 1970s and in the early to mid 1990s, hypnosis (especially hypnotic regression) was occasionally used on victims and witnesses to recover "lost" memories of crimes.

- Recent studies suggest that hypnosis cannot recover memories and may instead elicit the fabrication of false memories.

- Psychic detectives—civilian psychics who offer help to criminal investigators— have received much attention in the popular press.

- Veteran cops say all really good detectives are, in a sense, psychic; that is, they have "cop sense"—keenly developed intuition based on the perceptive interpretation of the subtle facts and clues most people miss.

Part 5

Crime in a Crystal Ball

The two chapters in this part look toward the future—the future of crime and the future of the police and scientific response to crime. Our outlook is based on current trends in crime, with an emphasis on the explosion of "cyber crimes," including identity theft, and the continued prospect of terrorism. So far as police work is concerned, the emphasis will be on the increasingly efficient acquisition and processing of information—intelligence—and the development of effective alternatives to deadly force.

We end with how, in the future, police and the society they serve and protect will have to continue to explore, improve, and strengthen their relationship with one another.

Chapter 21

Future Crime

In This Chapter

- Identifying crime trends
- Crime and the economy
- The emerging drug scene
- Data, computer, and identity crime
- Cyber terrorism and Internet child pornography
- Desktop counterfeiting

In the early days of organized police forces, the work of law enforcement was a business of reaction. A crime occurred; the police gave chase. Later, police departments attempted not merely to react to crime, but to prevent it, mainly by maintaining highly visible patrols on the streets. As police agencies grew increasingly sophisticated, they began to keep statistical records in an attempt to anticipate where and when crimes were most likely to occur. This allowed police administrators to deploy their forces more efficiently, putting more cops in high-crime areas during high-crime periods. The idea was to be proactive rather than merely reactive.

Most recently, police agencies have been applying similar principles to long-term planning in an attempt to anticipate crime trends and the nature of crime in the future.

Based on Current Statistics ...

Predicting the future is a highly seductive occupation. It's exhilarating to exercise the imagination, and no one can prove you wrong—at least not for years or decades to come. Criminal justice professionals try to base their predictions on extrapolation from hard statistical data rather than on unbridled imagination. Crime statistics are valuable as a measure of the current state of society and the current state of law enforcement. They also provide a valuable basis for projecting future trends.

Public Perception Versus the Numbers

As mentioned in the first chapter of this book, crime is very high on the list of our concerns. Ask most people about crime, and they'll tell you that it continually increases.

def•i•ni•tion

The **crime rate** is the number of crimes in a given period (usually a month or a year) among a fixed sample number of persons within a given population. The FBI reports the U.S. crime rate in terms of number of crimes per 100,000 persons.

This is a common popular perception, but over the past decade, the *crime rate* has actually declined. For example, in 1999, according to the FBI's *Uniform Crime Reports*, one of the standard digests of crime statistics in the United States, 11,634,378 crimes were reported. The number fell to 11,608,070 in 2000, a drop of 0.2 percent. This translates to a crime rate of 4,266.5 crimes per 100,000 inhabitants of the United States in 1999, and 4,124.8 in 2000.

After declining during the late 1990s, crime rates have been climbing modestly since 2001. If we take a truly long view, encompassing 50 years or so, crime rates today remain near their all-time highs since law enforcement agencies began recording reliable statistics. And it's no wonder that Americans are concerned about crime. Despite the modest (but significant) declines in the crime rate during recent years, the FBI's most recent (2005) "Crime Clock" reveals the following:

- One murder every 31.5 minutes
- One forcible rape every 5.6 minutes
- One robbery every 1.3 minutes
- One aggravated assault every 36.5 seconds
- One burglary every 14.6 seconds

- One motor vehicle theft every 25.5 seconds

- One larceny-theft every 4.7 seconds

In all, in the United States, one violent crime is committed every 22.7 seconds and one property crime every 3.1 seconds.

By the Numbers

The new century has brought a modest increase in the general crime rate. In 2001, 11,849,006 crimes were reported, a rate of 4,160.5 per 100,000 population. This was an increase of 0.9 percent over 2000. Nevertheless, even this represents a decrease in the crime rate of 26.5 percent since 1992. Preliminary data for 2006 showed some significant increases in the crime rate over 2005—for example, the number of robberies increased by 9.7 percent; murder, 1.4 percent; and aggravated assault, 1.2 percent (forcible rape was down 0.1 percent).

What's Hot

In the first year of the twenty-first century, 60 percent of all crimes committed were classified as instances of larceny-theft, which FBI crime statisticians define as "the unlawful taking, carrying, leading, or riding away of property from the possession or constructive possession of another. It includes crimes such as shoplifting, pickpocketing, purse snatching, thefts from motor vehicles, thefts of motor vehicle parts and accessories, bicycle thefts, etc., in which no use of force, violence, or fraud occurs." This is nonviolent, garden-variety theft, and while the writers of thriller cop fiction will never pay much attention to it, it is by far the most common type of crime. There is no reason to believe that it will be any less prevalent in the future.

In fact, most crimes are property crimes: burglary accounted for 17.7 percent of crimes reported in 2000; motor vehicle theft, 10 percent; robbery, 3.5 percent. Therefore, 91.2 percent of all crimes reported in 2000 were crimes against property.

What's Not

Murder, rape, and other violent crimes constitute a relatively small fraction of crimes reported: murder, 0.1 percent; forcible rape, 0.8 percent; *aggravated assault*, 7.8 percent.

def•i•ni•tion

Also called felonious assault, **aggravated assault** is an unlawful attack by one person against another for the purpose of inflicting severe bodily injury.

Yet if these are not statistically America's hottest crimes, they are nevertheless frighteningly prevalent. In a 1996 Scripps syndicated article, "Tracking the Crime Curve into the Future," Paul Akers reported that about 10 million violent victimizations occur annually in the United States. Americans, according to Akers, are twice as likely to be assaulted, robbed at gunpoint, raped, or abducted than they are to be seriously injured in an automobile accident.

Optimists look at the recent overall decline in crime (since the early 1990s) and attribute it to better policing and stricter law enforcement. Pessimists say that it is merely due to the aging of the baby boomer generation—older adults commit fewer crimes than youngsters—and they point out that, during the first decade of the twenty-first century, there will be a significant spike in the U.S. male population, ages 14 to 17. It is among this group that violent crime is most prevalent. Disturbingly, while the murder rate has generally declined during the 1990s, it has increased among teens. For example, during 1990 to 1994, the teen murder rate grew by 22 percent.

Statistically dwarfed by property crimes, violent crimes are likely to remain a very serious problem in the future, and if the violent activity among male teens is any indication, we may begin to witness an increasingly significant reversal of the decline in violent crime since the early 1990s.

Economy and Opportunity

For much of the 1990s, Americans enjoyed economically prosperous times, with unemployment levels at unprecedented lows—near 4 percent nationally, and in some areas even lower. Since most crimes are property crimes, some of the decline in crime during the decade of the 1990s may well be attributable to general prosperity.

Hard Times and Crime

As the twentieth century drew to a close, unemployment rose, the economy retreated somewhat, and the crime rate rose modestly. Several recent studies suggest that the rate of unemployment directly affects the crime rate. Higher unemployment means more crime.

Case in Point

Economists Steven Raphael (UC, San Diego) and Rudolf Winter-Ebner (University of Linz, Austria) published a report in 1998 indicating the impact of unemployment on crime. Analyzing statistics from 1970 through a portion of the 1990s, the authors noted a correlation between the economy and the crime rate. Especially dramatic was the period from 1992 to 1996, a time of falling unemployment that saw a decline in crime. The economists argue that a drop of two percentage points in unemployment can be expected to bring a 9 percent decline in burglary, a 14 percent decline in rape and robbery, and a 30 percent decline in assault. Raphael and Winter-Ebner claim that had unemployment been 1 percent higher in 1992, there would have been almost half a million more crimes in the United States.

New Opportunities

Economic conditions don't affect the crime rate alone (lower unemployment, less crime; higher unemployment, more crime); they also create new opportunities for criminals.

The FBI *Uniform Crime Reports* does not deal with so-called "white collar" crime—fraud, embezzlement, and the like—yet over the past 20 years or so these areas of criminal enterprise have seen significant growth. Many criminals have moved away from lifting physical merchandise to siphoning off information. This makes sense when you consider that, these days, money is less a physical thing than a set of digital records in a vast computer network. Cash doesn't change *hands*, it merely changes *number.* The typical business transaction isn't between a *you* and a *me*, but between a magnetic stripe on a credit card and a chunk of data stored somewhere in the electronic ether. Techno crime is an intense growth area in criminal enterprise, which we'll discuss in a moment.

By the Numbers

As of 2006, it is estimated that health-care fraud amounts to nearly $3 billion a year.

New Victims: Elder Crime

The tale of the especially despicable criminal who preys upon the elderly is at least as old as the two wicked daughters of Shakespeare's *King Lear,* but the fact that more people are living into advanced old age these days suggests that financial exploitation of elderly citizens by family members, fiduciaries, care givers, and acquaintances will continue to rise.

The special needs of the elderly also provide various unscrupulous individuals, especially in the medical, legal, and insurance fields, ample opportunity to rip off the federal health-care system, as well as private insurers.

The Drug Scene

Prior to the 1960s, illicit drug use was a problem confined to "poor neighborhoods" and "the criminal classes." During the 1960s, the use of such substances as marijuana, amphetamines, tranquilizers, cocaine, and hallucinogens (especially LSD) became widespread as drugs were increasingly perceived as "recreational" or even "mind expanding." Illicit drug use reached epidemic proportions during the 1960s, and it continues to be very serious, a powerful driver of organized crime on a national and international scale.

To gauge trends in illicit drug use, the U.S. Department of Health and Human Services closely monitors drug-related visits to the emergency rooms (emergency departments, or EDs) of U.S. hospitals. Of an estimated 106 million ED visits in the United States during 2004, the department reported that 1,997,993 were drug-related. (30 percent involved illicit drugs only; 25 percent involved pharmaceuticals only; 15 percent involved illicit drugs and alcohol; 8 percent involved illicit drugs with pharmaceuticals; and 14 percent involved illicit drugs with pharmaceuticals and alcohol). Although these figures suggest a high level of drug abuse, they are not significantly higher overall than they have been in recent years.

New Designs

If, on balance, drug use is not sharply on the rise, recent years have seen an influx of new so-called "designer drugs"—clandestinely produced drugs that are structurally and pharmacologically similar to controlled substances (federally regulated narcotics), but are not themselves controlled substances. Since 1987, federal statutes have prohibited the manufacture and use of these "controlled substance analogs."

In 2001, the most important designer drug was MDMA, popularly called Ecstasy, and also known as XTC, Adam, hug, beans, and the love drug. MDMA has stimulant (amphetamine-like) and hallucinogenic (LSD-like) properties and is chemically similar to methamphetamine, methylenedioxyamphetamine (MDA), and mescaline, all drugs known to cause brain damage. High doses can cause a sharp increase in body temperature (a condition called malignant hyperthermia), leading to muscle breakdown and kidney and cardiovascular system failure.

U.S. Department of Health and Human Services data indicated that while MDMA was once used primarily at dance clubs, youth parties—raves—and what the department described as "the college scene," it was reported in 2001 as more widely used and, in fact, was the most prominent stimulant used in Chicago. In Denver, many singles' bars were selling it illegally. It had become the drug of choice among white middle class young adults in Washington, D.C. In Miami in 1999, eight MDMA-related deaths were reported. Five were reported in Minneapolis/St. Paul. In Boston during the first three quarters of 2000, MDMA was the most frequently mentioned drug in telephone calls to the Poison Control Center.

The fact that the United States Drug Enforcement Administration (DEA) seized 13,342 MDMA tablets in 1996 and 949,257 in 2000 caused great alarm, indicating that the use of this dangerous drug would skyrocket in the twenty-first century and further suggesting that additional synthetic drugs would be rapidly developed and abused. In fact, by 2005, it became clear that 2001 was the peak of MDMA use, and in the first five years of the new century, use of the drug decreased significantly.

Even as MDMA use has declined, production and use of another "designer"—or synthetic—drug, one even more dangerous, has rapidly increased.

Methamphetamine is a highly addictive stimulant that resembles amphetamine but produces stronger and longer lasting effects that are more harmful to the central nervous system. It is produced in clandestine meth labs, the number of which have greatly increased in the United States in recent years, especially in rural areas. Not only is the drug dangerous, the manufacturing process, which involves toxic and potentially explosive chemicals, is extremely hazardous.

New Users

In recent years, it has become distressingly evident that illicit drugs have new users: the very young. From 1999 to 2000, the use of MDMA increased among eighth, tenth, and twelfth graders. Among eighth graders, MDMA use increased from 1.7 percent in 1999 to 3.1 percent in 2000. Among tenth graders, the increase was from 4.4 percent to 5.4 percent. Among twelfth graders, it rose from 5.6 percent to 8.2 percent. Alarming as these increases are, they seem to have leveled off from 2000 to 2001, and from 2001 to 2002.

What is true of MDMA use is generally true of other commonly abused or illicit drugs as well: abuse has become prevalent among increasingly younger groups; however, it does appear to be leveling off. For example, a 2003 survey of twelfth graders showed that 3.2 percent had used methamphetamine. In 2005, that figure had dropped to 2.5 percent.

Techno Crime

It is a cliché to remark that our lives these days are carried along on the endless stream of zeroes and ones that is cyberspace. Our personal and financial data is, it seems, everywhere. In the case of our homes and places of business, we know where the keys are—in our pocket or purse. In the case of our digital lives, well, who knows who has the keys?

Credit Card Crime

It is a rare day that most of us go to the mail box without getting an offer for a credit card. Most Americans carry upward of half a dozen cards; many have far more.

By the Numbers

In 1977, there were 8.2 million Visa and MasterCards in use. In 2001, there were 44.1 million. In 1982 (the first year statistics were kept), Visa and MasterCard reported writing off $15.88 million in fraudulent charges. In 2001, the companies reported a write-off of $142.27 million.

Unfortunately, credit cards are very easy to use fraudulently. All that is required is information—not even the physical card itself, just the number on it. This can be obtained from discarded receipts or from rifling through a person's mail. With more and more purchases being made online, a computer-savvy thief can obtain credit card numbers without having to get anywhere near the victim. An enterprising cyber thief can set up a website advertising some entirely fictitious product, include an online purchasing form, and then collect credit card numbers along with names and mailing addresses. Despite the development of various security countermeasures, this type of crime is likely only to increase.

ATM Spoofing

A whole generation of Americans may never see the inside of a bank. Automated teller machines (ATMs) proliferate across the landscape. One obvious risk of using these typically very exposed machines is getting robbed at gunpoint as you withdraw your cash. But no truly enterprising ATM thief uses a gun.

Unlike credit cards, ATM cards require a password—a personal identification number, or PIN—to work. This is an excellent security measure, but hardly unbreakable.

Recently, in a Connecticut mall, thieves set up a fake ATM, which looked and worked just like a real one. The only difference was that after you fed it your card and typed in your PIN, it reported itself out of order. However, it had recorded both the card information (account number and name of user) and the PIN. Using this information, thieves were able to withdraw funds from the accounts of various victims.

It is also possible to stake out a legitimate ATM, focus a video camera on the keypad, and record keystrokes. When a PIN is successfully recorded, the thief runs to the machine and looks for a discarded receipt—many people throw them down or even leave them in the ATM's dispenser slot. If he finds a receipt, he can put it together with the PIN and make a withdrawal.

Identity Theft

But why stop at fraudulently charging a few items with a credit card number or stealing a few dollars from an ATM? Increasingly, many techno criminals do not, in fact, stop at these.

Just what is *identity theft?* Here's an example. After obtaining someone's personal data, a convicted felon charged some $100,000 on fraudulent credit cards, obtained a federal home loan, and bought homes, motorcycles, and handguns in the victim's name. Then he decided, apparently just for fun, to give the digital knife a twist by taunting his victim with phone calls, telling him that he could continue assuming the man's identity for as

def•i•ni•tion

Identity theft, also called identity fraud, is a federal crime in which someone wrongfully obtains and uses another person's personal data in some way that involves fraud or deception, usually for economic gain.

long as he wanted because identity theft was not a federal crime (as it was not, at that time). Finally, the thief filed for bankruptcy—in the victim's name.

The victim and his wife had to spend some $15,000 and more than four years of their lives restoring their credit and reputation. The criminal, apprehended at last, served nothing more than a brief sentence for making a false statement to procure a firearm. It was this case, and others like it, that moved Congress in 1998 to create a new federal offense: identity theft.

It does not require a James Bond to steal the identity of another person. Nor does it even require picking the victim's pocket or breaking into his or her home or place of business.

Identity thieves may engage in shoulder surfing—surreptitiously looking over your shoulder as you punch in your telephone calling card number on a public phone or your PIN at an ATM. They may also eavesdrop as you give your credit card number over the telephone to a hotel or rental car company.

Case in Point

Discarded junk mail is a treasure trove for identity thieves, who pore through garbage looking for "preapproved" credit cards, which they may be able to activate. Word to the wise: cut up—in small pieces—any unwanted or expired credit cards, and consider purchasing a shredder to destroy any discarded junk mail or documents bearing your financial data.

An identity thief may also engage in dumpster diving—going through your garbage cans, dumpster, or trash bin looking for copies of checks, credit card or bank statements, or other records that bear your name, address, telephone number, and various financial account numbers.

Computer-savvy identity thieves obtain personal information of all sorts from the Internet, often setting up phony websites to capture victim information.

Once the identity thief has sufficient identifying information about an individual, the thief can effectively take over that person's identity and use it to make applications for loans and credit cards, withdraw money from bank accounts, use telephone calling cards, and so on. Identity theft is very clearly an alarming growth area in criminal enterprise.

Cyber Crime

As the Model T automobile transformed America's geographical landscape early in the twentieth century, so the development of the personal computer and the related evolution of the Internet have transformed the intellectual, commercial, and communications landscape. Something this sweeping, this pervasive, this important has to have a dark side. Right? Right.

Hacking It

A few years ago, when the Internet was in its infancy and when communication between and among computers was a highly esoteric field, a new kind of criminal came into being: the hacker. Actually, back then, many people did not consider the hacker a criminal, but rather a kind of merry prankster, a techno wit who delighted in tweaking the nose of big business and big government by sneaking into computer systems and leaving little calling cards, something in the nature of digital graffiti—nothing more, just a token to show he or she had been there. As the term is used today, a hacker is a person who surreptitiously and illicitly breaks into computer systems to disrupt them or to obtain data, usually, but not always, for financial gain.

Hackers may engage in industrial espionage or even espionage against the government. They may be identity thieves. They may commit credit card fraud. Some may be industrial or commercial saboteurs, disseminating computer viruses, worms, or other malicious programs to disrupt private and corporate computer systems. Or they may find ways to overload a commercial website, effectively bringing it to a halt and preventing any transactions from taking place (this is known as a "denial of service" attack).

Going Phishing

Phishing is a computer crime carried out not by phishermen, but by phishers. Typically, a phisher creates an e-mail or instant message that masquerades as a communication from some legitimate, trusted source, such as a credit card company, a bank, even the IRS. The recipient of the e-mail or instant message is instructed to click on a link to a website, which looks like a trusted corporate or institutional site.

The victim is typically asked to fill out an online form, which asks for such information as credit card numbers, bank account numbers, addresses, phone numbers, Social Security numbers, and the like on the pretext of updating account information or processing some special payment. In this way, the phisher acquires the victim's identity and can use it to open phony credit accounts in the victim's name and even raid legitimate bank accounts.

> **By the Numbers**
>
> It is estimated that between May 2004 and May 2005, about 1.2 million computer users in the United States suffered losses due to phishing schemes, representing some $929 million. American businesses lose an estimated $2 billion annually in phishing-related frauds.

Cyber Terror

Computer criminals may be pranksters, they may be vandals, they may be spies, they may be thieves. They may also be terrorists. The potential harm cyber terrorists might cause is truly terrifying. They could, for example, hack into the computer that controls the mix of ingredients in a pharmaceutical or food-processing plant. They could detonate explosive devices from remote locations. They could cause massive disruption of financial institutions and stock exchanges. They could hack into the computers at the heart of the air traffic control system. They could shut off city water supplies or regional electric service.

So far, the world has seen very little of this, but it is all too apparent that cyber terror offers a vast field for future crime.

Child Porn

The Internet has been compared to the Wild West, a digital Great Plains free of censorship and free of government regulation—a vast space in which anything and everything goes.

No freedom, of course, comes without a price. The anonymity of the Internet, the ability to plug into the world without being seen or heard or otherwise identified, has led to the proliferation of pornography on the World Wide Web. Some of this material is easy enough to take or leave as one wishes, but a portion of the Internet porn business exploits children and may lead to abduction, child rape, and even worse.

Who could have anticipated that the miracle of civilization embodied in the Internet would be used for such purposes? The only possible answer is that much of the future consists, precisely, of the unanticipated.

The New Counterfeiters

You've seen those gangster movies, circa 1940: the counterfeiting genius who has managed to engrave near-perfect plates, who has formulated near-perfect paper, who has compounded near-perfect inks. Ah, the counterfeiter! For years, he was the most exalted of criminals, highly skilled, practically a magician, and certainly a genius.

Today, just about anyone with a personal computer, halfway decent desktop publishing software, a modest desktop scanner, and a good color printer can counterfeit checks and currency. At least one government agency has called *desktop counterfeiting* the gravest threat to U.S. currency today.

def•i•ni•tion

Desktop counterfeiting is the use of readily available personal computer equipment, scanners, color copiers, and color printers to produce bogus currency, checks, and other documents.

But in addition to printing money, desktop counterfeiters have pulled off other feats of digital fakery. For instance: in 1989, an international counterfeiting ring bilked Los Angeles banking giant First Interstate Bancorp out of $750,000 by stealing a legitimate corporate dividend check, scanning it (including the authorized signature) into a computer, then electronically altering the amount and the name of the payee.

The fake was then printed out on a laser printer and successfully presented at the bank for payment.

Or this: in 1993, Ahmed Abdullah al-Ashmouny, a citizen of Egypt, was indicted in the United States for counterfeiting thousands of visas on a color copier and selling them to other Egyptians, including followers of accused terrorist leader Sheik Omar Abdel Rahman. (Rahman is a New Jersey–based Muslim cleric now serving a life sentence in the United States for conspiring to assassinate Egyptian President Hosni Mubarak and blow up five New York City landmarks, including the World Trade Center, which was bombed in 1993.) It is not known how many persons have used these visas to enter the United States illegally. Nor is it known how many were—or are—the associates, comrades, and colleagues of those who attacked America on September 11, 2001.

The Least You Need to Know

- Police agencies use current statistics to spot crime trends in order to formulate future law enforcement plans.

- The state of the economy appears to be an important predictor of the general crime rate: low unemployment is associated with lower crime rates, high unemployment with higher crime rates.

- The emergence of "designer drugs" and the widespread use of illicit drugs among younger people are two leading trends in drug-related crime.

- The Internet and the continued evolution of a digital economy offer expanding possibilities for such cyber crimes as credit card fraud, ATM fraud, identity theft, computer hacking crimes, phishing schemes, and even cyber terrorism and the exploitation of children through Internet-based child pornography.

- The universal availability of computer-based desktop publishing hardware and software has led to the development of "desktop counterfeiting," a serious threat to U.S. currency, as well as a challenge to all businesses and government agencies that rely on "authentic" documents.

Chapter 22

Future Cops

In This Chapter

- New developments, traditional values
- Crime prevention vs. the Constitution
- New emphasis on security
- Information: the most powerful police weapon
- Nonlethal weapons of the future
- Police and the community: a work in progress

Law enforcement planners think about the future, and they think hard. In 1991, the Society of Police Futurists International (headquartered at Eastern Kentucky University in Richmond, Kentucky) was organized to bring together some of the best thoughts.

The goals of Police Futurists International reflect the major concerns of law enforcement in the years to come: to encourage partnerships between law enforcement, the academic community, and private industry; to develop, analyze, and interpret long-range forecasts; to promote the use of technology; to research and promote creative, innovative, and proactive policing strategies; and to advance ethical behavior in law enforcement. Future police will be more thoroughly integrated into all aspects of the community; they will emphasize proactive and preventive strategies rather than reaction, they will exploit technology, and they will put increasing emphasis on ethics.

New Technologies and Traditional Values

In 1987, filmmaker Paul Verhoeven directed a vision of law enforcement in the near future. The city was Detroit, overrun with crime. Its police force was now managed by a private corporation, which transformed an officer, killed in the line of duty, into an armed and armored cyborg called Robocop. This futuristic vision of a bionic cop proved immensely popular, spinning off more than a few sequels, and it reflected the popular impression that urban crime had become so formidable that only a superhuman robot could fight it.

The fact is that cops really do use robots—right now, today. Well-equipped bomb squads use highly mobile remote-controlled robots, equipped with mechanical arms and capable of real-time video transmission, to investigate and handle potential explosive devices. Such robots can also be used in "urban warfare" scenarios, to seek out hidden gunmen and terrorists without exposing a live officer to gunfire. For that matter, video surveillance cameras, which are proliferating in many public buildings and public areas outdoors, may be seen as robotic extensions of the officers' vision. But police agencies regard all of these "robots," technical marvels though they are, as nothing more or less than tools to make the human cop's job safer and more effective.

Law enforcement is a social service, like government itself, and can never be automated. Cops are, first and foremost, people aiding other people. This requires and will continue to require human responsiveness and human judgment.

Some Things Just Don't Change

As discussed in the preceding chapter, technology, especially the information technology that has been enabled by the personal computer and the Internet, has opened new fields of techno crime and cyber crime. Yet while the modality of these crimes is new, the underlying nature of the wrongdoing is older than the Commandment: *Thou shalt not steal.*

Overwhelmingly, cyber crime or techno crime is property crime, theft of intellectual property, theft of identity, ultimately theft of money. Cops of the future will have to continue to develop the technological sophistication to foil and apprehend cyber criminals, but like the cops of today and the cops of 100 years ago, their principal business will be policing property crime. Second to this—in volume, but not importance—will be policing violent crime against persons, most of it associated with property crime.

Not all cutting-edge police work involves advanced technology. Special Investigator Guy Antinozzi and Sergeant David Aderhold demonstrate a blocking defense and elbow strike counterattack using the state-of-the-art law enforcement defensive tactics method known as Krav Maga developed by the Israeli Defense Forces.

(Photo by Rod Huene, DeKalb County [Georgia] Sheriff's Office)

Policing: From Reactive to Proactive

While the modalities of crime may change, the underlying crimes remain the same. Historically, police agencies have found that their greatest challenge has not been coping with new kinds of crime, but dealing more efficiently with the kinds of crime long familiar. From the very beginning of professional policing, the Bow Street Runners of eighteenth-century London (see Chapter 15), the effort has been to get the police force ahead of the crime curve, to transform the police from a reactive agency to a proactive one.

Future cops will most likely accelerate this drive toward anticipating crime and applying law enforcement resources wherever and whenever most needed to combat—

> **Sworn Statement**
>
> By trying to envisage what the crimes of the future may be, we are one step closer to preventing them.
> —Home Office (United Kingdom) Minister Charles Clarke, quoted by the BBC

and prevent—crime. Technologically, this requires creating ever more sophisticated means of gathering and analyzing intelligence. This means developing computer programs that can model reality in great detail, enabling police agencies to construct place- and time-specific pictures of crimes to come and to work through the implications of each scenario.

Nobody is likely to object to a technological wonder like this. However, such computer modeling will have to be built on present-moment, real-time intelligence, and that means increased systems of tracking and surveillance. It is at this point that police technology and the long-cherished rights of free people in a democratic society begin to clash.

An Ounce of Prevention ...

As the old saying goes, "An ounce of prevention is worth a pound of cure." But unlike so many time-worn sayings, this one still rings with solid truth. In general, preventing a bad thing is more efficient, easier, and cheaper than mopping up the mess that a bad thing makes.

Everyone agrees that crime prevention is a good thing. The disputes arise over methods of prevention. Our Constitution guarantees that we are presumed innocent until proven guilty by due process of law. This legal safeguard alone greatly limits the application of various means of crime prevention:

◆ The police cannot stop, search, or detain people without probable cause.

◆ Many forms of surveillance constitute an illegal presumption of guilt, invasion of privacy, or illegal search.

◆ *Racial profiling*, singling out individuals in the belief that members of their race have a high likelihood of committing or having committed a crime, has been found unconstitutional.

def•i•ni•tion

Racial profiling occurs when the police target someone for investigation or search on the basis of that person's race, national origin, or ethnicity.

Clearly, the police will always be limited in the type and degree of prevention they can exercise. And in a free society, we wouldn't want this any other way. In a free society, therefore, other means of crime prevention need to be developed and applied. In the future, society will likely look increasingly to criminologists and other social scientists to provide meaningful data on the causes of crime. Addressing these causes will not be a matter for the police alone, but for society as a whole. Crime prevention will doubtless require a willingness to restructure various aspects of society, to continue to increase economic opportunities for everyone, and to make room in our society for everyone—to ultimately create a society in which crime is perceived not only as dangerous, costly, and morally wrong, but as simply unnecessary.

Security Horizons

Upholding constitutional rights is of vital importance, as is working toward a more just and open society. But what should be done after events like the terrorist attacks of September 11, 2001? How can we preserve the Constitution and foster an open society when doing these things apparently leaves us that much more vulnerable?

The answer seems to be a compromise of some freedoms in certain, strictly defined settings. That is, we accept searches of our baggage and even our persons in airports. We agree to furnish identification when purchasing airline tickets. We tolerate delays. We try to be understanding and patient when a flight is cancelled because of security concerns. We relinquish the convenience of parking spaces close to the airport terminal. We ask that employees in sensitive areas be subjected to background checks. We ourselves willingly open our lives to inspection in order to get certain jobs.

In recent years, the most pervasive trend in law enforcement has been in the area of security, and since September 11, 2001, the security industry has burgeoned. It is likely that, as the future unrolls, many police duties will be assumed by private security personnel. Even more important, search and surveillance of a kind and degree constitutionally unacceptable on the street will be increasingly commonplace in many other public and semipublic places: airports, major events, even bars and restaurants.

Sworn Statement

We need a national ID card with our photograph and thumbprint digitized and embedded in the ID card.

—Larry Ellison, CEO, Oracle Systems, TV news interview, September 21, 2001

Violence and other crimes have become of increasing concern in schools and in the workplace. Doubtless, these venues will experience an increase in the presence of security personnel, in video surveillance, and in the use of personal identification cards to grant access to and track people.

Emphasis on Information

By definition, the future is an uncertain place, but within this unknown, at least one trend in criminal investigation is sure: information will be regarded as an increasingly valuable commodity, and law enforcement agencies will become information gathering, sharing, and processing agencies.

New Computers, New Networks

Just a few years ago, stand-up comics found much grist for the laugh mill in anecdotes about hopeless arguments with anonymous corporate or government computers—monologue bits about spectacular billing mix-ups with the electric company, grotesque IRS snafus, and the like.

Lately, comedians have been looking for new material. The reason? People are now quite accustomed to communicating with computers, and computers are much better than they were just a few years ago; more accurately, computer networks are better and far more extensive. The problem never really was one of people talking to computers, but of computers failing to talk to other computers.

> **Case in Point**
>
> Today, law enforcement computer networks are works "under construction." As extensive as the networks are, some experts have pointed to the absence of adequate computer networking among immigration officers, the FBI, and local law enforcement as one reason the September 11th terrorists were able to operate so easily, even taking flying lessons without raising suspicion.

Like the electric company, the IRS, and other big businesses, police agencies have also benefited from the quantum leaps in computer technology and computer networking. Today, criminals enjoy unprecedented mobility in geographical space, but they are increasingly hemmed in by cyberspace. Criminal records and suspect information are computerized, not tucked into a folder stuck in a detective's file drawer. Stored on computer, these records can be shared by virtually any law enforcement agency anywhere.

And not just shared, computer files can also be rapidly searched according to whatever criteria the investigator specifies. Let's say the investigator's looking into a rash of burglaries in which the perp always ensures that the home is empty, always enters through the garage, always strikes at night, always steals jewelry, and never leaves fingerprints. The investigator narrows the search through the computer files by specifying these and whatever other particulars he or she has. The computer returns a short list of suspects.

Communications and Access

Networking computer information is not just a matter of sharing information within and among law enforcement agencies. Look inside a modern police cruiser, and you're likely to see a computer screen and keyboard mounted on the dashboard or elsewhere in the front seat area.

Today's patrol officers do much of their communicating by computer. Files available at the station house may be summoned up in the patrol car. Dispatchers can make available more information (and more specific information) on the computer screen than they could in the space of a radio call, and they can continuously update the information.

For example: the computer inside the car beeps, signaling a call is coming in. The patrol officer glances at the screen. There he sees an incident report, which gives the nature of the call—a home burglary—and the address the officer's being dispatched to. The officer strikes a computer key, and a map of the city appears with the address location pinpointed. The officer types a message to the dispatcher, indicating that he is responding to the call.

More information comes across the screen: a description of the suspect, together with the street down which he was seen running. His description corresponds with a known criminal, and headquarters transmits a picture to the cruiser's computer. By the time of arrival at the scene, the officer has been more thoroughly informed en route than if he had been extensively briefed at the station.

This technology is appearing in police mobile units now, and it promises to become more sophisticated. The more a patrol officer knows, the safer that officer and the public are.

Artificial Intelligence

While police increasingly depend on computers and computer networks to store, process, and share hard information quickly and accurately, they have also begun to exploit the more speculative side of computing.

Artificial intelligence software is used in many scientific, commercial, industrial, and social-science fields to model certain real-world situations and to predict outcomes of various situations and combinations of factors. For example, an aircraft manufacturer might use artificial intelligence programs to study what happens to a certain wing if it is subjected to a specified set of stresses. How much can this or that design take before the wing fails? Asking a pilot to perform such tests in an actual airplane is expensive and potentially lethal. Computer modeling is cheaper and safer, and it enables designers to test a virtually limitless number of designs under a virtually limitless number of conditions.

def•i•ni•tion

Artificial intelligence uses computers and computer programs to emulate and extend human logical reasoning.

Police agencies have also used artificial intelligence to "age" suspects. A murderer has been on the run for 15 years. Police have nothing more than a 15-year-old picture of him. Using an artificial intelligence program, they "age" the picture, creating a reasonable prediction of how he might now appear. On a larger scale, police agencies use artificial intelligence to make long-term plans for deploying police personnel in order to address probable areas of crime as efficiently as possible.

In the future, it is likely that artificial intelligence will aid in solving actual crimes by helping investigators reconstruct events and predict the suspect's next moves.

Identification Technologies

The positive identification of suspects and others has always been important in police work (see Chapter 7). With the proliferation of identity theft and desktop counterfeiting (see Chapter 21), positive identification has become an even more urgent matter.

In recent years, several new biometric identification technologies have emerged and will surely play increasingly important roles in identification. These technologies analyze certain features of the human body, such as DNA, retinal patterns, iris patterns, or fingerprints, to provide positive identification of persons for security purposes. They include the following:

- **DNA technology.** This technology continues to undergo refinement and to find wider and wider application in criminal investigation as well as in the judicial process (see Chapter 14).

- **Retinal scanning devices.** Until recently these were the subject of science fiction, but they are now in use, typically in places where positive identification is required for access to sensitive areas. A digital camera images a person's retina, and a computer analyzes the distinctive pattern of retinal blood vessels, then compares it to patterns on file. No one can fake another person's retinal pattern.

- **Iris scan.** This simpler alternative to the retinal scan uses the distinctive patterns of the human iris to identify individuals.

- **Fingerprint readers.** These are also now commonly in use, and many more are likely to appear. An electronic scanner reads the individual's fingerprint pattern, and a computer digitizes and compares it to other patterns on file.

♦ **Odor detectors.** These are not yet in use, but some experts believe that electronic devices capable of identifying odors unique to an individual will soon be employed as the digital equivalent of that old analog standby, the bloodhound. The electronic devices could be used to track suspects who have fled.

Already, many states have adopted driver's licenses that incorporate a digitally encoded image of the driver's thumb print. In the wake of the September 11th attacks, serious consideration is being given to creating a national identity card that would probably include some mode or modes of biometric identification.

Big Brother?

Take a drive or go for a walk. Look up and around. Chances are, on lampposts, on building corners, you'll notice any number of long rectangular enclosures. They house video cameras. Five years ago, you'd have seen few outside of military bases and other high-security installations. Today, they are quite common everywhere. Over the next several years, they will become increasingly so, a fixture of city streets no more unusual, say, than a traffic light.

Video surveillance is here. Often, we welcome it. The sight of a video camera in a cavernous and deserted parking garage is highly reassuring. In some settings, we should welcome it. The "eye in the sky" at your local department store reduces losses from shoplifting, which ultimately helps keep prices lower for all of us. But in other settings (on city streets, for example) the presence of surveillance is more disturbing and has been subject to debate and court challenges. Nevertheless, the likelihood is that, little by little, more public areas will be deemed suitable for surveillance. In England, today, a number of small cities and portions of larger ones are extensively covered by on-street video surveillance. Freedom-loving Brits seem, for the most part, willing to trade some degree of privacy for a feeling of security.

By the Numbers

In 1998, the New York Civil Liberties Union counted 2,397 outdoor video surveillance cameras in use in New York City. Only about 300 of these were monitored by city authorities; the rest were maintained and monitored by private individuals or firms as part of their own security programs. The organization updated its count in 2005 to 4,468 outdoor cameras.

Another emerging technology with "Big Brother" implications is electronic tagging. For years, some persons sentenced to house arrest have been compelled to wear transmitters, usually around the ankle, which alert monitoring authorities if the convict ventures more than a prescribed distance from his home. Now under development are more sophisticated tagging devices, which may be used to track all persons who are on parole. No matter where the parolee goes, officials will be able to pinpoint his where-abouts.

Computer Forensics

Computers are already pervasive in our lives, and there is every reason to believe that they will become even more pervasive in the foreseeable future. This inevitably means that computer crime—especially identity theft and other computer-enabled financial crimes—will continue to be a serious problem, one that is likely to become increasingly widespread.

Police agencies already engage in *computer forensics*, but this area of criminal investigation will almost certainly expand significantly in years to come. Computer forensics is the use of specialized techniques for recovery, authentication, and analysis of electronic data in the investigation of crimes involving computer usage.

def•i•ni•tion

Computer forensics uses specialized techniques to recover, authenticate, and analyze electronic data in the investigation of crimes involving computer usage.

The computer forensics specialist typically focuses on data storage devices, including hard disks and other media. The specialist identifies sources of documentary or other digital evidence. He or she then preserves the evidence, analyzes it, and finally presents the findings.

Fragile Evidence

Today's computer forensics specialists contend with increasingly sophisticated cyber criminals, who often install countermeasures in their systems specifically designed to defeat forensic investigation. If the investigator works with a heavy hand, there is a real possibility that these countermeasures will destroy evidence. Electronic evidence is subject to viruses and electromagnetic and mechanical damage, as well as booby traps planted by the suspect.

Typical Procedures

A forensic computer investigation typically begins with a search warrant seizure of a suspect's computers and digital media. The data on the suspect's machines are copied;

analysis is performed using the investigator's equipment. The suspect's equipment and media is evidence, and it is important to keep it in as pristine a state as possible.

Like any other forensic investigators, those who specialize in computer crimes always look beyond the machines and carefully examine their surroundings, looking for written notes which may contain passwords and all recordable media.

Investigators take care not to shut down running computers. They take steps to preserve data that has not been transferred to a hard disk or other medium and that may be lost when the machine is shut down. Once the suspect's machines have been secured, all hard drives and other media are duplicated in their entirety.

Reading the Mail

In a few short years, e-mail has become a principal medium of communication, and a big part of the investigator's job is to preserve and analyze e-mail files, which may be stored on the hard drive of an individual computer, on some network device, or on a removable device.

Analysis of e-mail evidence highlights a major problem in computer forensics: the sheer volume of material that must be examined. Tens of thousands of messages—or even more—may present themselves at a suspect site. Increasingly sophisticated investigative software enables keyword searches that comb through mountains of data in search of incriminating words and word groupings that merit further investigation.

Beyond Investigation

Although the role of computer forensics is primarily investigative, knowledge gathered by investigators is being used more and more to understand cyber crime and therefore advise computer users—including individuals, businesses, and government agencies—and software engineers on how to prevent or defeat computer crime.

The Arsenal of the Future

As discussed in Chapter 17, the ready availability of military-grade assault weapons sometimes leaves police officers dangerously outgunned. The police arsenal of the future will doubtless include more assault-type weapons, but even more important will be the addition of an array of nonlethal weapons.

Guns and More Guns

During the 1920s and 1930s, the availability of the Thompson submachine gun—the "Tommy gun"—was a rude awakening for many police forces. Cops armed with revolvers found themselves going up against gangsters with high-powered automatic weapons. Accordingly, police agencies equipped themselves with automatic weapons as well as rifles fitted with sniper scopes, and the arms race between the bad guys and the good guys has escalated ever since. In the late 1960s, the high-stakes drug trade and various domestic revolutionary movements (for example, the Black Panthers) resulted in an influx of assault weapons. Over the past 40 years, despite assault weapon restrictions, the number of these high-powered weapons has multiplied dramatically. Police agencies across the country keep SWAT and other special weapons teams in a high state of readiness, anticipating situations in which officers will face formidable hardware.

Nonlethal Weapons

Even while police departments upgrade their firepower, as well as the training to go along with it, they also look for nonlethal alternatives. According to the U.S. Department of Defense directive, *Policy for Non-Lethal Weapons* (1995), "Non-lethal weapons are weapons systems that are explicitly designed and primarily employed so as to incapacitate personnel or material, while minimizing fatalities, permanent injury to personnel, and undesired damage to property and the environment."

> **Sworn Statement**
>
> So-called nonlethal weapons are still powerful and dangerous. They do not guarantee a zero probability of producing fatalities or permanent injuries, but they are designed to reduce that probability while incapacitating a suspect.

Tear gas, pepper spray, and other incapacitating agents have been around for many years, but they are not fully dependable because their performance—the degree of incapacity they induce—is not uniform against all persons in all situations. The great problem with nonlethal weapons is that, if they fail to incapacitate, they may provoke a suspect to respond with desperate and deadly force. Police agencies continue to look for effective, reliable, and consistent nonlethal weapons.

Nonlethal weapons in use or under development include ...

- **Acoustics.** A noise generator emits very low-frequency sounds that can incapacitate people by making them feel dizzy, vomit, or lose control of their bowels.

Another acoustic weapon system uses high-frequency "acoustic beams" to produce what experts describe as "blunt-object trauma like being hit by a baseball."

◆ **Chemicals.** Weapons experts are experimenting with sticky foam fired from a shoulder-slung dispenser. Strings of the foam expand on contact, stopping a person in his tracks. Another kind of weapon uses aqueous foam, a soapy substance that expands up to 500 times its original volume and prevents people from seeing, hearing, or moving. Police are even considering polymer agents that act like super glue to immobilize a suspect.

◆ **Electromagnetic devices.** The Taser is a low-powered hand-held device that can operate up to 15 feet away from a suspect. It fires a pair of dartlike electrodes into the suspect, which deliver 50,000 volts, inducing spasms and immobilization. Tasers are in use by some agencies, as is the stun gun, a two-pronged, handheld device that delivers a controlled charge of electricity to temporarily incapacitate a person. Unlike the Taser, which can operate from a distance, the stun gun requires close contact with the target.

◆ **Mechanical devices.** Rear air bag restraints were developed at the request of law enforcement agencies to subdue agitated assailants while they are being transported in the back seat of a police car. An officer can inflate the bag, thereby immobilizing the prisoner. Unlike the air bag that deploys in a front-end collision, the rear air bag inflates slowly and remains inflated. It is air permeable, so that there is no danger of suffocation. Another nonlethal mechanical device under development is a snare net launched from a canister attached to a rifle barrel. The net opens up over a fleeing suspect, entangling and immobilizing him.

◆ **Optical weapons.** Low-energy lasers can be used to blind people temporarily; an infrared laser can heat the skin sufficiently to cause incapacitating pain but not an actual burn. A newly developed argon laser beam can be aimed at a window or windshield and will turn the glass opaque green, thereby preventing a sniper from seeing his target or a driver from speeding away. High-energy pulsing strobe lights can be employed to disorient suspects, and optical hand grenades, like giant flash bulbs, can be used to create a flash that will blind a person for about 30 seconds.

A special class of nonlethal weapons is designed to be used against things—especially vehicles—rather than people. Police departments currently use various spike strips laid across a roadway to blow out car tires. On the horizon are "super-caustic" chemicals designed to "eat" vehicle tires, hoses, shoe soles, rooftops, and even road surfaces. Sticky foams are being developed to penetrate mechanical parts of vehicles or weapons, rendering them inoperative. At the other end of the spectrum are chemical lubricants nicknamed "slick 'ems," which are sprayed over pavement, stairs, and other surfaces to make them too slippery for people or vehicles to negotiate.

Policing for the People

Technology will certainly play an important role in the future of criminal investigation and police work. However, technology can carry law enforcement only so far. Most authorities believe that the future of effective policing depends on strengthening the ties between the police and the communities they serve. Many see the community policing idea as the way of the future, and all authorities agree that the police must represent the community, must embody its values, and must be perceived as acting on behalf of the community. This requires a commitment on the part of police leaders as well as individual officers, but it also requires the collective will of the community to support the work of the police.

The Least You Need to Know

- Although police work is being revolutionized by technological innovation, the underlying values of protecting and serving the community will remain unchanged.

- The most important technological innovations in police work will be in the area of information gathering, processing, analysis, and sharing.

- The future will see a continuation of the long historical trend toward preventing crime rather than merely reacting to crime; this trend, however, threatens to conflict with the constitutional guarantee of presumption of innocence.

- The field of security—especially identification and surveillance systems—will continue to grow; many basic security functions will probably be assumed by private agencies, freeing the police to devote more resources to investigating crime.

- The field of computer forensics will continue to become both more important and more sophisticated.

- Police arsenals will likely acquire a new array of nonlethal weapons in the near future.

Appendix A

Who's Who in Criminal Investigation and Forensics

Abberline, Frederick George (1843–1929). Chief investigator of the Jack the Ripper murders (1888).

Balthazard, Victor (1872–1951). French forensic scientist who pioneered the science of ballistics and the examination of hair evidence.

Barnard, Chester (1886–1961). Brought business management techniques to the modern police department organization with his 1937 book, *The Functions of the Executive*.

Battle, Samuel J. (1883–1966). First African American policeman on the NYPD; later, New York's parole commissioner.

Bayle, Edmond (1879–1928). French pioneer of the study of fiber evidence and the use of spectrography in criminal investigation.

Bertillon, Alphonse (1853–1914). The "Father of Scientific Detection"; French developer of the Bertillon System of applied anthropometry, the taking of key bodily measurements for positive identification of criminals.

Bril, Jacques L. (1906–1981). American pioneer and innovator in the field of polygraphy (lie detection).

Brussel, James Arnold (1905–1982). American forensic psychiatrist who pioneered the methodology of offender profiling; earned national fame in New York's "Mad Bomber Case" of the early 1950s and the "Boston Strangler" case of the 1960s.

Byrnes, Thomas F. (1842–1910). NYPD chief who created the "Rogues' Gallery," photographs of every suspect arrested and booked.

Caldwell, Charles (1771–1853). American physician, advocate of phrenology, and exponent of phrenological explanations of criminal behavior.

Canter, David V. (1944–). British pioneer of criminal profiling, specializing in profiles of serial killers and serial rapists.

Churchill, Robert (1886–1958). Introduced scientific ballistics to Scotland Yard.

Cicourel, Aaron V. (1928–). Pioneering student of juvenile delinquency in the United States; argued that coordination among police and the community could effectively reduce or prevent juvenile delinquency.

Cohen, Louis Harold (1906–1955). As co-author of *Murder, Madness, and the Law* (1952), was instrumental in establishing the modern criteria for evaluating criminal insanity.

Colquhoun, Patrick (1745–1820). British police theorist whose *Treatise on the Police of the Metropolis* (1796) is considered one of the founding documents of modern law enforcement.

Curphey, Theodore (1897–1986). First medical examiner of Los Angeles County; gained national celebrity for his controversial direction of the forensic autopsy of Marilyn Monroe (1962).

Dawson, Margaret Damer (1874–1920). Founder of London's Women's Police Volunteers, the first female police presence in the city.

Dew, Walter (1863–1947). Most famous chief inspector of Scotland Yard's CID (Criminal Investigation Division); apprehended the infamous Hawley H. Crippen, who had murdered and dismembered his wife in 1910.

Dondero, John A. (1900–1957). American forensics expert who greatly advanced the science of fingerprint identification.

Faulds, Henry (1843–1930). Scottish fingerprinting pioneer who developed techniques to make fingerprinting a practical means of criminal identification.

Faurot, Joseph A. (1872–1942). Called the American "father of fingerprinting"; won national acceptance of fingerprinting early in the twentieth century.

Fedle, Fortunato (1550–1630). First advocate of investigative autopsy in cases of mysterious death.

Ferracuti, Franco (1927–). Advocate of the creation of a medical-legal field of "criminological diagnosis."

Fielding, Sir Henry (1707–1954). Famed English novelist (*Joseph Andrews*, *Tom Jones*) who, as magistrate for the City of Westminster, created the Bow Street Runners, precursor of the modern police force.

Fielding, Sir John (1721–1980). Half brother of Henry Fielding and, like him, magistrate of the City of Westminster; led and expanded the Bow Street Runners.

Fodere, Francois-Emmanuel (1764–1835). An early French advocate of investigating the medical basis for crime.

Fosdick, Raymond Blaine (1883–1972). Historian and analyst of police systems in the United States and Europe.

Fuld, Leonhard Felix (1883–1965). New York author of the first comprehensive study of American police administration early in the twentieth century.

Gall, Franz Joseph (1758–1828). Viennese physician who codified phrenology, the basis for early medical explanations of criminal behavior.

Galton, Sir Francis (1822–1911). British amateur scientist who improved upon the work of Henry Faulds and William Herschel to revolutionize the classification of fingerprints.

Garofalo, Raffaele (1852–1934). Nineteenth-century writer on the "criminal thought process."

Gates, Daryl (1926–). Outspoken, abrasive, controversial LAPD chief who is credited with developing the SWAT concept.

Gettler, Alexander Oscar (1884–1968). New York City's pioneering chief toxicologist from 1918 to 1959.

Glueck, Eleanor (1898–1972) and **Sol Sheldon Glueck** (1896–1980). Wife-husband team who developed the highly controversial Glueck's Social Prediction Table during the 1950s; the table was intended to enable early recognition of incipient delinquency in children.

Goddard, Calvin Hooker (1891–1955). American ballistics expert who founded the Scientific Crime Detection Laboratory as part of Northwestern University (Evanston, Illinois); also started the *American Journal of Police Science*.

Gravelle, Philip O. (1877–1955). San Francisco-based inventor of the comparison microscope, principal tool of modern ballistics and firearms identification.

Hale, George (1855–?). Author/compiler of the first American encyclopedia of police work (1892).

Hamilton, Mary (active 1917–1930s). First female police officer to serve in a supervisory role; first director of the Women's Police Bureau, NYPD.

Hammurabi (ca. 1792–1750 B.C.E.). Ruler of Babylon and creator of the first important body of law in history, the Code of Hammurabi.

Harrington, Penny (1949–). First female police chief of a large American city, Portland, Oregon (1985).

Helpern, Dr. Milton (1902–1977). Famed medical examiner for New York City, 1954 to 1973, celebrated as "Sherlock Holmes with a microscope."

Henry, Sir Edward Richard (1850–1931). First fingerprint expert to devise a truly practical method of fingerprint classification and archiving.

Herschel, William James (1883–1917). British fingerprint pioneer, who concluded that fingerprints are unique to the individual.

Hilton, Ordway (1913–). Chicago-based founder of the science of forensic handwriting analysis.

Hindelang, Michael (1946–1982). Pioneered the idea of a relationship between low intelligence and delinquency.

Hoover, J. Edgar (1895–1972). Founder and life-long director of the Federal Bureau of Investigation; brought the bureau international acclaim and national controversy.

Inbau, Fred (1909–). American expert on the techniques of interrogating criminal suspects.

Jeffreys, Alec (1950–). British scientist who pioneered "DNA fingerprinting."

Keeler, Leonarde (1903–1949). American polygraph pioneer who founded the first private lie detection agency.

Kefauver, Estes (1903–1963). Tennessee senator whose televised congressional hearings in the 1950s exposed organized crime to the American public and helped shape the direction of law enforcement policy for decades to come.

Kersta, Lawrence George (1907–). New Jersey audio engineer who pioneered voice-printing technology.

Kirk, Paul Leland (1902–1970). An American pioneer in standardizing scientific techniques for analyzing physical evidence.

Koehler, Arthur (1885–1967). Famed as America's "wood detective"; an early expert in the analysis of wood evidence.

Kretschmer, Ernst (1888–1964). German psychiatrist who developed the "constitutional theory," arguing that one's physique has a bearing on behavior, including criminal behavior.

Lacassagne, Jean Alexandre (1844–1921). French pioneer in ballistics who first noted that the unique marks barrel rifling made on bullets could be used to match a bullet to the gun that fired it.

Landesco, John (1890–1954). Pioneering American student of organized crime.

Landsteiner, Karl (1868–1943). Austrian Nobel Prize winner who identified the four major blood groups, providing (among other things) the basis for a new method of forensic investigation.

Lange, Johannes (1891–1938). His *Crime as Destiny* (1931) studied criminal twins to explore the role of heredity in criminal behavior.

Larson, John A. (1892–1965). U.S. police officer, educator, and psychiatrist credited with inventing the polygraph in 1921.

Lavater, Johann Casper (1741–1801). Swiss founder of the pseudoscience of physiognomy, forerunner of phrenology.

Lee, Henry C. (1938–). Chinese-born American forensics expert, specializing in medical forensics at the crime scene; gave high-profile testimony in the O.J. Simpson case.

Leonard, V. A. (1898–1984). American pioneer in police education.

Levine, Lowell J. (1937–). Pioneer of odontology, the forensic identification of tooth imprints and bite marks.

Lohman, Joseph D. (1910–1968). American criminologist who advanced progressive programs on community relations and race relations within police departments.

Malpighi, Marcello (1628–1694). Italian physician who first described human fingerprints.

Marsh, James (1794–1846). British chemist who developed a laboratory test for arsenic in human tissue; a pioneer in forensic toxicology.

Maudsley, Henry (1835–1918). British author of *Responsibility in Mental Diseases* (1874), which challenged the belief that insane persons act without motive.

May, Luke S. (1886–1955). A private investigative consultant, May combined intuition with science to solve hundreds of cases and earn the nickname "the American Sherlock Holmes."

Mayne, Sir Richard (1796–1868). One of the chief founders of Scotland Yard.

McDonald, Hugh Chisholm (1913–). Associated with the Los Angeles Sheriff's Department, invented the Identi-Kit, an invaluable aid to making criminal identification sketches.

McKay, Henry D. (1899–1980). A Chicago-based pioneer in the field of juvenile delinquency.

Merton, Robert K. (1910–). Major twentieth-century sociologist who developed a model of crime and deviancy based on societal expectations.

Morel, Benedict (1809–1873). German-born French psychiatrist who was among the first to advance a legal definition of insanity.

Ness, Eliot (1903–1957). Chicago-based federal agent who organized the Prohibition-era "Untouchables," the most effective early force against organized crime.

Norris, Charles (1867–1935). New York City's first medical examiner (appointed 1918); created the model for American forensic pathology.

Orfila, Mathieu Joseph Bonaventure (1787–1853). Spanish chemist deemed the father of modern toxicology.

Osborn, Albert (1858–1946). American author of *Questioned Documents* (1923), the landmark handbook on examining document evidence.

Parker, William Henry (1902–1966). LAPD police chief considered by many to be one of the most effective chiefs in American history.

Parkhurst, Charles H. (1842–1933). Effective crusader against police corruption in New York City; raised the ethical standards of police agencies nationwide.

Peel, Sir Robert (1788–1850). British politician who established the London Metropolitan Police and made his "bobbies" (also called "Peelers") international models of professionalism.

Ray, Isaac (1807–1881). American author of the landmark *Medical Jurisprudence of Insanity* (1838), for many years the standard reference concerning the legal definition of insanity.

Reiser, Martin (1927–). Hired by the Los Angeles Police Department, he was the first psychologist ever employed full time by a United States law enforcement agency.

Reiss, Albert John Jr. (1922–). Author of the first definitive study of police brutality in major American police departments (1971).

Simpson, Cedric Keith (1907–1985). British pioneer in forensic dentistry and the first forensic pathologist to recognize and define "battered baby syndrome"; one of the world's leading forensic pathologists.

Smith, Sir Sydney Alfred (1883–1969). Author of major pioneering works on firearms and gunshot wounds.

Snyder, LeMoyne (1899–1975). U.S. pioneering advocate of forensic pathology.

Söderman, Harry (1903–1956). Swedish police official and principal founder of INTERPOL.

Spitzka, Edward Anthony (1876–1922). American neurologist who refuted the long-cherished belief that criminality resulted from a physical deformity of the brain.

Spurzheim, Johann Christoph (1776–1832). Early and influential advocate of the phrenological basis of criminology and criminal profiling.

Stas, Jean-Servais (1813–1891). Belgian chemist who refined the science of toxicology by developing a process for detecting vegetable alkaloids in dead tissue.

Stein, Robert J. (1912–1994). First medical examiner of Cook County (Chicago), Illinois; introduced many innovations into forensic pathology.

Stringham, James S. (1775–1817). Considered by many to be the founder of medical jurisprudence in the United States.

Sutherland, Edwin Hardin (1883–1950). American criminologist who originated the "white collar crime" concept and term; held that criminal behavior was learned through interaction with others.

Thrasher, Frederic Milton (1892–1962). Wrote the first major modern study of gang behavior, *The Gang: A Study of 1,313 Gangs in Chicago* (1963).

Torjanowicz, Robert C. (1941–1994). Michigan State University professor who was an instrumental advocate of the community policing concept.

Tyrell, John F. (1861–1955). Wisconsin-born expert on questioned documents.

Uhlenhuth, Paul Theodore (1870–1957). German forensic scientist who discovered a serum that enabled investigators to distinguish between human and animal blood evidence.

Vincent, Howard (1849–1908). First director of the Criminal Investigation Department of the London Metropolitan Police; expanded the detective force of Scotland Yard and built it into the world's premier investigative agency.

Vollmer, August (1876–1955). American "father" of the modern professional police force.

Waite, Charles E. (ca. 1874–1926). Pioneering American ballistics expert.

Wiener, Alexander (1906–1976). Co-discoverer of the Rh factor in blood; pioneered the study of blood and other body fluid evidence.

Wigmore, John Henry (1863–1943). Founder of the American Institute of Criminal Law and Criminology and author of the 10-volume *Treatise on the Anglo-American System of Evidence* (1904).

Milestones in Crime and Crime Fighting

Prehistoric: Humans include fingerprints in paintings and rock carvings.

700s: Chinese use fingerprints to authenticate documents.

ca. 1000: Quintilian, a Roman attorney, wins acquittal for his client by proving that bloody palm prints were intended to frame him.

1248: *Hsi Duan Yu* (The Washing Away of Wrongs), a Chinese text, includes a description of how to distinguish a drowning death from death by strangulation—the first recorded application of medical forensics.

1609: François Demelle (France) writes the world's first work on the examination of questioned documents.

1686: Marcello Malpighi (Italy) is the first to describe human fingerprints.

1784: John Toms (Lancaster, England) is convicted of murder because the torn edge of a wad of newspaper in the murder gun matched a piece in his pocket; this is perhaps the first documented instance of the physical matching of evidence.

1813: Mathiew Orfila (Spain) publishes *Treatise on Poisons*, thereby becoming the father of modern toxicology.

1823: John Evangelist Purkinji (Bohemia) publishes a work on the nature of fingerprints and suggests a classification system based on nine major types.

1830s: Adolphe Quetelet (Belgium) provides statistical evidence that no two human bodies are exactly alike, thereby laying the foundation for the later development of the Bertillon system.

1835: Henry Goddard (England) uses a mark (flaw) on a murder bullet to trace it to the mold that formed the bullet, thereby linking a suspect to the murder through ballistics.

1836: James Marsh (Scotland) is the first to present toxicological evidence (detection of arsenic poisoning) in a jury trial.

1851: Jean Servais Stas (Belgium) is the first to identify vegetable poisons in dead body tissue.

1856: Sir William Herschel (England) uses thumbprints to authenticate documents.

1862: J. Van Deen (Netherlands) develops a chemical test for human blood.

1877: Thomas Taylor (United States) proposes markings on palms and fingertips be used for identification in criminal cases.

1879: Rudolph Virchow (Germany) pioneers forensic hair analysis.

1880: Henry Faulds (Scotland) suggests that fingerprints recovered at the scene of a crime could identify the offender.

1883: Alphonse Bertillon (France) demonstrates anthropometry as a method of positive identification.

1887: Arthur Conan Doyle (England) publishes the first Sherlock Holmes story.

1889: Alexandre Lacassagne (France) attempts to match bullets to the gun barrel from which they were fired; founds modern ballistics.

1891: Hans Gross (Austria) publishes *Criminal Investigation*, the first comprehensive description of the use of physical evidence in solving crime.

1892: Sir Francis Galton publishes *Fingerprints*, the first major book on the forensic use of fingerprints.

1892: Juan Vucetich (Argentina) develops the fingerprint classification system widely used in Latin America.

1894: In a sensational case, French army captain Alfred Dreyfus is convicted of treason, in part as a result of a mistaken handwriting identification by Bertillon.

1896: Sir Edward Richard Henry (England) develops the fingerprint classification system widely used in Europe and North America.

1898: Paul Jesrich (Germany) uses comparison photomicrographs in ballistics analysis.

1900: Karl Landsteiner (Germany) discovers human blood groups, which, incidentally, greatly aids the field of forensic medicine.

1901: Paul Uhlenhuth (Germany) develops a test to distinguish human blood from animal blood.

1901: Sir Edward Richard Henry (England) of Scotland Yard replaces Bertillon's anthropometry with fingerprint identification.

1901: Henry P. DeForrest pioneers the first systematic use of fingerprints in the United States.

1902: R. A. Reiss (Switzerland) creates the first academic curriculum in forensic science.

1903: The New York State Prison system begins to use fingerprint identification; first U.S. law enforcement agency to do so.

1905: Theodore Roosevelt establishes the Bureau of Investigation, precursor agency of the Federal Bureau of Investigation.

1910: Victor Balthazard (France) publishes the first comprehensive hair analysis study.

1910: Edmund Locard (France) establishes the world's first police crime laboratory.

1910: Albert S. Osborne (United States) publishes *Questioned Documents*, the first major work on the forensic examination of documents.

1913: Balthazard (France) publishes the first major article on individualizing bullet markings.

1915: Leone Lattes (Italy) develops the first antibody test for ABO blood groups; he soon applies the test to criminal investigation.

1916: Albert Schneider (United States) develops a vacuum apparatus to collect trace evidence.

1918: Edmond Locard (France) suggests 12 key matching points for positive fingerprint identification.

1920: Locard publishes a landmark forensics text, which proclaims the chief principle of forensic science: "Every contact leaves a trace."

1920: Charles E. Waite (United States) catalogs manufacturing data relating to weapons.

1920s: Luke May (United States) develops striation analysis for tool mark comparison.

1920s: The American Calvin Goddard (with Charles Waite, Phillip O. Gravelle, and John H. Fisher) perfects the comparison microscope, the principal tool for bullet comparison.

1921: John Larson and Leonarde Keeler independently design polygraph machines.

1924: August Vollmer (United States) sets up the first U.S. police crime laboratory.

1925: Saburo Sirai (Japan) discovers the secretion of group-specific antigens into body fluids other than blood.

1929: Calvin Goddard is instrumental in founding the Scientific Crime Detection Laboratory at Northwestern University, Evanston, Illinois.

1930: *American Journal of Police Science* is founded.

1932: The FBI crime laboratory is established.

1937: Walter Specht (Germany) develops Luminol, which detects latent blood stains.

1940: Vincent Hnizda (United States) pioneers the forensic analysis of ignitable fluids, laying the foundation for scientific arson investigation.

1941: Bell Labs (United States) builds on the work of L. G. Kersta to develop voice-print identification.

1945: Frank Lundquist (Denmark) develops the acid phosphatase test for semen evidence.

1950: August Vollmer (United States) establishes the school of criminology at the University of California at Berkeley.

1954: R. F. Borkenstein (United States) invents the Breathalyzer for field sobriety testing.

1971: The U.S. Supreme Court rules that illegally obtained evidence is generally inadmissible at trial.

1974: A group of U.S. scientists use the electron microscope to analyze gunshot residue.

1975: Federal Rules of Evidence, originally promulgated by the U.S. Supreme Court, are enacted into law by Congress.

1977: Fuseo Matsumur (Japan) accidentally discovers the "Superglue fuming" method of latent fingerprint development.

1977: The FBI introduces the Automated Fingerprint Identification System (AFIS), the first fully computerized fingerprinting system.

1984: Sir Alec Jeffreys (England) develops the first DNA profiling test.

1985: The U.S. Supreme Court rules that police cannot use lethal force against an unarmed fleeing suspect who is not deemed dangerous.

1986: DNA evidence is first used to solve a crime; Colin Pitchfork is identified as the murderer of two young girls in the Midlands of England.

1987: DNA profiling is introduced in a U.S. criminal court; Tommy Lee Andrews is convicted of a series of sexual assaults in Orlando, Florida.

1988: American scientists develop a procedure for the analysis of drugs in whole blood by homogeneous enzyme immunoassay.

1991: Walsh Automation Inc. (Canada) begins to develop an automated ballistics imaging system, Integrated Ballistics Identification System (IBIS).

1998: The FBI establishes a DNA database, CODIS (Combined DNA Index System), which enables interstate cooperation in linking crimes.

The "Ten Code"

To facilitate radio communication, police officers use abbreviations and codes to save air time and reduce possible confusion. The so-called "Ten Code" is subject to local variation, but the Association of Police Communications Officers has standardized it and advocates its universal adoption.

Code 1: Your convenience

Code 2: Urgent, no red light and siren

Code 3: Emergency, use red light and siren

Code 4: No further assistance needed

Code 5: Stakeout

Code 6AD: Felony wanted, armed and dangerous

Code 6F: Felony wanted

Code 6M: Misdemeanor wanted

Code 7: Mealtime

Code 8: Box alarm

Code 10: Bomb threat

Code 20: Assist officer, urgent

Code 30: Officer needs help, emergency

Code 33: Emergency in progress, do not transmit

187: Murder

207: Kidnapping

211: Robbery

245: ADW (assault with deadly weapon)

261: Rape

288: L & L (lewd and lascivious) conduct

311: Indecent exposure

415: Disturbance

415F: Family disturbance

460: Burglary

480: Felony hit-and-run

481: Misdemeanor hit-and-run

487: Grand theft

488: Petty theft

502: Drunk driver

503: Stolen vehicle

505: Reckless driving

510: Vehicle speeding

647: Vagrant

647A: Child molestation

10-1: Receiving poorly

10-2: Receiving okay

10-4: Message received okay

10-5: Relay to

10-7: Out of service at

10-7B: Out of service, personal

10-70D: Off duty

10-8: In service

10-9: Repeat

10-10: Out of service at home

10-12: Visitors or officials present

10-13: Weather and road conditions

10-14: Escort

10-14F: Funeral detail

10-15: Have prisoner in custody

10-16: Pick up

10-19: Return to station

10-20: Location

10-21: Phone your office

10-21A: Phone my home, my ETA is

10-21B: Phone your home

10-21R: Phone radio

10-22: Cancel

10-23: Standby

10-25: Do you have contact with

10-28: Registration

10-29: Check for wanted

10-32: Drowning

10-33: Alarm sounding

10-34: Open door

10-35: Open window

10-39: Status of

10-40: Is available for phone call

10-45: Ambulance, injured

10-46: Ambulance, sick

10-49: Proceed to

10-50: Obtain a report

10-51: Drunk

10-52: Resuscitator

10-53: Man down

10-54: Possible dead body

10-55: Coroner's case

10-56: Suicide

10-56A: Attempted suicide

10-57: Firearms discharged

10-58: Garbage complaint

10-59: Malicious mischief

10-62: Meet the citizen

10-65: Missing person

10-66: Suspicious person

10-67: Person calling for help

10-70: Prowler

10-71: Shooting

10-72: Knifing

10-73: How do you receive?

10-80: Explosion

10-86: Any traffic for

10-87: Meet officer

10-91: Stray animal

10-91A: Vicious animal

10-91B: Noisy animal

10-91C: Injured animal

10-91D: Dead animal

10-91F: Animal bite

10-911H: Stray horse

10-97: Arrived at the scene

10-98: Finished with last assignment

11-24: Abandoned vehicle

11-26: Abandoned bicycle

11-54: Suspicious vehicle

11-79: Accident, ambulance en route

11-80: Accident, major injury

11-81: Accident, minor injury

11-82: Accident, property damage

11-83: Accident, no detail

11-84: Traffic control

11-96: Leaving vehicle to investigate an auto; if not heard from in 10 minutes, dispatch cover

Appendix D

Further Reading and Favorite Websites

Books

Axelrod, Alan, and Charles Phillips. *Cops, Crooks, and Criminologists: An International Biographical Dictionary of Law Enforcement.* New York: Facts on File, 1996.

Bennett, Wayne W., and Kären M. Hess. *Criminal Investigation.* Fifth edition, Belmont, Calif.: Wadsworth, 1998.

Douglass, John E., et al. *Crime Classification Manual.* San Francisco: Jossey-Bass, 1992.

Egger, S. *Serial Murder.* Westport, Conn.: Praeger, 1990.

Evans, Colin. *The Casebook of Forensic Detection.* New York: Wiley, 1996.

Fisher, Barry A. J. *Techniques of Crime Scene Investigation.* Seventh Edition. Boca Raton, Florida: CRC Press, 2004.

Fox, J., and J. Levin. *Overkill.* New York: Plenum, 1994.

Genge, N. E. *The Forensic Casebook.* New York: Ballantine, 2002.

Healy, William. *The Individual Delinquent.* Boston: Little, Brown, 1915.

Henry, A. F., and James F. Short. *Suicide and Homicide.* Glencoe, Il.: Free Press, 1954.

Herbert, David T. *The Geography of Urban Crime.* London: Longman, 1982.

Hickey, E. *Serial Murderers and Their Victims.* Belmont, Calif.: Wadsworth, 2002.

Hochstedler, Ellen, ed. *Corporations as Criminals,* Beverly Hills, Calif.: Sage, 1984.

Hooton, Earnest A. *The American Criminal.* Cambridge, Mass.: Harvard University Press, 1939.

Jeffery, C. Ray. *Crime Prevention Through Environmental Design.* Beverly Hills, Calif.: Sage Publications, 1971.

Jenkins, Philip. *Using Murder: The Social Construction of Serial Homicide.* New York: Aldine de Gruyter, 1994.

LaFree, Gary. *Rape and Criminal Justice: The Social Construction of Sexual Assault.* Belmont, Calif.: Wadsworth, 1989.

Liska, Allen E. *Perspectives on Deviance.* Englewood Cliffs, N.J.: Prentice Hall, 1981.

Lombroso, Cesare. *Crime: Its Causes and Remedies.* Boston: Little, Brown, 1911.

Lombroso, Cesare, and William Ferrero. *The Female Offender.* London: Fisher Unwin, 1895.

Mednick, Sarnoff, Terrie Moffitt, and Susan Stack, eds. *The Causes of Crime: New Biological Approaches.* Cambridge, England: Cambridge University Press, 1987.

Nettler, Gwynn. *Killing One Another.* Cincinnati: Anderson, 1982.

Platt, Richard. *Crime Scene: The Ultimate Guide to Forensic Science.* London: DK Publishing, 2003.

Rafter, Nicole Hahn. *Creating Born Criminals.* Urbana: University of Illinois Press, 1997.

Ragle, Larry. *Crime Scene: From Fingerprints to DNA Testing—An Astonishing Inside Look at the Real World of C.S.I.* New York: Avon Books, 2002.

Reiss, A., and J. Roth, eds. *Understanding and Preventing Violence.* Washington, D.C.: National Academy Press, 1993.

Russell, Diana E. H. *The Politics of Rape: The Victim's Perspective.* New York: Stein and Day, 1975.

Sanday, Peggy R. *Fraternity Gang Rape: Sex, Brotherhood, and Privilege on Campus.* New York: New York University Press, 1990.

Websites

Crime and Justice Statistics at www.fedstats.gov/programs/crime.html

Crimelibrary.com at www.crimelibrary.com

Crimetheory.com at www.crimetheory.com

Criminal Profiling Research at www.criminalprofiling.ch/introduction.html

FBI Laboratory Services at www.fbi.gov/hq/lab/org/labchart.htm

Forensic Science Web Pages at

www.aafs.org

www.cj.msu.edu

www.crimeandclues.com

www.criminalistics.com/abc/A.php

www.forensicpage.com

www.forensic-scinece-society.org.uk

www.forensic.to/forensic.html

www.kruglaw.com

www.nfstc.org

Metropolitan Police (London) at www.met.police.uk

New York City Police Department Timeline at www.nyhistory.org/previous/police/ptimeline.html

NYPD Official web page at www.nyc.gov/html/nypd/home.html

Police Chat: Law Enforcement Statistics and Facts at http://home1.gte.net/joking/lefacts.htm

Index

J-K-L

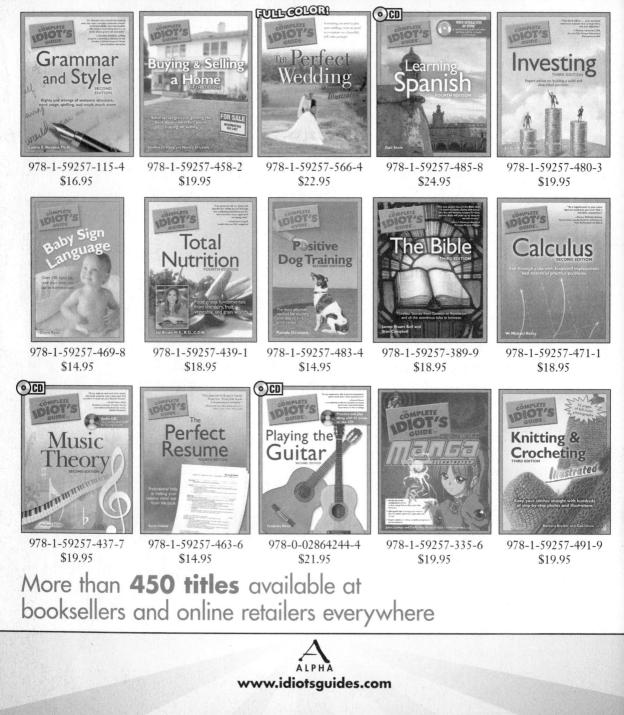